THE CLINIC AND THE CONTEXT

The History of Psychoanalysis Series

Professor Brett Kahr and Professor Peter L. Rudnytsky (Series Editors)
Published and distributed by Karnac Books

Other titles in the Series

THE CLINIC AND THE CONTEXT
Historical Essays

Elisabeth Young-Bruehl

KARNAC

First published in 2013 by
Karnac Books Ltd
118 Finchley Road
London NW3 5HT

British Library Cataloguing in Publication Data

A C.I.P. for this book is available from the British Library

ISBN-13: 978-1-85575-894-0

Typeset by V Publishing Solutions Pvt Ltd., Chennai, India

Printed in Great Britain

www.karnacbooks.com

CONTENTS

ACKNOWLEDGEMENTS

Chapter One: "Why psychoanalysis has no history" was published previously in German, in *Psyche* and is forthcoming in *American Imago*.

Chapter Two: "The trauma of lost love in psychoanalysis" was published previously in *On Freud's "Beyond the Pleasure Principle"* edited by Salman Ahktar and Mary Kay O'Neil (Karnac, 2011).

Chapter Three: "Civilisation and its dream of contentment: reflections on the unity of mankind" is forthcoming in *Psychoanalytic Inquiry*.

Chapter Four: "Psychoanalysis and social democracy: a tale of two developments" was published previously in 2011 in *Contemporary Psychoanalysis, 47*: 179–203.

Chapter Five: "A brief history of prejudice studies" was published previously in *The Future of Prejudice: Psychoanalysis and the Prevention of Prejudice* edited by Henri Parens, Stuart W. Twemlow, Afaf Mahfouz, and David E. Scharff (Jason Aronson, 2007).

Chapter Six: "Reflections on women and psychoanalysis" was published previously in 2001 in *Psychoanalytic Psychotherapy, 18*(1): 7–31.

Chapter Seven: "Sexual diversity in cosmopolitan perspective" was published previously in 2010 in *Studies in Gender and Sexuality, 11*: 1–9.

Chapter Eight: "Women and children first!" was published previously in 2010 in *Modern Psychoanalysis, 34*(2): 53–75.

Chapter Nine: "Psychobiography and character study: a reflection on *Hannah Arendt: For Love of the World* and *Anna Freud: A Biography*" was published previously in 2009 in *PINE Newsletter, 21*(2): 2–8.

ABOUT THE AUTHOR

Elisabeth Young-Bruehl (1946–2011) was a faculty member at the Columbia Center for Psychoanalytic Training and Research and a practising psychoanalyst in Manhattan. She was a member of the Toronto Psychoanalytic Society and the author of biographies of Hannah Arendt and Anna Freud plus many other books.

SERIES EDITOR'S FOREWORD

Professor Brett Kahr

Approximately fourteen years ago, the Philadelphia Society for Psychoanalytic Psychology, a branch of Division 39 of the American Psychological Association, kindly invited me to spend a weekend with them, giving a dinner lecture on the Friday night, followed by a day-long case discussion seminar on the Saturday. I flew to America with much excitement at the prospect of engaging in conversation with a group of experienced colleagues. Shortly after I arrived, I met the committee members—a very friendly group—who put me instantly at ease. I did not feel nervous at all.

But as I entered the reception room in Philadelphia's Adam's Mark Hotel, someone whispered, "Oh there's Elisabeth Young-Bruehl. She's only just joined our group." Within moments, my blood pressure had risen at the prospect of having to deliver an historical-biographical lecture on a hitherto unknown chapter from the life of Dr. Donald Winnicott in front of one of the world's leading psychoanalytical biographers. A longstanding fan of Young-Bruehl's masterful book, Anna Freud: A Biography, as well as of her many other formidable writings, I thought that I might not measure up to her exacting standards.

As I took my place at the podium, somewhat sheepishly, I must confess, I scanned the audience, and noticed Elisabeth at once, seated in the front row, her features instantly recognisable to me from the jacket photograph on the inside back flap of her study of Anna Freud. My anxiety level increased, and I had to remind myself that I had, in fact, already published a book on Winnicott, and that I had brought with me a well-researched, carefully prepared paper, full of new archival discoveries. So I tried to relax, and launched into the lecture. At times, everyone else in the room disappeared, and I kept turning towards Elisabeth, scanning her experienced face for signs of approval or criticism.

As soon as I finished my talk, I realised that I need not have worried about Elisabeth at all. She came bounding up to shake my hand, congratulating me with warmth and generosity. Still in my thirties, I had, at that moment, a strong reminder of the power of the transference; having learned so much from her work, Elisabeth had become such a towering figure in my mind that it had not occurred to me that she might also have the capacity to be ordinarily human and welcoming of a visitor from overseas!

Although Elisabeth outshone all of the psychologists in the room with her stellar academic career and publications, she had only just begun her psychoanalytical training and may have had her own anxieties about being the least clinically seasoned among us at that time. Fortunately, as the weekend progressed, I stopped worrying about Elisabeth's grand status as a doyenne of biographers, and I think that she, too, relaxed and began to immerse herself in the case discussion which followed. Elisabeth impressed me because in spite of her relative inexperience as a mental health practitioner, she comported herself in a most magnificent way as we talked about case material. She participated warmly and frequently in the conversations, but, in spite of her extraordinarily razor-sharp mind, she never boasted. But neither did she denigrate herself and keep quiet. She wore her brilliance in the most straightforward way, and I soon knew myself to be in the presence of a most exceptional person.

We had little contact, regrettably, after my visit to Philadelphia, though she did, most thoughtfully, refer a patient to me in London; and soon afterwards, I reciprocated with a referral for her. I continued to read her unceasing stream of wonderful writings, and to learn from this outstanding mind—one which had mastered a multiplicity of intellectual disciplines with breadth and with profundity.

When Elisabeth entered into negotiations with Oliver Rathbone, the publisher of Karnac Books, to produce this volume of her historical papers, Professor Peter Rudnytsky and I leapt at the chance to include Elisabeth's book in our collection. This sterling, wide-ranging set of papers, introduced affectionately, comprehensively, and eloquently by Elisabeth's great friend and colleague Professor Murray Schwartz, provides more than ample evidence of Elisabeth Young-Bruehl's stature as a leader in psychoanalytical thought, as an original thinker, and as a bold commentator, able to celebrate the successes of the psychoanalytical movement and to examine the causes of its often regrettable failures.

Few workaday clinicians have the time or the training to master historiography, biography, political theory, feminism, sexual politics, critical theory, queer theory, and sociology as well as Elisabeth has done, not to mention the sprawling literature of psychoanalysis itself. With a rich capacity for synthesis, which never dips into shallowness, Elisabeth had the unique ability to draw from these many reservoirs to marvellous effect. Psychoanalysis should be proud to claim her as an important political thinker who admired Freud and his followers, and appreciated the traumas which inhibited the field from developing in a more robust, influential, compassionate, and non-sectarian way.

Shortly before her death, Elisabeth flew to London for a brief research visit to the Wellcome Library, which houses many of the unpublished letters and papers of Donald Winnicott, and she invited me to meet her there to discuss our mutual interest in Winnicott, and to finalise arrangements for the publication of this book. Sadly, influenza prevented me from joining her for coffee and a chat, but I presumed, rather naively, that as Elisabeth had recently become the general editor of the proposed new edition of Winnicott's collected works, there would be many more opportunities for London visits. Cruel reality, alas, intervened, and robbed Elisabeth's family and friends of a much beloved person, and deprived the wider professional community of one of our most rich, engaging, effective, accomplished, and committed colleagues.

The Clinic and the Context: Historical Essays serves as a potent reminder of the power of Elisabeth's mind, of the breadth of her vision, and of the vibrancy of her authorial voice. Although she cannot be replaced or brought back to life, we hope that this selection of papers will keep the essence of Elisabeth Young-Bruehl's mind and spirit alive for many decades to come.

INTRODUCTION

The papers gathered in *The Clinic and the Context* were written for diverse audiences in the last years of Elisabeth Young-Bruehl's life, which ended without warning in early December 2011. She was in the midst of an enormously creative period, having married and moved to Toronto where she and her partner, Christine Dunbar, had founded Caversham Productions, a multimedia publishing enterprise devoted to psychoanalysis and the therapeutic goals of progressive politics. They had constructed an original design for their *One Hundred Years of Psychoanalysis: A Timeline: 1900–2000*, and EYB, as she signed herself, was preparing to celebrate the publication of the final phase of her massive studies of prejudices, her book on *Childism: Confronting Prejudice Against Children* (Yale, 2012). In her final months, as general editor of the collected writings of D.W. Winnicott, she had formulated the framework for twelve volumes that will now be completed by others. Through all this burgeoning activity, she continuously maintained her blog, "Who's Afraid of Social Democracy?", in which she promoted clear thinking in the face of what she saw as breakdowns of authentic politics in America. The clinic and its contexts were never separate in her mind. Like psychoanalysis in the clinical setting, her exceptionally erudite, varied, and wide-ranging work was always meant to transform the traumatic ruptures of individual and collective experience into integrated histories meant to enable a more meaningful future.

Taken together, these papers both recapitulate and extend the central themes of EYB's writing at least since the publication of her acclaimed biography of Anna Freud in 1988: the types and consequences of traumatic experience in individual and group development; the ruptures and continuities in Freud's work and their ramifications through the history of psychoanalysis; the evolution of feminist thinking and practice and its impact on both psychoanalysis and the broader cultures in which psychoanalysis had been both an obstacle and an agent of change; the promotion of "cosmopolitan" thinking in the interest of expanding democracy and more inclusive understanding of potential human identities; the relentless exploration of the prejudices that constrain, undermine, or destroy the acceptance of differences that are the basis of all authentic relatedness. In every area of her interests, a central strategy was to convert singularities and unitary explanations into pluralities and complexities, which, given her love of etymologies, she imagined as interwoven or confused strands, complications to be disentangled, unfolded in lucid narration. To continue the etymological play, we could say that EYB makes con-fusions into pro-vocative stories, theoretical and social histories that aim to speak for her central values. In today's concern with the ethics and efficacy of psychoanalytic thinking, she occupies a central position.

The first chapter, "Why Psychoanalysis Has No History", grew out of the deliberations of a multidisciplinary group of psychoanalysts and academic intellectuals that EYB and I organised in New York. From our different perspectives, our group discussed the ways histories of psychoanalysts have been written, especially their ties to Freud's biography and the repeated and tendentious summaries of theories under the mantle of one subsequent charismatic leader or another, mirroring the fragmentation of the field, which today suffers a crisis of identity like the dissociated condition of a victim of cumulative trauma. We saw in all this writing little "historiographical consciousness", that is, critical awareness of how the history of psychoanalysis has been written or how it ought to be written, a curious lack, given the historical focus and self-reflective nature of clinical practice and the contemporary emphasis on countertransference. Our paper outlines a "trauma history", which for psychoanalysis as a discipline is not merely metaphorical but may prove deeply consequential for its survival, at least in American culture. Implicit in this history is a historiographical question: What now would be the conceptual and rhetorical organisation of a pro-motional, future-oriented history of psychoanalysis?

A crucial juncture in Freud's thinking, "the great missed opportunity of psychoanalysis", opens the second chapter. For EYB, Freud's abandonment in *Beyond the Pleasure Principle* (1920) of separate status for the "ego instincts", the "affectionate current", or drive for nurturing relatedness—not his misunderstood "abandonment" of the seduction theory in the etiology of hysteria—marks the greatest error in his thought. In her reading, the "trauma of lost love" came about when Freud demoted self-preservation, self-assertion, and mastery to the status of component instincts that would guide the organism toward death, rather than recognising that compulsions to repeat are manifestations of precisely these drives when they have been thwarted or defeated. In the "trauma" of this historic moment, as Michael Balint called it, Freud's later drive theory diverged from the evolution of the Budapest School in the 1930s, after Ferenczi's death. EYB traces a "developmental line" for the "affectionate current" from Imre Hermann to Balint and the British Independent Group, to John Bowlby's Attachment Theory and the contemporary Freudians at the Anna Freud Centre, and she broadens the reach of the concept by linking it to the "commonsense of the European *eros/philia* tradition" as well as the Japanese term for the expectation to be loved, *amae*. All of these developments address aspects of a drive for attachment, security, love, and relationship, which, though intertwined with sexuality, seeks its own fulfillment throughout the life cycle. In recognising these interconnections, EYB orients psychoanalysis toward a democratic therapeutic politics based on "nourishment (trepho)", and a culture of generative affiliations.

With Aristotle's idea of *eudaimonia*, harmoniousness, "a word which invokes that growth principle in people and in nature", as its background, EYB's third chapter develops a bold thesis, her answer to Freud's *Civilization and Its Discontents*. She argues that in the violent, catastrophically disruptive course of the twentieth century, humankind has indeed become unified, but ours is a unity based on "common terror, shared traumatization". We think compulsively about the "unthinkable" potentials for the human species—suicide, political imprisonment, ecological disaster—but "we cannot really confront [these traumas] or put the fragments of memory into an integrated narrative." Characteristically,

EYB develops a typology of social traumas, drawing on Anna Freud's "identification with the aggressor" and, especially, Masud Kahn's concept of "cumulative trauma". If group traumas can unify people, the price we pay is "social-relationship harm" and the transmission of trauma histories to future generations.

As always, EYB's thought works its way through a great range of cogent readings of historical and theoretical examples, illustrating how breaches of the protective social shield have come to be experienced and defined, if not healed. She then asks: "Can a negatively attained unity that interferes with thought grow into a thoughtfully *chosen* unity?" And her answer, as always, is that an effective "therapeutic consciousness" should emerge from the characteristic structure of the trauma responses that prevail in each group. In all traumatised groups, the past is alive in the present, and "any therapeutic approach has to take into account this continuous condition, and its various forms, which are linked to the predominance of a particular dimension of the trauma in a given individual or traumatised society." Ultimately, the social macrocosm can only be repaired in the microcosm of childhood experience. Only by recognising and overcoming the reproduction of identifications with the traumatisers can the hand that rocks the cradle become "the hand that heals the world", she concludes eloquently.

In the fourth chapter, EYB gives us a masterful review of the ways in which psychoanalysts have engaged struggles for social democracy in theory and practice throughout the twentieth century and into our own time. Few psychoanalytic writers could condense so much interdisciplinary knowledge into one well-aimed argument. Sifting European political thought into two broad camps—Hobbesians ("control theory") and Aristotelians ("therapeutic theory")—she summarises the complex transnational interactions between theoretical developments and their political, economic, and institutional contexts from Freud through the variations on the "Marx-Freud synthesis" (e.g., Reich, Fenichel, and, later, Marcuse) to the post-WWII emergence of "epigenetic" thinking such as Erikson's and the deeply influential writings of feminists, to the evolution of progressive (and, at times, regressive) public policies that address the conditions in which the "basic human drive for attachment and security, for relationship" can be fostered. Her reading of this history cuts through the opposition of drive and object-relational thinking, and illuminates the common thread that links the psychoanalytic mission to "Aristotelian" democratic ideals:

> It is a short trip from this elaboration of the ego instincts (without
> the name "ego instincts") to the idea that human beings cannot
> live well or happily in their families and communities or politi-
> cal arrangements unless these do not thwart their ego instincts;
> and to the idea that this simple truth should be the basis for social
> psychoanalysis and its synthesis with socialism.

To complete her argument, EYB turns once more to Freud's "Libidinal
Types" (1931)—hysterical, obsessional, and narcissistic character
structures—as her way of mapping the particulars of prejudices that
impede social reform. "Emphasising the function and purposes of prejudices for prejudiced persons is, to my mind, the key to prevention",
she writes.

Mapping prejudices (in the plural) had been EYB's preoccupation
since the publication of *The Anatomy of Prejudices* (1996), and the following chapter both summarises the history of prejudice studies and brings
her thinking up to date. Ranging from the pre-Socratics through modern Europe and America to Osama bin Laden and his deviation from
the traditions of Islamic tolerance, EYB recapitulates and illustrates
the character structures and defensive strategies that enact particular
prejudices in the social field. Exploring a contemporary global scene
made dauntingly complex by instant mass electronic communications
and unprecedented immigrations among societies and cultures, she
concludes her brief history by focusing on the charges directed at the
targets of prejudices. Her major contribution is to define the questions
we can ask to avoid oversimplification and to sharpen programs for
amelioration. Are the victims of racism, anti-Semitism, sexism, homophobias, or childism seen as intruders? Sexual threats? Defective person? Threats to gender conformity and identity maintenance?

As a group, the three chapters that follow could stand alone as a
cogent analysis of psychoanalytic theories of sexual categorisation and
gender diversity in the twentieth century. In "Reflections on Women
and Psychoanalysis", EYB adopts an historiographical stance, asking,
"how and why the history of theories has been constructed as it has".
As the prejudgments of the past have led now to questioning of the
very categories Man and Woman, in the course of a century we have
seen a transformation of Freud's question, "What do women want?"
into a "pluralisation of psychoanalytic concepts" in which development
to maturity becomes "a quilt of traits, not a static condition". Theories

that emphasise superiority and envy have met with "reversals", counter-arguments that resist the hierarchic dimension of differences. Theories that emphasise "sameness" support "disavowal", "denying differences that are experienced as traumatic". Of course, Freud has been enlisted for or against each position, as the controversies within the psychoanalytic movement have yielded gradually and unevenly to abandonment of orthodoxies regarding the vicissitudes of sexual and gender differences.

A crux of EYB's narrative is the fixation on penis envy and the "masculinity complex" that took hold after Freud's 1914 essay "On Narcissism," and Abraham's affirmation of this doctrine, after which "any clinical or political protest ... whether in the mode of reversal or in the mode of disavowal, could be dismissed as a form of penis envy or wounded narcissism." EYB folds a host of major texts and theorists into her historiographical argument, with Horney, the Budapest School, Balint, Spitz, and Mahler playing crucial roles, and the next decisive turning point within psychoanalysis comes with the ascendance of object relational thinking and the focus on the mother-child dyad, developments propelled by the forceful critiques by psychoanalytically oriented feminists in the 1970s. The question of sexual differences then shifted on its axis to what Winnicott called "the fear of WOMAN", the figure of ambivalent infantile dependency unconsciously harbored by both men and women. To know this deeper territory remains the challenge today.

The "paradigm shift away from binarism and towards thinking in continua" is the focus of "Sexual Diversity in Cosmopolitan Perspective". In a fluent survey that reaches back to St. Paul, Christian Rome, and the Qu'ran, EYB summarises the homophobic and sexist prejudices typical of the equation of sexual diversity with sexual pathology. As Western binary thinking gave way to tolerance for multisexuality (already accepted in some other cultures and at other times) in the last third of the twentieth century, the paradigm shift has gained momentum globally, though anti-minority prejudices tenaciously persist in the "defensive asceticism" of groups that utilise "extreme splitting" as a strategy for identity maintenance, and which condone rape, "misopaedia" (child hatred), and persecution of homosexuals. Globalisation has facilitated sexual violence of all sorts, but the scientific study of sex has now identified about seventy intersex syndromes, and "quality of relationship" has increasingly become the measure of "perversions", not deviation from patriarchal norms.

The opening of psychoanalysis to pluralistic views of charac-ter development was not a linear progress, however, and "Women and Children First!" begins with an account of the "Freud Wars" of the 1980s and 1990s, in which charges and countercharges regarding "recovered memories" and child abuse deflected progressive thought. Nevertheless, acceptance of the sex/gender distinction, the depatholo-gisation of homosexuality, the rise of trauma studies and neuroscientific knowledge, and evolutionary studies of the animal kingdom have all contributed to a wider context for both theorising and political action. EYB recounts the rising politics of "a third wave of feminism" that has brought abuses of women and children to global awareness, despite strong reactionary forces, and has created new forms of community and economic empowerment for women in many countries. She argues, provocatively, that the International Psychoanalytical Association (IPA) has failed to participate robustly in this process. "Neither psychoanaly-sis as a cluster of institutions or as a theory, not even as a revised and pluralised theory of female developmental types, has been affected by third-wave feminism."

"Ruling over is the opposite of acting together", EYB declares, and in concluding evokes the power of women's groups. Freed from the historical distractions of hierarchy and rivalry, women can act together toward realising a "group ideal" of equality of opportunity and reward. Following Hannah Arendt's insight that violence emerges from the loss of power, she affirms the promise of generative maternity to contain and channel women's aggression, "rather than turning violent or self-destructive". In proclaiming this vision, EYB is giving voice to the ideal she lived by throughout her long, creative career.

The final chapter is the most personal, a reflection on writing biog-raphies in general and the writing of her two famous biographies of Hannah Arendt and Anna Freud. Committed to the tradition of classi-cal biography, in which exemplary lives are a form of intellectual his-tory, EYB became increasingly aware of the ironies of the biographer's role, the "explicit effort to do the impossible". Lacking free associations and the transferential dimension of the consulting room, the biogra-pher must construct "an imagined person, an imaginary person", making creative use of her countertransferential self while remaining anchored in a documented past. In a moving paragraph, she describes the place of contact between Arendt's character and her own:

> To me, Arendt's longing for recognition and continuity, her willingness to be loyal if loyalty was shown her, even if imperfectly, as well as her strong wish for a disruption of love to be overcome or miraculously repaired, seemed perfectly familiar. I have experienced variations on these themes in myself ...

In writing the Anna Freud biography, EYB tells us that her struggle was with her relation to her potential readers: "I backed away, particularly, from the psychoanalytic community's homophobia," she writes, "not because I was directly inhibited by it or intimidated by it, but because I was afraid of how furious it made me." In both biographies, the character development of her subjects, her own growing character, and our characters as readers come into complicate play.

Like her precursors and teachers, Hannah Arendt and Anna Freud, in these papers EYB enhances her legacy as a consummate teacher in both academic and psychoanalytic settings. She take us on a comprehensive intellectual journey, a journey meant to educate us in the potential for human self-realisation and community by confronting the obstacles to self-recognition and progressive political action in their myriad forms. For her, the clinic was the place where we live, and the context the pressure of history, our human condition.

Murray M. Schwartz
Amherst, Massachusetts
September, 2012

CHAPTER ONE

Why psychoanalysis has no history*

Elisabeth Young-Bruehl and Murray Schwartz

Introduction

No one who is concerned with psychoanalysis as a theory, a practice, and a cluster of local, regional, and international educational and scientific institutions would dispute that psychoanalysis is, today, in a profound crisis. The most obvious symptom of this crisis is comparable to the symptom most studied by contemporary psychoanalytic investigators of trauma, that is, dissociative fragmentation, loss of identity. There are now many versions of psychoanalytic theory; practitioners with the most diverse sorts of training perform the "talking cure" in the most diverse ways; and many of psychoanalysis's institutions are unable to integrate themselves or operate as communities even after intensely discussing everything about themselves, starting with "What is psychoanalysis?" Psychoanalysis is also in a critical relationship with the diverse societies and cultures worldwide, where its work is performed and where it competes with other mental health specialties for patients, for resources, for scientific status and control of

---

* Delivered on March 18, 2008 as the Gardiner Lecture, Yale University; presented to the British Psychoanalytical Society, September, 2008; revised 2009.

1

disciplinary boundaries, and for recognition of its particular qualities and appreciation of its illustrious past, when it grew from a marginal, revolutionary theory and treatment into a main source of all modern mental health specialties. As with individual traumatic experiences, working through the dilemmas of contemporary psychoanalysis is a slow and complex process, mixing advances, retreats, and iatrogenic effects as the doctors try self-doctoring and doctoring of their field.

Psychoanalysis's fragmentation is, we want to argue, connected to its trauma history, which reached a key culmination point with the death of its founder and organising force, Freud, in 1939, on the eve of the Second World War and the Holocaust, which generated the diaspora of surviving psychoanalysts mostly to England and to the Americas—a geographical but also a communal fragmentation. Behind this trauma cluster lies a pre-disposition to traumatisation connected to the fact that psychoanalysis was, from its inception, built up out of deep disagreements and internal splits. Each time there was a split, a valuable part-theory disappeared from consideration, impoverishing psychoanalysis and distorting its development. At the very origin of psychoanalysis, Freud sharply disagreed with himself, precipitating a depressive reaction, and decided that actual seduction in childhood was not the sole cause of hysterical neurosis. He responded with his essential initial formulations about the Oedipus complex and the power of unconscious fantasy. But a split between concern for external traumas and concern for unconscious fantasy took place in Freud and in his followers, to the eventual relative neglect of external traumas. After that, there were multiple splits in the early group around Freud in Vienna: Alfred Adler, for example, left, taking very important theories about the ego instincts and about aggression with him; Jung departed, taking with him his concern with spirituality and symbols, and his interest in treating psychotics with the talking cure.

The first trauma that Freud himself acknowledged as such was the First World War, about which he said in his "Thoughts for the Times on War and Death" (1915b): "We cannot but feel that no event has destroyed so much that is precious in the common possessions of humanity, confused so many of the clearest intelligences, or so thoroughly debased what is highest." His own response was to cut off any consideration of the ego instincts, submerging them in the life instincts as of secondary importance to the sexual instinct, and to posit the death instinct as the antagonist to the life instincts. Once again, the ego instincts disappeared from view, and were not available for his thoughts about narcissism; and human beings became creatures endlessly, repetitively condemned to being at war within themselves and with each other. Most of Freud's followers found the death instinct theory traumatisingly bleak and rejected it, disavowed it, and left themselves unable to explain aggression and unable to tolerate Melanie Klein's fervent embrace of the death instinct as the elemental drive.

In the late 1920s came the crucial disagreement that Michael Balint described in *The Basic Fault* (1968), which was a reprise of Freud's internal disagreement over the seduction theory. "The historic event of the disagreement between Freud and Ferenczi [which] acted as a trauma on the psychoanalytic world" (p. 152), Balint argued, had arisen when Freud considered the theory and especially the technique developed by Freud's colleague, analysand, and friend Sandor Ferenczi to understand and treat adults who had been abused as children. (And when Ferenczi was marginalised within psychoanalysis, his interest in the ego instincts went with him as well.)

This multifaceted, cumulative trauma story and its post-war sequelae are, on one level, well known. But we do not think that psychoanalysis as a discipline has really—or not yet—generated a collective historical consciousness that comprehends it as such, as a trauma history, a repetitive pattern of splits and consequent distortions. We want to suggest in this paper that psychoanalysis is without a history of this sort—a trauma history, a history of reaction to trauma—but we also want to argue that it is without a history in a further sense. It is without history-writing that has grown out of historiographical consciousness, that is, out of a reflective and diagnostic process in which writers say, first, "*This* is the kind of history that psychoanalysis needs," and then go on to say, "These are the internal and external forces, values, and ideologies that have shaped the histories that have been written, generating different types and forms of storylines, about which someone trying to write a more reflectively conscious—and perhaps more psychoanalytic—history must be aware." By this standard, which most professional historians would assume, the existing histories of psychoanalysis are without reflection on the form and function of narratives; they do not really rise to the level of history in the fullest sense; they are various kinds of often tendentious fragments, like the history of psychoanalysis itself.

Writing about psychoanalysis: a brief history

Before we pursue our two-step claim that psychoanalysis has no trauma history and that it has no historiographical consciousness about what kind of history psychoanalysis needs, we want to construct a brief history of how psychoanalysis's history has been written, and to view that existing history-writing as itself symptomatic.

However, as a preface to this history of history-writing we want to offer a more elaborate description of historiographical consciousness—the kind of consciousness that we are going to work with, work in. We need first to note that every field of science and art (or, more broadly, every domain of culture) comes to a moment in its development when it has accumulated a history—that is, histories of it have been written or constructed in some medium—and those histories then become an object of reflection and critique. The sources, methods, and development of the histories, individually and collectively, become the object of historical enquiry and narrative; the field or discipline enters into a period of self-consciousness or group consciousness. In the discipline of history itself, the Western founding fathers, Herodotus and Thucydides, outlined the historiographical task, although it was not fully taken up until the Enlightenment. The fathers of history not only wrote history but made explicit their decisions about what kind of stories they were going to tell for what reasons. They were not going to write myths (*mythoi*), nor mere hearsay and anecdotes. Rather, they would make enquiries into causes and into the nature of things; they were going to collect the facts, but also reflect on how versions of what had really happened had been constructed and handed down before them. Thucydides, further, reflected on what it meant to be a contemporary historian, writing about events unfolding around him, and writing as what we would now call a participant observer.

"Historiography" eventually became (in the Enlightenment) not just another word for "history" or history-writing but a word specifically designating enquiry and narrative about history-writing. The late nineteenth century German historians living in the land of Kant's *Kritik* wrote "histories of history". Recently, the American historian Hayden White added the term "meta-history" to the lexicon to indicate his idea that historiography should also include in its scope reflection on historiography itself, not just enquiry into the first principles of a discipline (like "meta-physics") and the methods (he emphasised narrative methods and rhetorical strategies) by which the discipline has accumulated its knowledge or made its claims to knowledge. This second order self-reflective dimension—meta-meta-history—involves examination of the historical representations themselves as motivated choices.

A central historiographical question is: "How is the representation of the past shaped by the desires of the present?" In psychoanalytic terms, historiography seeks to explore a transferential dimension of historical construction: "How are present desires, which are influenced by past desires, constructing this history?" The question is not—or not only—a biographical one, about a specific historian; it is a more general cultural one about what kinds of desires and stories are fostered or permitted in a given time.

Now, if we turn to the history of psychoanalysis, we can imagine or construct certain moments of change and/or crisis in which historiographical reflection and critique might have come about. One such moment could be constructed around Freud's death in 1939, when his movement was left leaderless and still wrestling with the unresolved controversy with Ferenczi, who had died in 1932. But the start of war—an external trauma—eclipsed that moment, or left it to a poet, W. H. Auden, who gave the world a famous phrase as a marker for future reflection on what psychoanalysis had become: "a climate of opinion" (1940), Another moment can be marked in 1956, the 100th anniversary of Sigmund Freud's birth, which was celebrated with events and publications sponsored by psychoanalytic institutes and societies around the world. These celebrations were obviously affected by the appearance of Ernest Jones's monumental three volume biography *The Life and Work of Sigmund Freud* (1953–1957), the first biography to have been written with access to Freud's private papers and correspondence. Similarly the celebrations were affected by the appearance of James Strachey's English translation (1956–1974) of *The Standard Edition of the Complete Psychological Works of Sigmund Freud* (incorporating the earlier *Gesammelte Werke*), which contained a scholarly apparatus that, for the first time, made it possible for readers to see the complete works chronologically, developmentally, as a story of ideas unfolding, being explored, changing, evolving. The high degree of Freud's own critical self-consciousness—his own historiographical consciousness—was apparent for the first time in a commentary on his *Works*. Strachey can be seen as like an Averroes to an Aristotle.

With these milestone works available, psychoanalysts and scholars, including intellectual historians, began to contemplate Freud's life and work *as a whole*—they began to assess, interpret, reflect. It was in this period that Freud's entire work became the basis of broadly influential books like (in America) Norman O. Brown's *Life Against Death*

(1959), Philip Rieff's *Freud: The Mind of the Moralist* (1959), and Herbert Marcuse's *Eros and Civilization* (1962). These works and others like them, written by non-analysts, developed narratives of the internal evolution of Freud's thinking and its impact on twentieth-century Western culture. The alliance of Freud with the culture of the humanities was also advanced by works that followed in the footsteps of Lionel Trilling's *The Liberal Imagination* (1950). By the end of the 1950s, psychoanalysis began to have a history comparable to the histories of other disciplines in which a founding figure or figures have done the work of establishing the discipline (and sometimes of training the immediate successors); the discipline's key evolved concepts and techniques have become available to frame the history; and a reflective, historiographical dimension has grown up. (A moment in sociology could be noted comparatively: Auguste Comte had initiated the field, and then, with Max Weber, a flag had been planted on it as a modern field, historiographically conscious, and with a key text: "Science as a vocation".)

Psychoanalysis had, of course, been written about historically before the 1956 centenary moment. But, like everything else in psychoanalysis's history up until that moment, the history-writing had been completely dominated by Freud himself, and specifically by such texts of his as "On the History of the Psychoanalytical Movement" (1914d) and "An Autobiographical Study" (1925d). But the main history-writing method used by Freud and then by his early followers was what he came to call "psychobiography". That is, Freud had tried to psychoanalyse his own and his collaborators' psychological dispositions to theorise and practise in the ways they did. (Freud thus went further than Nietzsche, who had simply proclaimed that all philosophy is unconscious autobiography). Correlatively, psychobiography became the main psychoanalytic genre for writing both history and historiography, no matter whether the history was focused on intellectual and theoretical developments, rather than biography proper, or not. Even long after Freud's death, really until the late 1980s, the history of psychoanalysis was available predominantly in the medium of biographies—especially biographies of Freud himself, but, by the late 1980s, biographies of the second generation Freudians like Anna Freud and Melanie Klein as well. And this biographical mode correlated with the way in which psychoanalysis was handed down among psychoanalysts themselves—as a kind of oral tradition focused on relationships among analysts, on who analysed whom, on who agreed with whom or quarrelled with whom, who led and who followed in the various groups. Psychobiography was like a tribal history or a chronicle in which the stories of the chief and the chieftains dominated—like "the begats" in the Bible, but with psychoanalytic markers.

As we noted before, there was a brief period in the late 1950s and early 1960s in which some non-biographical historical works written with emergent historiographical consciousness appeared. For that moment, Jones's biography functioned as a memorial for Freud, a way of keeping him on after his death, and keeping his followers unified in their mourning for the larger than life figure of genius they found in the biography and in the *Standard Edition* with its apparatus. But at the same time Ernest Jones's work—particularly because it was so idealising—also provoked a vein of critical writing. The psychobiographical approach was adopted by the critics, as well, but in a mode that the philosopher Paul Ricoeur was to call "the school of suspicion" (1965).

During the 1960s, the critics of Freud began to generate controversy about how to view Freud. Not his greatness, but his detrimental effect on individuals—particularly women—and on cultures began to be stressed. Paul Roazen published *Freud and his Followers* (1975), a kind of multibiography emphasising the pathologies of Freud and the various Freudians. This critical, de-idealising development was contemporaneous with and related to the post-war history of psychoanalysis as a field of contending individuals and contending schools of thought, some of which were schismatic (that is, fully split off), but most of which stayed uneasily under the broad label "Freudian psychoanalysis", even if they had identifying designations of their own, like "Kleinian psychoanalysis". It was in this period of the late 1960s that the controversy over Lacan's "return to Freud" built up and then erupted in Paris, a controversy at the crossroads of institutional, clinical, and theoretical psychoanalysis.

Looking historiographically at the period after Jones's biography, we can summarise by positing that two dominant storylines about psychoanalysis developed. The first was the one laid down by Jones, and it featured a heroic Freud, complex but noble, whose views, although much contested from within the ranks of the early analysts, triumphed and achieved the status of foundational knowledge, needing development and elaboration but not, ultimately, revision. This story could reference the encyclopaedic compendium of psychoanalytic thinking to be found in every analyst's library, at least in North America, Otto

Fenichel's *The Psychoanalytic Theory of Neurosis* (1945); and it could offer as evidence of itself a great many synthetic ego-psychological works, especially Erik Erikson's (now almost unread) *Childhood and Society* (1950). This storyline served all the so-called "classical Freudians" who treated Freud's work as received wisdom. Freud did not die in this developmental line; the trauma of his death was disavowed. This was a story of expansion (of the sort envisaged by Erikson in his famous paper on Freud's specimen dream) and of struggle, but not of fragmentation.

The second storyline, developed by Freud's critics, including those like Eric Fromm who became known as neo-Freudians, was that Freud's authority, which was often called authoritarian, made it very difficult for fundamentally divergent knowledge claims to be heard, and the authors of those claims—chiefly Ferenczi, Klein, Fairbairn, Bowlby, and then later, Winnicott, Sullivan, and Kohut—remained marginal until groups of their followers were able to bring them forward. This second line has more recently been updated to indicate that each of the divergent authors (except Winnicott) was the font of a group or school until the collective influence of the divergent authors produced a paradigm shift within psychoanalysis, so that now all the schools can be heard, sometimes in discord and controversy, and sometimes—as in the so-called "relational" school—in accord or in a kind of amalgam. Also during this recent period, psychoanalysis extended its influence—always controversially—into a very broad range of humanities and social science disciplines, including literature, art history, history, philosophy, sociology, and anthropology, and some interactions arose between the non-medical academic teaching of psychoanalytic theories and the institutional training of analysts. In this critical storyline, Freud's death can be seen as an event that exposed all kinds of fault-lines and fissures. But this story is also not a "confusion of tongues", a fragmentation trauma story; it is something like a contested succession story, an Elizabethan history play about contending princes and princesses after the passing of a Richard or a Lear.

As we noted before, even in the post-Jones biography period, when these two storylines were developing, the main method of history-writing (and what little historiographical writing there was) remained what it had been all along: psychobiography. The appearance of many memoirs by analysts and many biographies of Freud's collaborators and critics reinforced this tendency. But, although nearly every article would begin with a little "review" of the history of psychoanalysis since Freud, there were very few intellectual or institutional histories, and, until quite recently, very few efforts to place psychoanalysis as an institution (or, in Freud's term, a movement) in a broader social, political, and cultural context, despite its profound influence on thinking in these areas. When the broader context was portrayed, it tended to be national, not international (with the rudimentary exception of Edith Kurzweil's *The Freudians* (1990)). Psychoanalytic centres had developed all over the world as the European analytic diaspora settled, particularly in England, America, and South America, but most histories of psychoanalysis were national histories; there is not yet a worldwide context or a "cosmopolitan intent" (in Kant's phrase) in the histories or historiography. Further, histories of psychoanalysis (still mostly in biographies of psychoanalysts) were written exclusively by analysts from the 1960s until the late 1970s, when the role of psychoanalysis in broader social, political, and cultural movements did finally begin to become a compelling topic for academic historians (seldom for analysts).

In academic circles in the Americas and Europe, the 1970s was a period of interdisciplinary flowering, when a variety of psychoanalytic theories were at play simultaneously. There was an open, exploratory dimension to the teaching of psychoanalyses (now plural), a kind of comparative psychoanalysis. For example, differing and conflicting theories of infancy were taught and evaluated in relation to one another. In general, during this period, there were marked differences between three approaches to psychoanalysis and its history: (1) the various orthodoxies of the training institutes, which were sometimes internally split; (2) the more "cosmopolitan" reception in segments of academia; and (3), most vociferously, the antagonisms that developed out of the tendency to criticise or attack Freud's character and motivations, which became the so-called "Freud Wars" in the late 1980s and 1990s. Academic efforts to evaluate the meaning, the importance, and the significance of psychoanalysis—and particularly of the key concept, the unconscious—in the broader context launched these Freud Wars, both within psychoanalysis and among those academic historians and critics who wrote about it. But the Freud Wars have hardly been more than a grand polemic over the person of Freud (as the war metaphor implies), not a discussion; and, as though calling out for psychobiography, they have been conducted by a large number of pseudo-scholars as well as by actual scholars. (The Freud Wars have yet to have their David Lodge, much less a mere historiographer.) Nevertheless, in cultures that had already become increasingly receptive to nosological and pharmacological approaches to mental disturbances, the Freud Wars contributed to the decline of psychoanalysis as both theory and practice. Where Freud had studied what Richard Wollheim called "the deafness of the mind", and the Freudian émigrés, survivors of catastrophes of the wartime, had dwelt in the darkest continents of the unconscious, the focus in other brands of therapy and theory was shifting to the more positive features of human development and less time-consuming technologies of symptom removal.

Reflections on this brief history in the current moment

In retrospect, the moment in the late 1950s when psychoanalysis might have begun to have a "normal" history and historiography, comparable to what other disciplines have produced as their founding figures have been succeeded, was probably too Freudian to be sustainable; that is, too under the still powerful influence of Freud and Jones's Freud and the tradition of psychobiography. Criticism, controversy, and struggle to win a hearing for voices other than Freud's finally swept the discipline, preoccupying both analysts and non-analyst historians (and contributing to the second storyline we described before). Histories of psychoanalytic theory frequently were constructed (often still in the medium of biography) to lead with a sense of necessity from Freud to the author's preferred new leader.

Psychoanalysis was not alone in this respect. Many disciplines began to undergo internal rifts and fissures in the 1960s, and the phenomenon was international in scope. Charismatic offerings by theoretical gurus swept academia, encouraging discipleship rather than openmindedness. Deconstruction and distrust of received opinion often led, ironically, to idealisation of new authorities. Unlike academia, however, psychoanalytic institutions often proved incapable of containing public dissent and diversity within their institutional structures; hence institutional as well as conceptual splittings began again—as they had in the 1920s—to impede a "normal" historiographical development.

It is interesting to compare what happened in the history of medicine after the 1960s. It was still being sustained worldwide by the huge launch it had been given in London, when Henry Wellcome established the Wellcome Institute in 1931 as—and this is crucial—simultaneously a historical and research library, a museum of medicine, a museum of human culture, and a current medical research foundation. In its multifunctionality, the Institute was the fullest definition of history incarnate, a model for other institutes. Further, after the 1960s it was directed by Roy Porter, who had a specialty in the history of medicine, but who was also a prolific historian in many cultural areas; a man who could connect the history of medicine to cultural history and to contemporary developments in historiography, and who could also connect the Wellcome Institute to more fractious university history departments all around the world. By contrast, psychoanalysis had the secretive Sigmund Freud Archives and, after Anna Freud's death in 1982, the Freud Museum in Hampstead, which was just that, a museum about Freud, a kind of psychobiography in many media, centred on the master's consulting room and his library and collection of antiquities. While popular culture was Hollywoodising Freud in every possible way, the Freud Museum was a shrine or a mecca for Freudians in the midst of a ramification of theories and techniques. It was deeply defensive, a shrine to fear of fragmentation.

Once psychoanalysis began its post-war fragmentation after the 1960s, the possibility that history and historiography of psychoanalysis might grow beyond Freud biography writing faded further and further as partisans appropriated the biography-dominated history of psychoanalysis to advance their schools. Then, as the institutional power of psychoanalysts peaked, and as the generation of analysts who fled Europe in the 1930s began to retire, the wars within psychoanalysis were caught up in, and in many ways overshadowed by, externally generated wars against psychoanalysis originating in social movements. These cast into question Freud's views on female psychology, on homosexuality, on aggression, and—most complicatedly, because the unresolved Freud/Ferenczi disagreement was involved—on childhood trauma and repressed memory. Historical study of Freud himself and of psychoanalysis came from within sociopolitical movements—from within Marxism, feminism, and the gay liberation movement, and later from within the academic disciplinary clusters, cultural studies and post-colonial studies. These "external" movements and their historians were mostly antagonistic. However, they also generated a great number of new and revised views within psychoanalytic circles. (Splitting can be a generative process as well as a defensive one.) At the same time, both the antagonistic and positive effects of these movements made it more difficult to discern the boundaries of psychoanalysis. The "traumatic" process was ironic: it overwhelmed the sense of coherence while simultaneously opening avenues of growth.

Only in the late 1990s, after the external wars against psychoanalysis had subsided—having had enormous and in some respects progressive reforming impact upon both theory and practice in all the various schools of psychoanalysis—did there open up another moment in which a historiography of psychoanalysis could flourish. This moment, the current moment, which is also, not coincidentally, an extremely rich moment in the history of historiography, could be described as one in which the Jones story featuring Freud the invincible authority has completely ended—Freud has really died—but so has the polemically critical counter-story of the pathological and harmful Freud. Theoretical and practical pluralism has established the revisionary paradigms. However, these paradigms can be outlined in terms of what they have rejected of Freudianism more easily than they can in their own terms, which are an orchestration (more or less harmonious in different judgments) of the once marginalised or sidestage theoreticians' views.

In the last decade psychoanalytic history-writing and historiography (aided by the derestricting of the documents that had been gathering in the Sigmund Freud Archives since the 1950s) have begun to emerge from their long period of domination by biography, and then of internal partisanship and external embattlement. This has happened not only in one-volume histories of psychoanalysis like (non-analyst) Eli Zaretsky's *Secrets of the Soul* (2004), by far the most historiographically conscious history to date, but in societies for the history of psychoanalysis like the International Association for the History of Psychoanalysis (Paris), journals for the history of psychoanalysis, and exhibitions (both in the museums specifically dedicated to psychoanalysis in Vienna and London and in the Library of Congress), especially around the 2006 celebration of the 150th anniversary of Freud's birth. For the fifty years between 1956 and 2006, psychoanalysis really had no history in the full sense we have been trying to describe, but it is possible that the conditions are now right again.

One of the most obvious signs of this shift is that so much of the historical work is now being done by non-analysts, that is, by historians who approach psychoanalysis as a field, as a cultural phenomenon, as a theory and a clinical practice (or a group of theories and practices) that have had a defining impact on modern life in much of the world.

That is not to say that such events as the acrimonious controversy that broke out over (and influenced the final form of) the Library of Congress exhibition "Sigmund Freud: Conflict and Culture" are now anomalous. Historical study of Freud and psychoanalysis is still fraught with controversy. But this controversy, although it retains unique features, is at least comparable to the kinds of controversy that are to be found in the historical study of other disciplines (even though no other discipline has had a history comparably organised around a cumulative trauma). This normalising trend in psychoanalytic historiography means—very importantly—that it is now possible to ask questions about what light the history of psychoanalysis can shed on current developments in psychoanalysis and on the relations psychoanalysis has both with other fields and disciplines and with social issues and world contexts.

A story of cumulative trauma

Moving from period to period, from the 1950s to the 1960s and 1970s and then the 1980s and 1990s, we have been constructing a brief history of writing about psychoanalysis's history. Into this history, we have woven strands suggesting that psychoanalysis and historical writing about it were both shaped crucially by the early schisms within psychoanalysis, by Freud's death, and then the diaspora of European psychoanalysis, a trauma history which precipitated a fragmentation or dissociation. We have noted how psychoanalysts have tried to master that trauma with story-telling, history-writing, at certain moments with a degree of historiographical consciousness. But, we noted, psychoanalytic history-writing kept regressing into biography writing, memorialising or criticising Freud himself, not the science, and we offered the judgment that even the more historiographically conscious history-writing of the last few years has not yet made psychoanalysis a discipline with a history, comparable to other scientific disciplines in this respect (although not with respect to the traumatic content of the history, because, as we noted, no other discipline was traumatised by dissension, death, and loss in the way that psychoanalysis was). It is our assumption, as we said at the outset, that psychoanalysis needs, like a traumatised individual, to be able to tell reflectively the story of the group trauma. That is, like a curative personal narrative (or a curative analytic process) this reflective story would involve both telling what happened and reflecting upon how the telling is being done and what it means for the tellers and in the wider world. In psychoanalysis's own terms, it needs to be both analytic (psychoanalytic) and synthetic.

Now, to be historiographically conscious in the way we have been recommending and saying is normal among historians and historians of other disciplines. We should be able to say why we think that the as yet unwritten history of psychoanalysis should be a reflective trauma story and why it makes sense to speak of group processes in the traumatisation terms that have been developed for individuals. After all, the people and events of psychoanalysis's past could be shaped into another kind of story, another narrative—as we are saying they have been.

First, we see the need for a trauma history in the shared symptoms of psychoanalysts, by which we mean something simple: psychoanalysts around the world, but particularly in Europe and in the Americas, North and South, where European émigré psychoanalysts founded colony-like institutions after the Second World War, now routinely speak of their profession as one in search of an identity—or as multiple professions in search of an author. Their stories are not usually written, they are much more frequently present in conference speeches, the platforms of candidates running for psychoanalytic offices, and online discussions. Our sense (as participant observers) is that these stories come in basically three varieties or variations, each a continuation of the critical second storyline we described before, the one that variously acknowledges the plurality in psychoanalysis. Further, our sense is that the shared stories are the unifying stories of three groups or three types within psychoanalysis, but these are not institutionalised groups; the groups exist more or less influentially in each institution, and they are defined most obviously by shared character type or characterologically rooted affinities for types of group. None of the pluralism storyline variations *explicitly* acknowledges the traumatic loss of the great leader or the traumatic losses of the diaspora colonies—losses of life and losses of home and culture—but they are not understandable without this submerged reference

The first of these three commonly heard stories reflects a stance that is depressive. Psychoanalysts drawn to this story acknowledge the fragmentation of their discipline but, rather than look for its cause, they throw up their hands, convinced that Humpty-Dumpty will never be put back together again, even if there were kings and horses and not just well-intentioned but undistinguished foot soldiers to come to his rescue. The past, unexplored or even explored to a degree, simply looms like a ghost or an intruder, often representing Freud or another great contributor. All the great contributors, like the great founder, are gone, and publishing is now all full of sound and fury signifying nothing. This was the theme that recurred insistently in last year's online discussion with the psychoanalytic publisher Paul Stepansky, to give an example.

A second stance, which is manic, generates a forward-looking, optimistic story, again without an explanatory past: out of chaos, a new paradigm will certainly come, either a new unifying idea or a clear common ground. Some people of this persuasion will go so far as to announce that the redemptive new psychoanalysis is at hand: object relations theory or attachment theory will embrace all disparate strands; or psychoanalysis will make an alliance with neuroscience that will, finally, dispel any charge that the polyglot psychoanalysis is not scientific. To cite an example, Joseph Schwartz in his *Cassandra's Daughter* (1999) is a psychoanalyst historian in this vein, who celebrates the triumph of relational psychoanalysis, of which he is a partisan.

Finally, a kind of middle way position, cautious and sometimes obsessional, embraces diversity and tells a very present-oriented story of groups in dialogue, meetings, fruitful pluralism. People of this inclination organise case conferences, for example, in which clinicians of different orientations or schools all comment on a single case, or they plan issues of their journals in which a variety of perspectives is represented. From the work of Fred Pine, embracing diversity (e.g., 1998), through Lewis Kirshner's more recent *Having a Life: Self Pathology After Lacan* (2004), efforts to negotiate and translate differences have seemed to lose more in power of revelation than they have gained; even when careful attempts at "translation" between and among different psychoanalytic conceptual vocabularies are offered, they have not generated a large following. For practical as well as more deeply rooted psychic reasons, most analysts adhere to and continue the orientation of a local group or subgroup, at least in public. It is difficult for clinicians who do not identify with an orientation to have a presence in such an identity-typed world; they are like stateless people. Few can be what Donald Winnicott was clinically, a loner who never became the source of a school, although his influence, after some decades, pervaded many schools; and even fewer can be what Hans Loewald was theoretically, a pluralist who specifically focused on the tensions in psychoanalytic theory with a synthetic intent. But both Winnicott and Loewald, in their quite different ways, demonstrate the power of being a pariah in a world dominated by parvenus and negotiators.

We view these three modes as symptomatic, as defences against recognising the traumatic past or reliving it in acknowledging it. They all insist that some key feature of Freud's legacy must be discarded—and thus they repeat the trauma of splitting and dissociation that has marked psychoanalysis as it banished split off theories. Among the depressives who think that the current fragmentation is unhealable, who do not think that any integration is possible, it is Freud's structural theory and his notion of the ego as a synthesiser that must be abandoned—and with it everything that is known as ego psychology. Lacan, for example, set himself up as the great critic of ego psychology and the one who could endure psychoanalytic life without any of the stultifying reifications of ego psychological theory or technique, without synthesis. Interestingly, it is the Lacanians who most oppose the notion of adaptation that ego psychology promoted, for they think that adaptation must result in stultifying conformity.

Among those hoping that the object relations tradition, in its British beginnings or in its American development, perhaps in combination with attachment theory, will be the new paradigm or the new common ground, it is Freud's instinct theory that must be discarded, as Stephen Mitchell insisted so forcefully (and argued as a historian in *Freud and Beyond* (1996), which he co-authored with Margaret Black). An implicit antithesis prevails: either instinct theory or an object relations theory. Either there is a "one person" therapeutic situation in which the analyst analyses conflicts between the instincts and the defences or there is a "two person" therapeutic situation in which the focus is on the relationship of the analyst and the analysand. Thinking in terms of an *ancien regime* that must be overthrown requires, for its forward thrust, a basic old/new duality—and the instinct theory is the old. For theorists of this type, Ferenczi, even though he subscribed to Freud's instinct theory and developed it in his own way, is the most important theorist of Freud's generation because he stressed object relations and real world experiences, particularly of trauma.

Among those who promote pluralism—those who are eclectics or who, above all, want the voices of each school to be heard—what must be discarded is Freud's focus on the Oedipus complex as the nucleus of the neuroses, for this blocks out the basic orientations of the Kleinians, the self psychologists, the object relations theorists of different sorts, the attachment theorists, all of whom focus on the pre-Oedipal.

And the Oedipus complex, a story about rivalries, a story about parricide, also brings to the fore rivalries among schools, and that makes it quite problematic to argue for the vision of a triumphant theory or even a common ground.

Concluding remarks

Each of the three positions we have been sketching has generated a certain degree of historiographical consciousness. But, we have been suggesting, the appearance of these positions, and the attractions of them, has not been analysed. We are, of course, assuming that such an analysis should be psychoanalytical, and connected to the psychoanalytical analysis of psychoanalysis's traumatic history. But, by that, we do not mean that psychobiography should be the mode of analysis, because we are describing group or shared images of psychoanalysis and its history, and to analyse group consciousness a psychoanalysis of groups is required. As with everything else in psychoanalysis, Freud gave the original impetus for this requirement with his *Group Psychology and the Analysis of the Ego* (1921c), a text that reached for generalities about the father-son, intragenerational, Oedipal dynamics of *all* groups. We, by contrast, think of group dynamics in more characterological terms, assuming that there are fundamentally different dynamics operating in different characters and in groups of different characters (that is, groups in which different character types dominate and determine the dynamics of the group).

But it has not been the purpose of this chapter to suggest how the three positions we have sketched and constructed as responses to a trauma history, which reflect that history, can be worked through (in a process that would have features in common with the working through in an individual analysis). Nor has it been our purpose to develop the history we are imagining or to explore the theory that would be needed for its elaboration—although we have called historiographical consciousness to the task, and to the aid of psychoanalysis itself. But we do want to suggest, in closing, that there is also something that psychoanalysis can give historiography: perhaps the most profound contribution that psychoanalysis can make to historiography lies in its recognition of the inevitable investment we make in any construction of the past, and the interminable process of becoming conscious of the structure and purposes of that investment. In this respect, psychoanalysis is potentially the most historiographical of disciplines.

References

Auden, W. H. (1940). *In Memory of Sigmund Freud*. In: *Another Time*. New York: Random House.

Balint, M. (1968). *The Basic Fault*. New York: Brunner/Mazel.

Brown, N. O. (1959). *Life Against Death*. Middletown, CT: Wesleyan University Press.

Erikson, E. (1950). *Childhood and Society*. New York: W. W. Norton.

Fenichel, O. (1945). *The Psychoanalytic Theory of Neurosis*. New York: W. W. Norton.

Freud, S. (1914d). On the history of the psychoanalytical movement. *S. E. 14*. London: Hogarth.

Freud, S. (1915b). Thoughts for the times on war and death. *S. E. 14*. London: Hogarth.

Freud, S. (1921c). *Group Psychology and the Analysis of the Ego. S. E. 18*. London: Hogarth.

Freud, S. (1925d). An autobiographical study. *S. E. 20*. London: Hogarth.

Jones, E. (1953–1957). *The Life and Work of Sigmund Freud*. New York: Basic.

Kirshner, L. A. (2004). *Having a Life: Self Pathology After Lacan*. London: Routledge.

Kurzweil, E. (1990). *The Freudians: A Comparative Perspective*. New Haven, CT: Yale University Press.

Marcuse, H. (1962). *Eros and Civilization*. New York: Vintage.

Mitchell, S. A., & Black, M. J. (1996). *Freud and Beyond*. New York: Basic.

Pine, F. (1998). *Diversity and Direction in Psychoanalytic Technique*. New Haven, CT: Yale University Press.

Ricoeur, P. (1965). *Freud and Philosophy: An Essay on Interpretation*. D. Savage (Trans.). New Haven: Yale University Press, 1970.

Rieff, P. (1959). *Freud: The Mind of the Moralist*. New York: Viking.

Roazen, P. (1975). *Freud and his Followers*. New York: Knopf.

Schwartz, J. (1999). *Cassandra's Daughter*. London: Allen Lane.

Trilling, L. (1950). *The Liberal Imagination*. New York: Viking.

Zaretsky, E. (2004). *Secrets of the Soul*. New York: Knopf.

CHAPTER TWO

The trauma of lost love in psychoanalysis

Most historians agree that in the history of psychoanalysis Freud's *Beyond the Pleasure Principle* (1920g) marks a juncture, even perhaps *the* juncture. Until 1920, no one could be a Freudian without subscribing to his libido theory—in its evolving formulation—and to the centrality of the sexual instinctual drive in the aetiology of the neuroses. Non-subscribers left the movement. Adler's and Jung's withdrawals became like traumas that Freud kept trying to master in writing about them. But in *Beyond the Pleasure Principle*, Freud himself brought into question the defining position of the libido theory. He disagreed with himself, and the disagreements his internal debate provoked among his followers have, to this day, not ceased reverberating. But, because the master's revision was so problematic, and got no less so as he elaborated his new theory in some later works while rejecting it in others, his followers have felt free to disagree without needing to become schismatics. *Beyond the Pleasure Principle* was more a statement of intense theoretical need than a diktat.

To me, the text seems like the great missed opportunity of psychoanalysis, a moment when an elementary form of love—long known and named—might have been described in dynamic psychoanalytic terms: it might have been shown to have a developmental course, growing to be foundational for mature human relations and political life. To make this argument briefly, I am going to pay particular attention to how this form of love slipped away, became nameless, as Freud proposed his startling hypothesis that there is a "death instinct" in all humans and, indeed, in all nature—a hypothesis of *Naturphilosophie*, not a psycho-analytic hypothesis.

* * *

Let me begin with a few remarks explicating the text's overdetermined title: *Jenseits des Lustprinzips*. All the psychoanalysts who read Freud's *Beyond the Pleasure Principle* in 1920 were familiar with his (1911b) paper called "Formulations on the Two Principles of Mental Functioning". They knew Freud's claim that the *Lustprinzip* operates on a newborn's sexual drive or libido with few constraints as long as the newborn is cared for. That is, the well-cared-for newborn's sexual drive produces tensions and excitations which the newborn can discharge unconstrain-edly, with libidinal *wishes*—hallucinations—attached to memories of pleasures past. By contrast, there are drives, like the prototypical drive hunger, that cannot be satisfied for more than a brief while with a wish but are dependent for their satisfaction on real food, a real breast, a real carer's responsiveness to baby communications. These drives are more governed by a second *Prinzip*, called the *Realitätprinzip*. The sexual drive always retains some of its initial capacity to be satisfied, so to speak, "beyond [or before] the *reality* principle"—or to be satisfied by phan-tasy. Libido's initial manifestations are like a tribe living without any constitution, and its later manifestations may be like anarchists who hark back to the state of nature and reject constitutions as constraints.

The self-preservative drives need reality from the start (as Ferenczi pointed out, even *in utero* they need the reality of the mother's whole body's functioning) and thus they come to adapt more to reality at every stage of the child's life; they become tamed by reality, educated to work with it, to postpone satisfaction while real (or perhaps better) satisfactions can be found. These drives were called by Freud the ego instincts because they preserve the baby's developing "I" (as well as its life) and because the developing ego allies with the reality principle to satisfy the ego instincts (and the sexual drive, too) in a progressively more "civilised" way, using thought, judgment, imagination, and, ulti-mately, scientific reasoning. The self-preservative drives, and the ego, can come, thus, into conflict with the phantasy-prone sexual drive, and then the ego becomes the director of repression of the sexual drive and its phantasy objects. In *Beyond the Pleasure Principle* Freud invokes this opposition and remarks (p. 10) that the *Realitätprinzip* is "under the influence of the ego's instincts of self-preservation". But that is all that Freud says about the ego instincts in the opening pages of *Beyond the Pleasure Principle*—thus missing the opportunity to keep them in his view and in psychoanalysis.

His 1911 theoretical picture of two basic drives—libidinal and ego instinctual—and two basic governing principles was quite clear and unproblematic to Freud, although he had ended his summary statement with a host of questions that needed exploring. His theoretical house seemed in order and consistent with what he had been thinking for years, frequently announcing his agreement with the poet Schiller, and with the great Darwin, and with common psychological sense and language since the Greeks. Human beings are ultimately moved by sex and hunger, that is, by a sexual instinct that eventually leads them as they mature to reproduce (to preserve the species) *and* by an instinct that moves them to preserve themselves—initially, to satisfy their hunger, but also to live in safety, security, with healthy functioning of all organs, in a state of well-cared-for-ness or psychic holding. Crucially, Freud acknowledged that self-preservation requires the affection or love or socialisation of real (not phantasy) preserving carers, that is, it is a relational drive. Human beings are, as Aristotle had said long before, *by nature* sociable and desiring to live together in polities. Affection cannot be obtained by a baby from a hallucination, or from a wire mother with a bottle, as Harlow's little experimental monkeys knew; it cannot even be satisfied—as Ferenczi's pupil René Spitz (1945) showed experimentally—by a well-intentioned hospital nurse with a bottle who shows no warmth or affection for her baby charge and thus causes the baby to suffer from and even die of what he termed "hospitalism".

In the early editions of "Three Essays on the Theory of Sexuality" (1905d), Freud had declared that the libidinal energy in children should be called "the sensual current" and the self-preservative drive energies should be called, collectively, "the affectionate current". Similarly, he distinguished sensuality—*Sinnlichkeit*—from tenderness or affection—*Zartlichkeit*. Both currents of desire have as their first object the maternal breast, but when a baby is nursing, the affectionate current leads the way and the sensual current leans upon it (or is "anaclitic" on it). The breast is the "anaclitic" object, *Anhanglungsobjekt*, literally the object leaned upon, depended upon, by the affectionate desire, because the baby cannot survive without the breast (or as Freud would later stress, because the baby is helpless without it). Winnicott put the matter more wittily by saying "There is no such thing as a baby"—there is only a baby-and-mother. For the sexual instinct the breast is an erotic object, pleasurable but not essential to life.

As a child develops, Freud argued, the sexual instinctual drive (the sensual current), at first so strong in the mouth, concentrates in the site of the anus, then in the genitals. But he did not note a corresponding stage development or site-specificity for the self-preservative drives, although he sometimes associated a self-preservative drive with each of the major bodily organs. Generally, he left these drives very little explored once he had described their satisfaction as getting physiological needs met and getting affection.[1] Crucially, Freud did not explore an object relational line of development for the affectionate current, even though he had said clearly that it is object-related before the sensual current is.

When Freud wrote about sex and hunger, he always interpreted sex very broadly, using the Greek word *eros*, as the qualitative dimension for what he would describe quantitatively as tension reduction. But he never assigned hunger a general name comparable to *eros*—although such a word was available in ancient Greek, where *eros* was always contrasted to but entwined with *philia*, affection or love of the sort that exists first between parents and children, but later between children and mentors, between friends who care for each other, citizens who appear before each other in councils and are bound by respect or *philia politike*, and so forth. *Philia* refers to all bonds without which humans do not survive or do not survive *as humans*.[2] In all the European languages with which Freud was familiar it is very obvious that a distinction between libidinal desire and needs that require loving care is registered as fundamental. Further, that lexical line separates desire—chiefly sexual desire—which you must actively reach out to satisfy (even if only to touch your own body) or go after, from desire which is satisfied by taking in or binding to yourself and which originally came *to you* in your helpless, dependent infant state. It is from the taking in or binding desire that the higher capacities of people in their relations with each other derive. The two forms of desire are analogised with words like "appetite", which you can have for sex as well as for food, but the satisfactions are understood to be quite different. *Eros* and *philia*, desire directed actively outward and desire directed inward (as incorporative, receptive), are in non-technical German *Begierde* (*sinnliche*) and *Wunsch*, in Italian *concupiscenza* and *desiderio*, in Spanish *lujuria* and *deseo*. These distinctions are like the one in English between lust and desire, where lust indicates acquisitive sexual desire (and also inordinate activity, avidity, greed) and desire is closer to need.

But, even though Freud's first instinctual drive theory had the virtues of clarity and simplicity, the weight of poetic and scientific authority, and the wisdom of common speech to recommend it, he renovated it. The period of Freud's thought between 1911 and 1920 can be characterised in many ways, but for the argument I am making here it is most important to note that this is the period in which the self-preservative instinctual drives were unexplored, then marginalised, and finally redefined into unimportance. From 1911 to 1920, Freud's attention was on the emergent ego as intently as it had been, until then, on the sexual drive, and, even more, it was on the relationship of the ego and the sexual drive (not the self-preservative ones). His burning question was how does the ego form (and also deform) and grow *in relation to the sexual drive*? This striking de-emphasis on the self-preservative drives came just after Freud had geared up to defend his libido theory against Adler, who had been very concerned with the ego instincts (which he thought included an aggressive drive), and just as he was beginning to realise that he had to get ready to argue with Jung, who thought (monistically) that there was but one type of energy moving human beings. The Jungian single energy was not specifically sexual—indeed, it was more self-preservative, more affectional (even though Jung had the impertinence to call it "libidinal"). It may well be that Freud (consciously or unconsciously) steered away from the ego instinctual drive territory where he thought his opponents had set up their theoretical camps in order to attack his libido theory. They seemed more concerned theoretically with security (or, in Adler's case, insecurity) and social power than with sex.

As he realised that he and Jung had substantial and potentially irreconcilable differences, Freud was also very concerned to clarify his own thinking about obsessiveness and particularly about psychosis, that is, about ego distortion and pathology, Jung's specialty. So it was his work on Schreber (1911c) that led Freud to the hugely consequential work "On Narcissism" (1914c). This paper is too complex to go into in detail here, but for my purposes its final declaration that there are but two kinds of love is the nub. Freud described the sexual drive, under the direction of the ego, as going to objects and hanging on them, that is, as directed towards the "anaclitic object" (which, of course, had once been the ego instinctual drive's object). And he described the sexual drive (not the ego instinctual) as directed towards the ego itself, both in the ego's initial emergent state ("primary narcissism") and in later states subsequent to the sexual drive having gone out towards an ana-clitic object and then retreated, either unable to hang there or suffering a loss of the object. The ego has either anaclitic objects or a narcissistic object (itself). In a normal developmental course, the child grows from narcissistic love to love of another. If the normal child must retreat into narcissistic love after a loss, it can do so without "narcissistic neurosis" (which basically means that it manages to master its loss of an object and is able to go forth again to love others, not getting stuck in patho-logical mourning but being strengthened by reinvesting its salvaged libidinal investment in its ego).[3]

After 1914, when Freud had added to his theoretical edifice these ideas about normal primary narcissism and psychotic retreat into narcis-sism, he offered a crucial redefinition of the self-preservative "affection-ate current". In his last revision of the "Three Essays", the affectionate current lost its distinctiveness from the sensual current and changed into inhibited *sexual* desire. It became sexual desire that cannot proceed to full object love but remains fixed in self-investment or retreats to narcissistic love of the self. The theory of narcissism really erased the independence and the importance of the self-preservative drive as it demoted affectionate love to a kind of narcissism. The new develop-mental theory (from primary narcissism to object love) then required a slight renovation or development of the *Lustprinzip*: auto-erotic tension reduction normally gives way developmentally to alter-erotic tension reduction (and this vastly increased the pathological significance of masturbation and of the perversions, which fall short of alter-erotic ten-sion reduction). The helpless newborn baby's need for, search for, and reception of sustenance and affection in relation to its caregivers (partic-ularly the mother) was replaced by primary narcissism conceived of as an explanation for the newborn's search for pleasure in auto-eroticism, which requires no dependency, no other, no mother. There is such a thing as a baby, alone.

So, when Freud came in 1920 to looking "beyond the pleasure prin-ciple", it was hardly to be expected that he would find a new version of the old ideas that had been demolished during the years when he was extending and broadening in every way that he could his "libido theory", his postulation of the omni-causality and centrality of the sexual instinct, in general and in the development of the ego. Freud was not going to return to or reconsider or rebuild the old idea that there are two instincts, sex and hunger, particularly as such a return might have weakened his ability to distinguish his theory from Adler's or Jung's. And, besides, the self-preservative instincts were not at all what Freud thought he needed in order to deal with the pieces of evidence he catalogued in *Beyond the Pleasure Principle*, claiming that they did not fit with even the revised *Lustprinzip* postulation. Apparently, it did not occur to him that the pieces of evidence he was cataloguing were without a theoretical place because he had been so busy demolishing their place—the self-preservative instinct theory.

* * *

Let me turn now to the pieces of evidence. They are of different sorts, but all have in common that they involve repetition—what Freud called "the compulsion to repeat"—of painful activities, some of which do finally end in pleasurable relief, but some of which bring discharge but no relief, and some of which bring only perpetual pain. He noted that children play games in which they repeat actions, over and over. This seems to have the function of allowing them (usually) to cope with or master loss, particularly separation from the mother (in the instance of the "fort-da" game he describes in detail). Then Freud noted that people who suffer traumatic injuries, as well as soldiers who suffer from war neurosis (where no physical injury is involved), dream repeatedly of their traumas—seldom to any relief. In psychoanalytic treatments, he adds, returning to a feature he had noted in his papers on technique, neither interpreting the content of patients' free associations nor analysing their resistances to interpretations brings about a cure. Cure must arise from allowing the patient to repeat in the analytic situation their childhood experiences of defeat, loss, rivalry with parents or siblings, or failure to fulfil their wishes because of physical immaturity or prohibitions. Repetition of painful childhood experiences takes place in treatment and with the analyst (where it is called the "transference neurosis"), but it also takes place in the lives of some normal people, who "give the impression of being pursued by a malignant fate or possessed by some 'daemonic' power" (1920g, p. 21). They have a character trait or formation that produces repetitive patterning or "perpetual recurrence of the same thing" (p. 22).

Every analyst knows that compulsive repetition is evident in every treatment, crucially, and is everywhere in people's lives (and, many would say, as Freud himself later did, in the collective lives of groups). The quarrel over *Beyond the Pleasure Principle* that began in 1920 and continues is not over the commonness of the repetition compulsion or its paramount significance, but over the explanation. For Freud, the phenomenon points to the limits of the *Lustprinzip*, which cannot regulate and reduce the tension these games and dreams and enactments are themselves trying to contain or master. The *Lustprinzip* cannot, as Freud puts it, "bind" the energy—so far unnamed—that *must* be invidiously active in these activities, which have run unchecked, he suggests, because the precipitating traumas have broken through the mind's "protective barrier" against shocking stimulation and overstimulation. The traumas have, so to speak, returned the mind to formlessness and void, like pre-life. The mind has to be somewhat regulated, somewhat constant, before it can carry through the process of finding peace and quiet; internal chaos cannot bring about the end of chaos produced by trauma or returned to in trauma. So these traumas must release an instinctual drive lying deep in the mind, there *before* the *Lustprinzip*.

At this point in the argument, Freud of the first instinct theory might have been able to say: what is released by a trauma is the self-preservative drive, screaming, so to speak, "Let me live! Help me! Take me in your arms!" But that is not the step Freud took in 1920. Rather he took one that caused the trauma to the psychoanalytic community that it has been repeating compulsively ever since.

His thoughts about traumatic breakthrough had been propelled by the question: if the compulsion to repeat can override the *Lustprinzip* ("to which, after all, we have hitherto ascribed dominance over the course of the processes of excitation in mental life" (p. 23)), does that not mean that this compulsion is "more primitive, more elementary, more instinctual than the pleasure principle which it over-rides"? Freud then asks (p. 36): "But how is the predicate of being 'instinctual' related to the compulsion to repeat?" His next, fateful, cluster of questions was: Does the compulsion to repeat express an instinctual drive towards an earlier state of things, towards a state of dissolution, breakdown—ultimately, towards death? Does it express an inertia inherent in organic life? And might this instinctual drive towards dissolution even have brought the ego into being in the first place—that is, might the ego have grown up to try to control this dissolving energy (not to try to preserve itself by getting love and care)?

A fragile ego trying to control this dissolving energy would have to have its own energy, of course, and that would, of course, have to be an energy of binding and building up. Such an energy would have to be, Freud argued, none other than the sexual instinctual drive, the species preservative drive that eventually brings sperm to ovum, creating new life. Eros. So Eros, which had once been the source of disruption in the psychic economy, the source of ego pathology, because it resisted the reality principle and maintained its phantasy-proneness following the *Lustprinzip*, becomes now the redemptive force of binding, unification, building up (on its eventual way to reproduction).[4]

The biological speculations and reviews of contemporary biologists' speculations that Freud offered as he took up his questions and began to construct his theory of "the death instinct" (later to be called Thanatos in contrast to Eros) are not, I think, of great interest now. What seems to me most important in the theory construction is the act of demolition required to make way for it. Specifically, the self-preservative instincts, long under threat of theoretical superfluity, had to be completely broken up and recycled. Remarkably, they do not appear with Eros as forces of binding and building up, but as forces that serve the death instinct! Freud himself seemed shocked at this strange development:

> The hypothesis of self-preservative instincts, such as we attribute to all living beings, stands in marked opposition to the idea that instinctual life as a whole serves to bring about death. Seen in this light, the theoretical importance of the instincts of self-preservation, of self-assertion and of mastery greatly diminishes. They are component instincts whose function it is to assure that the organism shall follow its own path to death, and to ward of any possible ways of returning to inorganic existence other than those which are immanent in the organism itself. We have no longer to reckon with the organism's puzzling determination (so hard to fit into any context) to maintain its own existence in the face of every obstacle. What we are left with is the fact that the organism wishes to die only in its own fashion. Thus these guardians of life, too, were originally the myrmidons of death ... . (p. 39)

As they struggle against dangers and threats to life, the self-preservative instincts may *seem* to serve life—as the sexual instincts actually do, Freud believed, by leading to unification, reproduction. But, in fact, self-preservation serves only to stave off any externally dealt death blow while the death instinct follows its inevitable immanent or interior course, which is so inexorable that it does not even require a *Todesprinzip*, a regulatory principle (although, in effect, it follows a principle of inertia). As we compulsively repeat, we struggle mightily to take *our own* path to death.

Not surprisingly, this idea soon seemed to Freud himself to be far-fetched, and he eventually redeemed the much-diminished self-preservative drives somewhat by saying that, really, they must serve the sexual instinctual drive—they must be *its* guardians.[5] But he did not then, as he might have, realise that the compulsion to repeat can very well be seen (as I suggested before) to be manifesting these very "instincts of self-preservation, of self-assertion and of mastery" as they go about trying to heal the effects in children and adults of traumas (which may be traumas primarily affecting the sensual current or the affectionate current or, more usually, both). He did not say that if reality is traumatic to a sufficient degree, reality will overcome the *Lustprinzip*, reality itself will be beyond the pleasure principle. And the self-preservative drive, rather than serving the reality principle, will have to fight it; survival will depend upon the self-preservative drive not being knocked completely out of commission. If, in a manner consistent with Freud's first instinct theory, in which his notion of the "protective barrier" was framed, we describe a trauma as an event (or series of events) that, producing psychic chaos, cuts a person off from carers, security, safety, allegiances, comrades, civility—all the aims of the affectionate current—as well as from any sexual desire satisfaction, then a compulsion to repeat is a compulsion on the part of the drives for preservation to heal, to overcome, to make a different outcome, to reconnect. The compulsion to repeat is attempted self-caring or solicitation of caring from others. The traumatised person wants her own *path to life*, which has been obscured, demolished.

In fact, this line of argument that I have imagined had been taken by Freud himself back in the 1911 Schreber case, where Freud had described the psychotic's symptoms as manifestations of an effort to return to a benign reality and to other people, a self-preservative effort or an effort at self-healing. And the line of argument was also taken *after* 1920. It shapes the 1926 text *Inhibitions, Symptoms and Anxiety*, where Freud constructed a brilliant definition of anxiety as—in effect—a signal that an elemental expectation of love had been or was about to be disappointed. He even constructed a developmental line for anxiety. This definition and this developmental line obviated the need for a death instinct theory.[6] But Freud compulsively repeated the theory anyway.

* * *

In the history of psychoanalysis since *Beyond the Pleasure Principle*, two roads eventually parted in the woods. At first, there was some agreement. All Freudians were impressed with the emphasis that Freud put after 1920 on aggression, because everyone who survived the First World War realised that aggression and aggression against the self (masochism) had been underemphasised and undertheorised in psychoanalysis. But there agreement ended. And most subsequent psychoanalysts have either followed Klein and Lacan in elaborating the death instinct theory in various ways, or followed Hartman and Fenichel and others among the ego psychologists in repudiating the biological theory while accepting the idea that sex and aggression are fundamental drives. (Anna Freud stood diplomatically aside: speaking of sex and aggression as fundamental drives, but neither embracing nor rejecting the biological death instinct theory, which she said needed to be confirmed or disconfirmed by empirical research.)[7]

In only one camp did refusing the death instinct theory flow from recognition that the theory had cost psychoanalysis its path to exploring the self-preservative drives or the ego instincts and thus to developing a philosophy of love and a moral-political theory: this was the Budapest School, starting in the 1930s, after Ferenczi's death.[8] Ferenczi himself had opened the way for his trainees with his asides in Thalassa about a self-preservative longing for the nourishing protective enclosure of the womb. But he had also emphasised a *sexual* drive for return to the womb and accepted a version of the death instinct theory. Most significant for his trainees were his efforts to theorise about protective, affectional love in the therapeutic situation, although these efforts were disturbing when they veered off into reflections on eroticism in the therapeutic situation and to dangerous experiments with "mutual analysis".

The most empirically oriented Hungarian explorer of the self-preservative relational drives was Imre Hermann, a researcher well-versed in ethology and primatology, who wrote a famous 1936 paper on the self-preservative drive pair, "to cling" and "to go in search".[9] Michael Balint recognised that the original affectionate current had a developmental history that needed exploring (and he eventually thought that the developmental history might be clearest in group relations, hence the Balint groups). As children grow more complex, they do so on the basis of an original relational love, which he called "primary passive object love" or sometimes just "primary love" (Balint, 1937). Depending on the reality—the traumas—they encounter and how they react, children become characterologically "ocnophile" (loving to cling to objects) or tend towards "philobatism" (orientation towards open spaces that are free of dreaded, anxiety-producing obstacles). Balint's first wife Alice Balint spoke of "archaic, egoistic object love" in a 1931 book called *The Early Years of Life*, which, when it was finally translated into English in 1954, contained an appreciative preface by Anna Freud.

To my knowledge, the difficulties of finding an adequate single noun for the affectionate current (as a range and development of drives, not just in its prototype, hunger) have been considered only by a psychoanalyst who did not think in the lexicon that Freud inherited from German philosophy and physics. Takeo Doi notes that in his mother tongue, Japanese, there is an everyday noun, *amae*, which means "the expectation to be sweetly and indulgently loved". *Amae*, Doi argued (and Michael Balint accepted the argument in his 1968 book *The Basic Fault*), is Freud's old ego instinctual "affectionate current" and it is a template for all later affectionate love, in children and in adults and societies. But neither Michael Balint nor Takeo Doi recognised, it seems to me, that the distinction Freud drew in his early work between "the sensual current" and "the affectionate current", like the one he drew between the sexual instincts and the ego instincts, actually represents the commonsense of the European *eros/philia* tradition as well as of the Japanese.

The relative silence in psychoanalysis over the lost ego instincts has not been recognised in recent years because those who have felt the need for an "affectionate current" have thought that such was supplied by John Bowlby's Attachment Theory, which was developed by Mary Ainsworth but also by the contemporary Freudians at the Anna Freud Centre, like Peter Fonagy and Mary Target. Bowlby had posited an attachment drive which must be satisfied for normal development, while pathology flows from its frustration or its traumatisation by environmental factors. Others have felt that Winnicott's distinction between the object mother (recipient of erotic love) and the environmental mother (supplier of vital needs and protector from trauma) recognises the love that had no name other than hunger. These are crucial contributions, which have inspired most of the fruitful work in child analysis in recent decades, but the Bowlbyan line really has no theory of the unconscious, and the Winnicottian line has no drive theory.

So, it seems to me, what was lost in 1920 has not really been refound, and psychoanalysis remains relatively unconnected to the ethical and political insights first articulated in the West by the Greek explorers of *philia*. The ways in which we are supplied with the necessities of life— the ways in which we are lovingly fed and cared-for tenderly—set the developmental stage for mature life when people are no longer under the sway of necessity, no longer helpless and dependent, and can tend to others, including their parents, in a well-regulated polity that guarantees their freedom to act, or to direct their own actions according to worthy principles like courage and magnanimity. Affectionately reared children, Aristotle says in the *Nichomachean Ethics* (IX. ii.8), will later impart to their parents "nourishment" (*trophe*), and find this care more beautiful than they find caring for themselves. Receiving affectional love is the root of altruism.

And in our world it would be a great benefaction, it seems to me, were altruism to be understood this way, as the great life-sustaining attainment of our inborn expectation of love.

Notes

1. Sandor Ferenczi noticed this absence, and wrote a paper in 1913, after the *Prinzip* concept had entered the Freudian lexicon, called "Stages in the Development of the Sense of Reality". He set out a preliminary sketch for a line of ego instinctual development that had great influence in the Budapest School, particularly upon Michael Balint.
2. *Philia* was the word used by Aristotle to reflect an earlier Homeric system of words focused around the verb *trepho*, to cherish or nurture, which was translated as *colere* in Latin, the verb underlying the noun *cultura*. The *philia* bonds are the cultural bonds, encompassing child-rearing methods, education, mentoring from older to younger citizens, and creating cultural objects, monuments, and cities (cf. Young-Bruehl & Russo, "*Amae* in Ancient Greece", 2003).
3. In the technique papers contemporary to his work on narcissism, Freud recommended to analysts who felt erotically drawn to their female patients that they withdraw, mastering their "counter-transference" (a new term) and enhancing their ego-strength thereby. This was another matter on which he and Jung disagreed, particularly as they both treated an incurable extreme obsessional patient, Elfriede Hirschfield (cf. Falzeder, 1994).

4. In his writings on sexual development after 1920, Freud emphasised the normality and importance of reproductive sexuality and heterosexuality more than he ever had before, because homosexuality and the perversions made no contribution to opposing the death instinct. The consequences of this emphasis were disastrous for psychoanalytic understanding of homosexuality and the perversions.

5. In the unfinished *An Outline of Psychoanalysis* (1940a, p. 148), Freud wrote: "The contrast between the instincts of self-preservation and the preservation of the species, as well as the contrast between ego-love and object-love, fall within Eros."

6. Anna Freud seems to have understood this significance of signal-anxiety and its developmental line, as she built it into the framework of her *The Ego and the Mechanisms of Defence* (1936), in which she did not need to make mention of the death instinct theory.

7. Then, in 1971, upon her first return to Vienna after the war, speaking about aggression to the IPA Congress, Anna Freud (Writings, VIII, p. 174) asked her colleagues to "agree to acknowledge the gap between clinical fact and biological speculation instead of enforcing direct causal links between the two fields".

8. There was American interest in the ego instincts after WWII, but that interest focused on the ego instincts as instincts of mastery or "effectence" (Robert Knight's word), not on their modality of love. This was a kind of pragmatist Darwinism.

9. Hermann has a contemporary advocate in the Belgian analyst Tomas Geyskens, but Geyskens does not see the ego instinctual line of development outlined in Hermann's work.

References

Balint, A. (1931). *The Early Years of Life: A Psychoanalytic Study*. New York: Basic, 1954.

Balint, M. (1937). Early developmental states of the ego: primary object love. In: *Primary Love and Psychoanalytic Technique*. London: Karnac, 1994.

Balint, M. (1968). *The Basic Fault: Therapeutic Aspects of Regression*. London: Tavistock.

Doi, T. (1973). *The Anatomy of Dependence*. New York: Kodansha.

Falzeder, E. (1994). My grand-patient, my chief tormenter: A hitherto unnoticed case of Freud's and the consequences. *Psychoanalytic Quarterly, 63*: 297–331.

Ferenczi, S. (1913). Stages in the development of the sense of reality. In: *First Contributions to Psychoanalysis*. London: Karnac, 1980.

Freud, A. (1936). *The Ego and the Mechanisms of Defence.* London: Karnac, 1992.

Freud, A. (1971). *The Writings of Anna Freud, Vol. 8*, p. 174. Presentation to IPA Congress, Vienna.

Freud, S. (1905d). Three essays on the theory of sexuality. *S. E. 7.* London: Hogarth.

Freud, S. (1911b). Formulations on the two principles of mental functioning. *S. E. 12.* London: Hogarth.

Freud, S. (1911c). Psycho-analytic notes on an autobiographical account of a case of paranoia (dementia paranoides). *S. E. 12.* London: Hogarth.

Freud, S. (1914c). On narcissism. *S. E. 14.* London: Hogarth.

Freud, S. (1920g). *Beyond the Pleasure Principle. S. E. 18.* London: Hogarth.

Freud, S. (1926d). *Inhibitions, Symptoms and Anxiety. S. E. 20.* London: Hogarth.

Freud, S. (1940a). *An Outline of Psychoanalysis. S. E. 23.* London: Hogarth.

Geyskens, T. & Van Haute, P. (2007). *From Death Instinct Theory to Attachment Theory.* New York: Other Press.

Hermann, I. (1936). Sich anklammern—auf Suche gehen. In: *International Zeitschrift für Psychoanalyse und Imago, 26*: 252–274.

Spitz, R. A. (1945). Hospitalism—an inquiry into the genesis of psychiatric conditions in early childhood. *Psychoanalytic Study of the Child, 1*: 53–74.

Young-Bruehl, E. & Russo, J. (2003). *Amae* in ancient Greece. In: E. Young-Bruehl, *Where Do We Fall when We Fall in Love?* New York: Other Press.

CHAPTER THREE

Civilisation and its dream of contentment: reflections on the unity of humankind

Introduction: the dream of contentment

Aristotle systematised or made a *theoria* out of a train of thought that was common among his contemporaries who composed tragedies, as it had been among his predecessors, the first Western philosophers, called the Pre-Socratics. The thought train had been especially clear in the teachings of Heraclitus, even though the Ephesian was known as "the Obscure" for representing it in cryptograms or aphorisms like *"ethos anthropo daimon"* (in a human, character is destiny). These Greeks believed that human beings are microcosms and their societies macrocosms within the great macrocosm, which is all of *physis*, all of nature, so beautiful to contemplate.

Through the same phases and patterns, human beings and their societies are born, grow, develop a mature character, and decline. When they pass away, new ones are born to replace them, and these, in turn, grow, develop a mature character, and decline. The cycle is ceaseless. But there is incremental evolution in it, despite episodes of devolution or regression or missing the mark or the goal (such a miss being attributed to a *harmartia*, sometimes translated as "a tragic flaw"). Slowly, the maturation of human beings and of societies comes closer to the

35

goal that Aristotle named *eudaimonia*, harmoniousness, happiness, or, literally, wellness of the *daimon*, a word which invokes that growth principle in people and in nature which is the future of the whole and the destiny of each. Growing from little groups to bigger families to polities and eventually commonwealths, human societies are incrementally approaching unity and peace, as some magnanimous humans are approaching apprehension of the unity of mankind by swelling their minds up, as it were, to embrace the macrocosm.

Human beings, Aristotle observed, imagine *eudaimonia* or dream of contentment in different ways, because they have grown to have somewhat different characters (and thus destinies). Some think that *eudaimonia* consists in pleasure and some in the accumulation of material goods. Quite different from the hedonists and proprietors are the moralists for whom *eudaimonia* is exercise of their moral faculty (*dianoia*); and even more different are those rare, maximally evolved individuals for whom exercise of mind (*nous*) in contemplation is *eudaimonia*. It is the contemplatives who can envision the future unity of mankind, civilisation's contentment. Aristotle's teacher Plato had discussed these character types in terms of the functions they would have in an ideal eudaimonic polity: they would be craftspeople and workers and merchants; warriors and guardians; and philosopher kings. Aristotle, however, wanted the contemplatives to have the leisure and safety to contemplate, not to rule—for in ruling they would run the risk of missing the mark and devolving into tyrants.

Down through the Western tradition, the microcosm/macrocosm analogy[1] offered basic guidance for understanding nature and the characters of human beings and their societies. But by the end of the nineteenth century, confidence that there was a slow progressive trend—an incremental evolution—towards the eudaimonic unity of mankind was challenged by great nay-sayers like Nietszche and then by less great but very forceful devolutionists like Spengler. Sigmund Freud declared himself an ambivalent heir of the tradition, a pessimistic optimist. When he wrote *Das Unbehagen in der Kultur* (*Civilization and Its Discontents*) (1930a), which might have been Greekishly entitled *Dysdaimonia in Culture*, he announced with the grandeur of an Aeschylus that Eros is always at war with Thanatos, the sexual instinctual drive with "the death instinct". But whether Eros could advance in the cycle of his era, or the unity of mankind come any closer, Freud declined to predict. It was as though he had produced only two parts of an Orestia-like trilogy: would the ferociously punishing Erinyes, wanting vengeance on Orestes for his guilty aggression against his mother, give way to the Eumenides?

In the tradition within which Freud—ever so precariously—thought, the coming unity of mankind had always been envisioned as a triumph of the human spirit, which Hegel had invoked during the Napoleonic campaigns as a triumph of the *Weltgeist*. Freud was far less "Prussian" when he declared (1930a, p. 69):

> ... civilization is a process in the service of Eros, whose purpose is to combine single human individuals, and after that families, then races, peoples and nations, into one great unity, the unity of mankind. Why this has to happen, we do not know; the work of Eros is precisely this. These collections of men are to be libidinally bound to one another. Necessity alone, the advantages of work in common, will not hold them together. But man's natural aggressive instinct, the hostility of each against all and all against each, opposes this programme of civilization.

Not surprisingly, Freud's conviction—a speculation which over the course of the decade from 1920 to 1930 became a conviction—that human beings have a natural aggressive instinct, a derivative of "the death instinct", has been the crux of all controversy among psychoanalysts since his death in 1939. Gradually, the controversy diffused and came to encompass the whole of Freud's theory of the instinctual drives, which had evolved over his career. To some psychoanalysts the theory of instinctual drives is a legacy that must be rejected; to others it must be retained—perhaps reformulated or refined—as a necessary foundation. And as this controversy has ramified and grown in scope, it is not surprising that no one who calls herself or himself a Freudian has been ready, willing, or conceptually able to write about the microcosm/macrocosm analogy or the evolution of human beings and societies or the unity of mankind. "The death instinct" challenges the basic assumption about human beings that subtended the Western philosophical tradition which Freud himself inherited, and which Aristotle had summarised with his aphoristic definition of a human being as *zoon politikon* (a *polis*-dwelling animal); that is, a being *by nature* designed for bonding with others in a polity, for acting with others similarly moved by *philia politike*, political affection or friendship, respect. A being by nature seeking contentment in civilisation.

The unity of humankind after the Second World War

To my way of thinking, while this controversy over the instinctual drive theory was developing within psychoanalysis, and especially during recent decades when the controversy linked up with a postwar tendency—deeply indebted to Nietszche—to pour "post-modernist" deconstructive scorn on all "master narratives" that rest on the microcosm/macrocosm analogy (as all master narratives not involving a transcendent deity do), something has been happening in reality, unremarked, to mankind. It seems to me that humankind (as we ought now to say, acknowledging women, so absent from the prejudiced philosophical tradition) has really become, since the Second World War, united. The unity of humankind is not in the future, it is not a possibility (of libidinal purpose or any other). It is present, factual, and it has come about in an unforeseen way: humankind has been united in and by common terror, shared traumatisation.

There was a period of preparation for this phenomenon, so unprecedented in depth and scope. In the first three decades of the twentieth century, many thinkers observed that modern technologies were "shrinking" the planet, even as imperialists were criss-crossing it, leaving their corseting tracks of ruthless exploitation and cultural suppression on every part of it. New modes of transportation on land, sea, and—most astonishingly—air, brought regions of the world into proximity and peoples into contact as never before. New modes of communication shrank space and time. Peoples who were, in the old microcosm/macrocosm terms, living in the childhood of humankind, isolated in small families and tribes, were "discovered" by those (sometimes anthropologists, sometimes imperialists) who called themselves maturely "civilised", so that the whole history (and common ancestry in prehistory) of humankind could be studied. Even though study of humankind was biased by moralistic and prejudiced versions of evolutionary assumptions and analogies to individual development, it was, nonetheless, universal in scope.

Crucially, new modes of warfare and weaponry erased the boundaries of battlefields, so that the First World War extended out around the globe but also no longer stopped at civilian areas or spared women and children. And in this context, after the First World War, ideas learned from Roman Stoics, heirs of the Greek tradition and its vision of the unity of humankind, were taken up—filtered through Kant's oeuvre—to found the League of Nations, a grand adjunct to the peace treaty that concluded the terrifying First World War. The effort to make that horror and that flawed treaty into a step forward for humankind was doomed, however, by the ethnic nationalism it permitted—even promoted.[2]

Again, after the Second World War, when technological developments and group conflicts had gone even further towards shrinking the world, an organisation for imagining the unity of humankind had been sought in the United Nations. But this postwar context was different—and remains different. The changes that had preceded the Second World War continued and cumulated to such an extent that a discontinuity in human history was registered in many domains with use of the word "unprecedented"—now so hackneyed, but then, itself, unprecedented, for human history and the human condition had not been thought to admit events and changes without precedent. Throughout the tradition, *Natura non salut* (nature makes no leaps) had been held to be a principle of both microcosm and macrocosm evolution.

The world-shrinking technological developments had turned out to have sinister consequences that were novel: they had made possible or supported grandiose bids for power and methods of war that were without precedent. A form of human governance had arisen in Germany and in the Soviet Union, to be given the new name "totalitarianism", that did what no tyranny, monarchy, or oligarchy had ever done: in its bid for world conquest, it had attacked all political life, destroying all genuinely political institutions and ruthlessly suppressing and killing its own citizens like an omnivorous monster eating itself. Totalitarians invented methods for this killing—concentration camps, crematoria for millions—that were the Industrial Revolution turned totally malignant. To fight the Nazis, and then the Soviets, the Americans had invented an atomic bomb, which they used on Hiroshima and Nagasaki in 1945, incinerating those cities, turning them into crematoria. It became apparent that genocidal warfare could have ecocidal consequences, as it became (more slowly) apparent that the Industrial Revolution, unrestrained and carried everywhere by expansionary capitalism or communism, could have both genocidal and ecocidal consequences as it polluted and corrupted all of human nature and nature, the macrocosm.[3]

The Second World War—if we take that title to embrace the war itself, the apex of full-blown totalitarianism, the Holocaust, the use of the A-bomb—was traumatic for all involved, which eventually meant for all humankind because images and stories of it reached those not directly involved (especially via the new media of television and news reels). In the years immediately after the War, the trauma linked to traumatising events around the globe, especially as the surviving empires dissolved and new nations were created. Events like the 1948 War of Independence in Palestine, the partition of India, the institution of apartheid in South Africa, the Long March launching a Cultural Revolution in China—all shaped the histories of the peoples, countries, and regions involved, and still reverberate in intra-group conflicts that threaten the world. Each of the nations that gathered at the United Nations was compromised by a trauma history as all engaged in new forms of treaty-making to try to heal from the cluster trauma of the Second World War. Debates over the Universal Declaration of Human Rights and the Convention on Genocide were filled with echoes of the traumas the various national populations had endured, and also inflicted.[4]

The UN Declaration's aspiration to "save succeeding generations from the scourge of war" reflected the realisation that human beings had become capable of destroying human life in the mass, that is, the potentiality existed that *all* human life could end, become extinct. The species was capable of suicide; of producing what came to be called "nuclear winter", and of creating political institutions that could eliminate politics. Or, more accurately, the Declaration's framers realised that one people, even a single leader of one people, possessing nuclear weapons and infected with totalitarian elements, could bring about the death of all. Rightly, this realisation was immediately dubbed "unthinkable" and it remained "unthinkable" right through the Cold War that kept the threat of nuclear war and totalitarianism continually in the minds of everyone. No matter which camp they aligned with politically or ideologically, everyone agreed that trying to "think the unthinkable" was necessary for survival (and the same phrase has now been extended to the ultimate environmental catastrophe or ecocide that was vaguely envisioned after the war).

One way to define a trauma is: an experience (or a series of experiences) that is, for those who suffer it, unthinkable. "Unthinkable" may mean that a person thinks compulsively about the trauma but cannot really confront it or put the fragments of memory into an integrated narrative or even an integrated neuronal memory. Often such compulsive thinking produces "worst possible case scenario" thinking that has little connection to present reality or realistic assessments of the future. On the other hand, "unthinkable" may mean that the traumatic experience is denied, dissociated, disavowed, and the traumatised person is left psychically split or disintegrated. Either way, traumatised people become "stupid" in the sense that their ability to think is compromised by the anxiety-ridden compulsiveness which grips them. Specifically, they are "stupid" as judges of future possibilities, for all they experience is the traumatic past laid out in front of them. Judgment—including good political judgment—presupposes freedom of mind, freedom to range imaginatively and see matters from many points of view, imagine many outcomes of events, many causes of events. Traumatised people, whether compulsive ruminators on their trauma or compulsive deniers of it, easily become "fundamentalists", that is, they embrace a pre-existing thought system with a fundamental event in it that explains all of history, polarising all humankind into all-good and all-bad. The thought-system also plots an endpoint at which ultimate judgment is delivered by a forgiving or punishing deity, ruler of the macrocosm, who is outside the macrocosm, transcendent.

I am suggesting that traumatisation, with these consequences for human thought and judgment, was a collective experience of humankind in the Second World War and its aftermath, so that this type of unification into a traumatised mass is the currently existing factual unity of humankind. We have the task before us of grasping this unification and thinking, therapeutically, how it can be turned into a unification that is not based on what traumatologists call "psychic numbing". Can a negatively attained unity that interferes with thought grow into a thoughtfully *chosen* unity? If it is so that there has been one trauma, repeating itself in many forms and degrees, but many ways of responding, which ways of responding are most conducive to overcoming it? Can those help who are least trapped in this collective traumatisation or most able to analyse it because they have struggled free of it?

It seems to me that it is not Freud's contested theory of instinctual drives, or Freud's speculation about Eros locked in battle with Thanatos, that we need in order to understand this development in the human condition and what it means for the future unity of mankind. Rather, we need the Freudian theory of trauma, propelled by Sandor Ferenczi's interest in trauma (first among war neurotics and later among abused children) and elaborated by many postwar Freudians. For this theory brings out a dimension of human experience that had been obscured: it was first obscured by the emphasis on human evolution in the Western philosophical tradition, which so often degenerated into facile worship of automatic progress; and then it was obscured again by Freud's own hypothesis about a devolutionary counter-force to Eros, misidentified as innate aggression, not trauma. But, at the same time, I think we need to rescue from Freud's late emphasis on the Eros and Thanatos battle his very important—and now neglected—continuation of the old philosophical tradition of character-oriented microcosm/macrocosm thinking. Minus its distortions,[5] this train of thought can be used to explore the idea that there are social traumas that operate analogously to individual traumas, and that we have been living inside such a shared trauma since the Second World War (more than half a century, the entire lifetime of my generation, that is, of people born around my birth year, 1946).

Theory of social trauma

A second way to define a trauma is: an event (the actions of a person or groups of persons) rends the psyche of an individual or the interpersonal fabric of a society in such a way that the ingredients of the event are compulsively repeated within the individual or the society, which come, then, to resemble the traumatising event. This definition references a phenomenon known to psychoanalysts since the 1920s and elaborated by Anna Freud in her *The Ego and the Mechanisms of Defence* (1936). An individual who is traumatically aggressed can—and usually does—"identify with the aggressor" or the aggressive event and do unto others as has been done unto her or him. That is, the person will imitate the ingredients of the aggression suffered, including not just acts but the ingredient of motivation. (Later, after child abuse was more thoroughly studied, this phenomenon between children and adults was called "intergenerational transmission of trauma".)

The elaboration of this definition for social traumas depended upon work done on trauma after the Second World War, and very crucially on a classic 1963 paper by Masud Khan, "The Concept of Cumulative Trauma." This paper had as its purpose the delineation of a particular trauma type, "cumulative trauma", and a comparison of it with other types of trauma—a first attempt at a typology of traumas. Clearing a path for this pioneering typology, Khan noted that the complex history of "trauma" in psychoanalytic theorising began with Freud's shift away from making sexual trauma central to his aetiological theory of the psychoneuroses (particularly seduction trauma in hysteria) towards emphasising fantasy (especially Oedipal fantasy) and intra-psychic experience—a move Ferenczi protested. Later, as Freud reconsidered his instinctual drive theory and his theory of anxiety in the 1920s, he attempted several different syntheses of his first concern for traumatising events and his second with the intrapsychic experience of being traumatised. But this project remained incomplete (and it was quite derailed by the "death instinct hypothesis", which minimised external trauma).

In the absence of a clear synthesis, subsequent theorising oscillated back and forth between emphasis on event and emphasis on intrapsychic experience. Having noted this pattern, Khan made a synthesising proposal that the basic Freudian definition of traumatisation—as a process involving breaching a protective stimulus barrier and subsequent efforts to repair or remedy the breach—be retained, but that the protective barrier be understood not as a "stimulus barrier" but as, basically and primarily, the relationship that a helpless baby has with its carer (usually the mother). Every individual's trauma history—and every individual does have such a history—begins with a history of infant and childhood growth in the matrix of the protection provided (to some degree) by the carer. All subsequent traumas reference this beginning and are experienced as repeating it. This is the universal situation, the human condition, Khan argued, and in order for a description of the universal situation not to become a launch for over-generalising, attention must turn to types of traumas, which will each have a relation to types of failures of the protective shield of the carer-infant relationship.

Khan first noted the two forms of traumatising failure best known to Freud. The first form included traumas of separation, abandonment, or loss (including fantasised loss of the phallus, castration anxiety); the second, particularly explored by Ferenczi, included traumas of excessive intrusion into the infant's mind of the carer's psychopathology (or the psychopathology of another significant person, or, I would like to add, a society). For simplicity's sake, I suggest that these be called rupture traumas and break-in or abuse traumas. A third type of protective shield failure noted by Khan occurs when some problem in the child—physical handicap, constitutional sensitivity, illness—is overwhelming to the carers, who then cannot provide a protective shield. A fourth type of failure is the one Khan designated "cumulative trauma" (and related to the "strain trauma" that Ernst Kris (1956) had earlier distinguished from "shock trauma").

The cumulative trauma is a cluster of experiences and events, over the years of infancy and childhood, no one of which entirely destroys the protective shield of the infant-mother relationship, but each of which contributes to strains, distortions, and attenuations of the protective relationship and of the character of the infant's emerging ego (eventually resulting, he might have added, in character traits and a character clued to the cumulative trauma). A cumulative trauma is usually not even visible until its ingredient events have become so woven into experience that we say (for example) "He has a schizoid character," marked by futile, repetitive preoccupation with his trauma. By contrast "He has a dissociative character" would more likely be said of someone whose trauma history included salient events of rupture or break-in that had been sealed off. Khan did not go on to use Freud's own characterological scheme, which consisted of three types, hysterical, obsessional, and narcissistic, and ask about the experiences of trauma typical of them. But he might well have, and I think we should take this cue.

It is important to note that the kind of review and clarification of types that Khan was undertaking in the 1960s was part of a wider shift within psychoanalysis to correct for Freud's original pendulum shift away from traumatic events. This correction came particularly from child analysts, especially Winnicott, who was Khan's analyst and mentor, and it represented a critique of the extreme emphasis on intrapsychic experience (especially of the death instinct in aggression) among the Kleinians. The correction coincided with a movement within child studies to use new techniques of observation (like film) and new observational situations (like parent-infant play groups, the "strange situation" set-up, and simultaneous analyses of mothers and infants) in order to focus on early (pre-Oedipal) growth environments and the mother whom Winnicott had called "the environmental mother" (in contrast to "the object mother"). The Ferenczi-trained émigré analyst René Spitz made films of hospitalised children—children suffering traumas of separation, abandonment, loss—and then American colleagues of Spitz's in Colorado, led by C. Henry Kempe, developed techniques for empirically studying children suffering from break-in traumas of physical abuse ("the battered child syndrome"). The phrase "child abuse" came into common use in the 1970s, with both clinicians and policy commissions trying to define it for both clinical and legal purposes. By the 1980s there was a surge of paediatric procedure and of legislation to protect children from abuse: the development, as it were, of a social protective shield, with a therapeutic component, a social matrix in which children could be protected from the failures of their parental relationship shields.

A social protective shield could be defined as a relational network of people and institutions that grows up to enwrap basic social units—like families, but also states—in customs, programmes, and ideas of *eudaimonia* that prevent the units' failure and remedy their ills medically and psychotherapeutically. Social shields of all sorts develop in societies as different needs and "social ills" are discovered and addressed. Sometimes great effort has to be expended to construct them, as was the case with the child abuse initiatives in America; sometimes they generate more spontaneously, as in villages where it is taken for granted (to use an African proverb popularised in the 1990s) that "It takes a village to raise a child." Or they may result from political movements that build "from the ground up", maximising citizen participation and emphasising human rights.

In the same period during which "child abuse" emerged and was refined, the diagnostic category post-traumatic stress syndrome (later PTSD) was formulated, and much work was done by neuroscientists to examine forms of trauma memory. This work brought together two decades of child study with contemporaneous clinical observation of "war neuroses" in the specific forms encountered among Vietnam War veterans.

But, interestingly enough, the convergence of child study and adult PTSD study did not include the more widespread, and less acknowledged, social trauma phenomenon that I am considering: all children born during or at the end of the Second World War were raised by adults who had been collectively traumatised, that is, by adults who were to one degree or another and in one way or another united as the terrorised survivors of the Second World War. "Intergenerational transmission of trauma" emerged as a category specifically applied to children who had been abused and neglected in the clinically and legally defined sense; but it did not refer to the transmission of a trauma experience from a group to a next generation.

In the 1980s, however, the concern with PTSD did bring into the burgeoning trauma literature another form of typological distinction relating to traumatic events—one according to degree or scale. The phrase "catastrophic trauma" appeared to indicate that traumas most immediately and physically devastating to the protective barrier of the infant-carer relationship could affect groups. "Catastrophic trauma" was used for individuals—in considering severe in degree, life-threatening physical abuse, for example—but the term more often referred to traumas on a large scale involving large groups: force of nature traumas like fires, earthquakes, and floods; technological traumas like airplane crashes, chemical spills, and nuclear reactor meltdowns; and traumas of war.[6] More and more frequently, study of catastrophic traumas of war focused on civilian populations in addition to veterans, for it had become widely acknowledged that the nature of war itself had continued to change since the unprecedented Second World War changes. The traditional barriers (topographical and legal) distinguishing battlefields and civilian areas continued to erode. War and genocide became blurred as civilian casualties mounted in both high technology and low technology war zones. Similarly, particularly in the 1990s, war and terrorism became blurred as the purpose of so many war efforts, which employed civilians, became to terrorise civilian populations and create waves of refugees, and this, in turn, inspired terrorists who were not soldiers. By the time Americans declared "war on terrorism" in the days after the 9/11 terrorist attack, many around the world, organising massive protest demonstrations against a retaliatory invasion of Iraq, realised that "war on terrorism" was going to mean state terrorist attack on non-state terrorist attackers. Again, the phenomenon of a state identifying with its aggressor and aggressing back in its mode was apparent.

Despite the work of Masud Khan and others in delineating types of traumas, psychoanalytic theorists made little contribution to the study of catastrophic traumas experienced by groups because their concern remained so decidedly with individuals and the interplay of individuals' subjective experience (their histories, their fantasies, their reactions to trauma) and traumatic events of different types.[7] But that lack of contribution has also stemmed from not filling in the conceptual or theoretical blank between individuals' experiences of being traumatised and experiences that individuals have as members of groups with group trauma histories. The microcosm/macrocosm thinking frame has been left unused, as though it were obsolete, in the old Freudian closet.[8]

Taking as a cue Masud Khan's adaptation of Winnicott's notion that the protective shield breached by a trauma repeats or reactivates earlier breaches in the child-carer relationship, this conceptual blank could be filled with the analogous notion I suggested before: a society provides the individuals who constitute it with a protective shield or shields, and there are traumas that breach these shields of existential belonging and social care or service and political union. A social shield can be broken through in many ways and degrees that are analogous to traumas of rupture, of break-in, and—perhaps the most common—of cumulative social erosion and deterioration and failure over time. The profound—unprecedented—rupture and break-in trauma cluster of the Second World War became a cumulative trauma as the generation suffering it transmitted it to their children, and as the events it set in train continued to traumatise both the adults and their children and grandchildren—thereby setting off more traumatic events.

To this thread of reflection about social trauma and particularly cumulative social trauma, I want to add one more thread before returning to the question of how shared social trauma as a type of unification of people might be worked through (as we say in clinical work) and transformed into constructive unification. So let me add a third definition of trauma to the preceding two. A trauma is a social-relationship harm that is compounded in the person or society harmed (and in the harmers as well). It reactivates older childhood relationship traumas, and it sets off a process of accumulation in which its own consequences, mingling with the consequences of the older childhood traumas that were woven into it, become traumatic. The mix of traumas influences the ways in which subsequent traumatic experiences are experienced. All traumas are, in this way, cumulative traumas. People and societies develop characters out of their trauma histories, and those characters are their destinies.

Are there characterologically typical trauma experiences? I think there are, and want to make a suggestion in this direction by using the Freudian theory of defence mechanisms and character-structuration. When Freud began to think in terms of the analogy between individuals and societies, microcosms and macrocosms, repression was the defence he had his attention focused on. Hysteria and obsessional neurosis both seemed to him pathologies of repression—the first more common in women, the second in men; the first more connected with oral and genital (Oedipal) repression, the second with anal; the first involving more passivity, the second more activity, and so forth. Both seemed common in and typical of societies in which sexual repression was obvious enough to be held responsible for "modern nervous illness" generally (as Freud had argued in his 1908 paper "'Civilized' Sexual Morality and Modern Nervous Illness", a premonition of things to come in *Civilization and its Discontents* (1930a)). During the 1920s, as much of the overt

Victorian sexual repression lifted, hysteria and hysterical characters of the type Freud had studied became much less common in the clinical population (although obsessional characters remained common). All Freud's followers observed this diminishment of *fin de siècle* hysteria, but only some—particularly Otto Fenichel, Wilhelm Reich (1970), and others of socialist formation—responded by making the microcosm/macrocosm analogy more dynamic: as societies change, so do illnesses and so does the preponderance of one kind of illness over others in a society, marking that society's "social character". Many analysts who survived the Second World War noted that the prewar "Prussian" character of German society, even during the upheavals of the Weimar period, had meant that narcissistic obsessiveness[9] was the "social character" of the period when Nazism was articulated as an ideology and a way of life and a way of warfare. It was, to use Reich's phrase, "the mass psychology of fascism".

Narcissism was the third kind of neurosis and character disorder Freud identified. "Narcissistic neurosis" received much attention among the "ego psychologists" after the Second World War, for they, of course, were concerned as Freud had been in the 1930s with pathologies of the ego. Eventually, when narcissism was intensely studied in America in the 1960s, and work by Heinz Kohut, Otto Kernberg, and others built upon earlier work by Sandor Ferenczi, Franz Alexander, Melanie Klein, Ronald Fairbairn, Harold Searles, Harry Stack Sullivan, and others, the idea began to form that America was becoming more narcissistic and more promoting of narcissism in individuals. This idea was fully formed as far as American society was concerned by the time Christopher Lasch published *The Culture of Narcissism* in 1979.

To my mind, the development in America of a "culture of narcissism" was connected to the way the Second World War traumatisation developed in America, which was characterologically different from the way it developed in other parts of the world, and particularly in European societies that had been the main wartime battlefields and had been physically devastated and depopulated. At a greater distance from the actual land campaigns and bombings, America became a "Never again!" society: being resolute about never being traumatised again was as close as the society came to acknowledging that it had been traumatised, even though it had been victorious in the war and had emerged "a superpower". There were many facets of this rigidity: assertions of territorial and military invulnerability;[10] assertions of moral rectitude (most obvious in the nationwide pact not to question the rightness of Truman's decision to use atomic bombs or of the earlier decision to "blitz" Germany's cities as Germany had blitzed English cities); rejection of anything that could be called "appeasement" in foreign affairs, assertions of "exceptionalism"; celebrations of American individualism (often gendered as "rugged individualism" and thus indistinguishable from *machismo*); and triumphalism (particularly as the Cold War was "won"). These social defences became so normal that individuals with these forms of narcissistic character armour could not recognise them as such. (Thus a central contribution of feminism was to recognise these defences in men and to make an effort to analyse them in terms of the way American men were "socialised", starting with their socialisation in the protective matrix of child-parent relations.)

Also characteristic of America during and after the Second World War was the appropriation of Nazi and Soviet institutions—the creation of American identifications with the two aggressors' institutions. America manufactured a bomb fit for "total war"—a Nazi military ambition—and then engaged in an arms race with the Soviet Union that made the two countries imitators of each other's scientific and military institutions. They shared a belief in "mutually assured destruction" (MAD) and a commitment to "deterrence". America also developed a secret police, or several secret polices, and secret intelligence agencies like the CIA and the NSA, all using techniques developed by the Gestapo and the KGB. Through the Cold War, a concept of "national security" evolved that rationalised these agencies, which were billed as protective but which became more and more aggressive. The American military even created a "School of the Americas" training programme for the police and military forces of its client states in Latin America, most of which developed into dictatorships with American help. Within the US government, a slow but steady shift began, away from the basic constitutional republican assumption that the legislative branch of the government should lead, representing the people. The new assumption developed that the executive branch, and the president as commander-in-chief particularly, was the leadership branch of government, sanctioned to appoint the judiciary branch along ideological lines. To the president was given authority to use the nuclear armoury, as the nation learned so vividly during the 1962 Cuban Missile Crisis. The ultimate species-extinguishing trauma can be inflicted by one person—and this knowledge is itself traumatising (as it has become assimilated through all kinds of Dr Strangelove images and scenarios).

Another specificity of the American experience of the shared Second World War trauma was the society's development of an acute vulnerability to any experience that could be viewed as or actually was a national defeat. The school experience of my generation was as profoundly shaped by the launch of the Soviet satellite Sputnik in 1957—a great "defeat" for America—as it had been by the constant rituals of preparedness against Soviet nuclear attack that started in 1951. But the major defeat—or narcissistic wound—of the Cold War period was, of course, the Vietnam War, which was a rite of traumatic passage for my generation. After years of being threatened with a "domino effect" in all of South-East Asia if the Vietnamese Communists were not defeated, Americans found their military defeated by a nation that had turned itself into a guerilla force and won the war by hiding its actual soldiers in the civilian population, which the American military attacked by sea, by land, and by "saturation" aerial bombardment. Vietnam was bombed almost to the point of using nuclear weapons, polluted almost to the point of having its land and natural resources irreversibly devastated–all to no avail, and to the widespread moral corruption of the American air force, army, and navy. The sons of "the greatest generation" who had fought Nazism—and endured the terrorisation of totalitarianism, the Holocaust, the bombings of Hiroshima and Nagasaki—were demoralised and disgraced and terrorised by an experience particular to them but part of a cumulative trauma. Most Americans, to this day, if asked whether America "lost" the Vietnam War would be unable to acknowledge that, in fact, yes, it did; the most that is admitted is that America got "stuck in a quagmire", without "an exit strategy".[11] So this anal-obsessional language has overshadowed every word said about the Gulf War, the invasion of Iraq, and now the war in Afghanistan. These wars are all talked about against the background of the ritualistically invoked but still not fully acknowledged trauma of Vietnam.

It was not until the Vietnam War that America fissured along the line marked by struggle between "hawks" and "doves", which eventually morphed into a broader struggle touching on social and cultural issues between red or Republican conservatives and blue or Democratic liberals. Through the decades a split along generational lines recurred as some young people—over two generations—longed to exit the collective trauma condition. That is, within these groupings the two typical responses to a cumulative trauma played out: one, most common in the Second World War generation (quite obsessional as well as narcissistic, and ruminating on the trauma of the Second World War) emphasised being moralistically in control of bombs and being willing to use them; and the other, more common among the Vietnam War generation and its children, wanting to exit the trauma and struggling not to dissociate from it, emphasised disarmament, pursuit of peace by peaceful means, and reassertion of hedonistic and proprietary *eudaimonia*. The young called not just for—to use Freud's terms—Eros over Thanatos, but for avoiding or diminishing the anxiety of war, the anxiety of terrorisation.[12] In the social domain, many among the traumatised who were "hawks" associated the loss in Vietnam to a change in American society that featured a women's liberation movement, a revived civil rights movement, and a gay liberation movement, all of which signalled loss of power, loss of privilege, loss of patriarchal authority—in short, narcissistic vulnerability.

Therapeutic consciousness

The fact—it seems to me a fact—that societies develop different characters in their responses to trauma, which reflect their prior histories of trauma as well as the conditions under which they experienced the trauma and transmitted it, is crucial to acknowledge in thinking about what might be called social therapy. The unity of humankind in terrorisation that I have been broadly describing seems to me to have three obvious dimensions, registered in each and every postwar society, although each society has been particularly marked by one or more of these dimensions.

The first form comes from the period of the Second World War, and it is terrorisation in the face of the existence of totalitarian forms of government in Nazi Germany and the Stalinist Soviet Union (and its Eastern Bloc colonies) and the mass deaths those regimes engineered, known later as the Holocaust and the Gulag. Terrorisation in the face of the existence of atomic weapons and the threat of their use for "mutual assured destruction" followed as the Cold War heated up, invoking again and again as it did the bombings at the close of WWII of Hiroshima and Nagasaki, the mushroom cloud. Terrorisation in the face of global pollution and, eventually, global warming grew, as the threat of ecocide joined the threat of genocide. The theme of this dimension of terrorisation is: mass death is coming or is growing all around us; we are besieged. The theme is narcissistic, all about preventing defeat and death.

The second dimension compasses all the ways in which the world has become boundary-less. To the "shrinking" planet phenomenon has been added the massive postwar movements of peoples: first, the European refugees and displaced persons, then stream after stream of political and economic refugees from all around the world to all around the world. These movements were unprecedented in comparison to any population upheavals that had preceded the Second World War. Although the world is still a world of nation states, every state (particularly in the developed world, the destination of immigrants) is now a complexly multinational entity. All states have had to confront the problems of their diversity or multiculturalism, so civil wars of one form or another—sometimes "cultural war"—have dotted the globe, increasing as the Cold War came to an end or morphed into global cultural war of more or less progressive states and entities against anti-modernists and reactionaries of various sorts. None stop short of using torture and terrorism. Some historians have spoken of a "conflict of civilisations" with the implication that the Muslim world is regressive and the developed, Westernised world progressive and freedom-loving, when it seems obvious that there are progressive and regressive groups within every nation state, as there are terrorists in every nation state—often in uniform—as well as in non-state or transnational alliances. The most assiduous boundary protectors and creators are obsessional.

In the boundary-less world, only the Americans, relatively bordered by two oceans and with a relatively sedentary ruling group, the WASPS, could continue to debate whether isolationism and/or anti-immigration policies could sustain a foreign policy. No other people had the luxury of being isolated in any way or the luxury of continuing or developing notions of individualism for individuals or absolute sovereignty for nations. The European nations, invaded, bombed, occupied, devastated, emerged from WWII more community-minded and more dependent on government programmes in the areas of social development and family support, more "social democratic", more convinced that they had to work towards multi-state unity—as they eventually did in forming the European Union, the first postwar multi-state regional political entity to have emerged out of a collective sense of danger. America has also been more and more hostile towards the United Nations, although immediately after the war it was committed to the United Nations and to the Universal Declaration of Human Rights.

The third form of terrorisation has resulted in various kinds of panics and moral panics—what Gustave Le Bon had named mass hysterias. This form could be described as terrorisation in the face of unpredictability. Or terrorisation in the face of constant anxiety. Freud concentrated his attention on the ways in which repression had produced a certain predictability or continuity in human affairs by keeping sexual energy and aggressive energy bound, for examples in monogamous families or authoritarian institutions like churches and armies. Similarly, he had studied the ways in which the task of repression had been unsuccessful or had needed all kinds of consolations to work at all (consolations of substance abuse, of worldviews promising postponed gratification, etc.). He noted that as religions, with their traditions of repression, were losing power, insecurity was rising, and he suggested that only for a return of security in some form would people repress their instinctual needs. He did not foresee (and nor did anyone else, even after WWII) a religious revival of the sort that has swept the world since the end of the Cold War, promising security and return to a (quite mythical) tradition-bound time of security. Nor did he foresee the apocalyptic nature of some of the current fundamentalisms, which promise that security in the next world is imminent. This religious revival points, I think, to the changed nature of the unpredictability fear: it is no longer fear that instinctual drive energy will break out of bounds, but fear that there are no bounds—so fundamentalisms are desperate efforts to reinstate lost bonds, lost traditions.

The phenomenon I am describing (and analysing as having three key dimensions) is not a collective post-traumatic stress disorder, but a collective cumulative-traumatic stress disorder or retraumatisation stress disorder. There were mid-century traumas which we now refer to as "past", but each of these has continued in its original form or in a variant form; there has been a continuous and cumulative collective retraumatising. So any therapeutic approach has to take into account this continuous condition, and its various forms, which are linked to the predominance of a particular dimension of the trauma in a given individual or traumatised society.

Trauma therapy in the clinic begins with identification and description of the trauma: in the context of a safe, secure, protective relationship matrix, the story can be told and explored in all its dimensions. Why it has been unthinkable—what is unthinkable about it—can be slowly thought through. The emotions involved in it—the fear, the anger, the guilt, sometimes the survivor guilt—can be recovered, and the trauma's relation to early breaches of the protective shield explored. These processes have their analogies in the social world, where stories *can* be told in the course of political campaigns, deliberations, policy discussions, and, most important, treaty-making and convention drafting, which are the key acts of reconciliation and unification.

In my estimation, the clearest and most encompassing collective articulation of the shared trauma of the Second World War and what is needed to master it took place in the decade after the International Year of the Child in 1979, when the UN Convention on the Rights of the Child was being drafted. This has been the most progressive and sweeping of the UN's postwar conventions, and the one that has garnered the most signatories. All the UN members have signed except Somalia, which has had no legitimate government for decades, and the United States of America, which is stubbornly committed to its absolute sovereignty and which has had successive governments that have judged children's rights to be threatening to traditional parental rights. And this convention has been the one that really addresses the postwar world in which children—the children of the wartime generation and their children—have grown up and needed (in the Convention's terms) provision, protection, and participation (to the extent of their "evolving capacities" in decisions affecting their lives).[13]

The framers of the Convention, many of them psychologists of the Vietnam War generation that so desired exit from the collective accumulating human trauma, understood that the crucial developmental period up to the age of three must be a period of relational matrix, a protective shield capable of sustaining a child through its maturation so that the child can become an active participant in his or her community and the world community, as a world citizen. Families, societies, and world organisations that are able to give children's rights priority, that is, to make them, as the Convention says, "paramount", do not live in the past, identifying with their aggressors, repeating their traumatisation, handing it—rather than good mothering—on to their children. They have been able to grasp the nature and dimensions of the traumatising past and "master the past" rather than identifying with the traumatising elements and repeating them.[14] The future unity of humankind depends upon how widely and deeply the peoples of the world can see the significance of this exemplary kind of unifying action. The old dream of contentment in civilisation, similarly, depends upon adding to the post-American Civil War insight, "The hand that rocks the cradle is the hand that rules the world,"[15] something more contemporary: the hand that rocks the cradle is the hand that heals the world.

Notes

1. The Greeks would not have spoken of an analogy in the rhetorical sense: the sameness of microcosmic and macrocosmic processes and patterns was a fact to be represented in a theory, a kind of language picture (in the sense that a Chinese character or ideogram is a language picture).

2. The European who most clearly grasped the implications for the unity of humankind of the pre-WWII preparatory period was Karl Jaspers, trained as a psychiatric neurologist, in his post-WWII *The Origin and Goal of History* (1949). But Jaspers had also been courageously prescient in his 1931 book *The Spiritual Situation of Our Time*, which won him the enmity of the Nazis, who later scheduled Jaspers and his Jewish wife for deportation to Auschwitz on the day the American Army entered Heidelberg.

3. Naturalists had warned of the destructive effects of human technologies since the eighteenth century, but Rachel Carson's *Silent Spring*, published in 1962, was epoch-making for taking the warning into the realm of genetics and for considering how nature can be not just cultivated or shaped by humans, but genetically altered.

4. The Cold War was incipient when the Soviets rejected the Declaration for its refusal to support absolute state sovereignty and to guarantee not just political but social, economic, and cultural rights. The first argument was a regressive, nationalistic one designed to prevent interference with Soviet expansion into Eastern Europe; the second a progressive, universalistic one. Ironically, over time it was American governments that refused regressively to sign declarations and conventions and accords that they viewed as infringements on state sovereignty. Thus did American governments imitate the worst in Soviet opposition to the unity of humankind, which is what assertion of absolute sovereignty implies.

5. The worst distortion of the analogy appeared in the nineteenth century when it was used to identify white Europeans as the most evolved and mature of people and societies, in contrast to the dark-skinned primitives—that is, it served race-thinking and imperialism. One of the most powerful counters to this distortion appeared right after

WWII in the anthropological studies of Claude Levi-Strauss, who was so respectful of *la pensée sauvage* and so sensitive to the corruptions of colonialism.

6. A fascinating entry into this literature has been made this year by Rebecca Solnit, whose *A Paradise Built in Hell: The Extraordinary Communities that Arise in Disaster*, describes communities built up or reconstituted after natural disasters like the San Francisco earthquake and Hurricane Katrina, by ordinary people acting together and helping each other in extraordinary ways. In effect, this is a study of the immediate reassertion of human *"polis*-dweller" nature, the triumph of sociability; but it is not a study of what happens over time to such resilient communities, when the traumatisation settles in and the traumatised must sustain their communities or their socially created protective shields. Veterans with PTSD will often describe how they functioned superhumanly during and immediately after a traumatising event and then "crashed" when they had to return home and live a "normal" life. Making a revolution "sustainable" similarly involves translating it and its initial violence into a phase of consolidation and constitution making.

7. This generalisation should be qualified with acknowledgement of the psychoanalytic literature on the Holocaust as a social trauma for the Jewish people, which includes some contributions on the children of Holocaust survivors, although it does not include much on the painful topic of identification with the aggressor in the survivor generation or among its children, or on the ways in which the Jews in the diaspora and in Israel were united with humankind in their trauma, as opposed to being distinguished by it, exceptional in it.

8. The major exception to this generalisation is the "Culture and Personality" school of psychoanalysis, led in the immediate post-war period by analysts and anthropologists at Columbia University (Abram Kardiner, Ralph Linton, Franz Boas, Ruth Benedickt, Margaret Mead, etc.), although the emphasis in this school was on how culture (chiefly child-rearing practices) shapes individuals, not on how individuals and cultures might be shaped by traumas. At the same time, the culture critic Richard Hofstader (1955) used "culture and personality" ideas to frame his extremely astute study of the "paranoid style in American politics", a delineation of individual paranoids and the paranoid groups they dominated during the rise to prominence of the Right in the anti-Communist 1950s and during Barry Goldwater's leadership of the Republican Party.

9. In his 1931 essay "Libidinal Types", Freud sketched his three character types—hysterical, obsessional, and narcissistic—and noted defence mechanisms characteristic of each. He also noted that they seldom appear in pure form. Most people are mixtures, for example,

narcissistic-obsessional—a combination in which grandiosity and moralistic rule-boundedness are the salient character traits.

10. America's postwar destiny has been deeply influenced by the fact that the Second World War (in the broad cluster-trauma meaning I suggested above) was not fought on American soil—with the extremely consequential exception of the offshore Pearl Harbor attack in 1941 that precipitated America's entry into the war. How crucial our territorial inviolability has been to our defence against trauma was immediately obvious when Pearl Harbor was invoked after 9/11, across the political spectrum but especially by those who wanted to use the terrorist attack as a *causus belli* for making war on Iraq, a nation that was said—falsely—to have nuclear weapons ready to use, and to be totalitarian and to be led by a Hitler.

11. Both President Johnson and President Nixon and their advisors were committed to preserving the image of invincible America even after they realised that the war could not be won: American "credibility" was said to be at stake. They assumed (in their worst possible case thinking) that a defeat in one location, Vietnam, would necessarily pave the way to other defeats in other spheres of interest around the world.

12. The Freudian text that most influenced the anti-Vietnam War student movement was Herbert Marcuse's *Eros and Civilization* (1955).

13. The Convention is organised to present the child's rights as "the three Ps": rights to provision, to protection, and to participation—the last the most radical for it denies that children are owned by their parents and under unqualified parental authority, and it affirms that children have "evolving capacities" (Article 5) that eventually fit them to actively engage in decision-making in matters affecting them (an empowerment, in effect, for citizenship). UNICEF has developed a detailed analysis of programmes that promote these three Ps, and all the signatories to the Convention submit to UNICEF biannual reports on their progress in the agreed-upon directions. That the United States does not hold itself to these standards and measurements is one of the key policy reasons why the condition of American children has deteriorated so drastically since the early 1970s, when a Comprehensive Child Development Act was vetoed by Richard Nixon during the Vietnam War.

14. I think the fact that the so-called Golden Rule has been formulated within every known religious tradition is a universal acknowledgement of the power of identification with the aggressor (or, as I prefer to say, the traumatiser) and acknowledgement of the healing power of confronting and defusing trauma (which may, but need not, entail forgiveness). But the Golden Rule has appeared in two different forms—one more therapeutic than the other. "Do unto others as you would have done unto you" is typical of the Abrahamic monotheistic religions where

an elite of believers (or non-sinners) is said to be able to do rewarding deeds, and thus be rewarded by being distinguished from the rest of humankind by God's ultimate judgment. They are "the chosen". By contrast, consider the restraining rule offered by Confucius: "Do not do unto others what you would not have done unto yourself," which presumes that humankind's peaceful unity will come if humans restrain themselves. In the Confucian form, which is quite psychoanalytic, you must think what would harm you if it were done to you—you must imagine yourself being traumatised or remember your traumatisation and on the basis of your empathic insight not become a traumatiser, identified with your traumatiser.

15. The popular poet William Ross Wallace published the famous poem entitled with this line in 1865, as America began its healing—still in course—from the Civil War.

References

Carson, R. (1962). *Silent Spring*. Boston: Houghton-Mifflin.

Freud, S. (1908d). "Civilized" sexual morality and modern nervous illness. *S. E.*, *9*: London: Hogarth, p. 177ff.

Freud, S. (1930a) *Civilization and Its Discontents*. *S. E. 21*. London: Hogarth, p. 59ff.

Freud, S. (1931a). Libidinal types. *S. E. 21*. London: Hogarth, p. 215ff.

Hofstadter, R. (1955). *The Paranoid Style in American Politics*. New York: Knopf.

Jaspers, K. (1931). *The Spiritual Situation of Our Time*. (In English under the title *Man in the Modern Age*.) New York: Henry Holt & Co., 1933.

Jaspers, K. (1949). *The Origin and Goal of History*. New Haven, CT: Yale University Press, 1953.

Khan, M. (1963). The concept of cumulative trauma. In: *The Privacy of the Self*. New York: International Universities Press, 1974.

Kris, E. (1956). The recovery of childhood memories in psychoanalysis. In: *Selected Papers of Ernst Kris*. New Haven, CT: Yale University Press, 1975.

Lasch, C. (1979). *The Culture of Narcissism*. New York: W. W. Norton.

Lévi-Strauss, Claude. (1955). *Tristes Tropiques*. New York: Atheneum, 1973.

Marcuse, H. (1955). *Eros and Civilization*. Boston: Beacon Press.

Reich, W. (1970). *The Mass Psychology of Fascism*. New York: Farrar, Straus & Giroux (from a 1942 German original manuscript).

Solnit, R. (2009). *A Paradise Built in Hell: The Extraordinary Communities that Arise in Disaster*. New York: Viking.

CHAPTER FOUR

Psychoanalysis and social democracy: a tale of two developments*

Elisabeth Young-Bruehl

fter World War I, Freudian psychoanalysis was approached
by reformers and revolutionaries in the Marxist tradition who
hoped to find in its theory and practice a psychological foundation for the future they envisioned. A "Freud-Marx synthesis" was
also an ideal for the democratic socialists among the younger psychoanalysts trained by Freud and his first followers. After World War II,
a second version of that "Marx-Freud" synthetic ideal began slowly
to emerge while both psychoanalysis and socialism were undergoing
profound changes. That synthesis powerfully influenced the "social
democracies" emergent in Europe and in other parts of the world. But
when the European social democracies began to respond in the 1980s to
the decline of the Soviet Union and to the rise of globalising capitalism,
which brought new immigrant populations to Europe and surges of
prejudice against them, the synthetic ideal needed reworking. In particular, psychoanalysis needed to be able to offer the "Freud-Marx synthesis" an updated analysis of aggression and prejudice.

---

* This article is based on the inaugural Freud Lecture, which I gave on October 13, 2010
at University College London, in the Psychoanalysis Unit, chaired by Juliet Mitchell. My
thanks to those who commented on it then and who have commented on it since.

Both sides of the synthesis have continued to develop, and a third version of the "Marx-Freud synthesis" is now a work in progress, not just in Europe but throughout a rapidly changing world. In this context, I want to contribute a brief—and necessarily schematic—history and some reflections on what might be done theoretically on the "Freud" side of that work in progress.

Throughout the European tradition, political thinkers who have hoped to guide their visions of ideal political arrangements with a theory of human nature have generally gone down one of two broad theoretical roads. The first road, mapped by Plato and remapped in the Enlightenment by Hobbes, assumes that humans are born with something disruptive inside them that is ignorant, wild, bad, rebellious, or patricidal: some original bent towards violence and sinfulness. This disruptive element needs containing or controlling by those who recognise it so that humans can live together in harmony or at least stability. In other words, humans need to be dominated and ruled. Those who have travelled the second road, as did Aristotle and Rousseau, believe that humans are born sociable and desirous of community; they assemble in gradually larger and larger communities, becoming more harmonious, but often relapsing, particularly when they defeat themselves with their learned *hubris,* their developed character flaws, and their acquired immoderation. People need to be helped to understand what they may be contributing when they fail to free themselves from external obstacles or fall short of their shared desires. Let me call these two theories, for short, "the control theory" and "the therapeutic theory".

Neither Marx nor Freud, the two most influential theorists on human nature in the twentieth century, were purely of the "men are born unfit for living together and need to be ruled" (control theory) nor the "men are born sociable but are vulnerable to failure" (therapeutic theory) type. Rather, Marx and Freud were full of contradictions, and exerted contradictory influences, providing their followers with justifications for all kinds of splits and factions, and all kinds of control practices as well as therapeutic practices.

The problem Freud's socialist followers had with him was that he started out Aristotelian and socially therapeutic and ended up a Hobbesian strong-government Platonist. To Wilhelm Reich, Siegfried Bernfeld, Otto Fenichel (and his so-called "Children's Seminar" associates in Berlin), to Erik Erikson, Erich Fromm and the Frankfurt School, and even to the not-very-Marxist members of the neo-Freudian group led by Karen Horney and the anthropological cultural-Freudian group at Columbia University, Freud was a theorist whose early work was perfectly suitable for the therapeutic ideal of sexual liberation. These political Freudians imagined sexual liberation as either the catalyst for broader social liberation or the first consequence of such a broad liberation. Freud once identified himself in a letter to Jung as a "liberator of youth", and the Marxist young of the 1920s embraced him as such—their therapist.

Freud did, however, think that sexual restraint, although productive of "modern nervous illness" (as he had said in 1905) when excessive, was in some form necessary. Nevertheless, in the 1920s, he largely left this topic to be developed by those around him who were involved in child development studies, education, and child guidance. He was supportive of their work, especially of August Aichhorn, once a schoolteacher, who was not only an analyst but the socialist Viennese government's supervisor of youth guidance clinics; Siegfried Bernfeld, a socialist Zionist youth leader; Willi Hoffer, who wrote on creative play in education; and by his daughter Anna, who was trained as a schoolteacher and ran several progressive children's centres and schools, one with her companion Dorothy Burlingham. Although others were concerned with the "Marx-Freud synthesis" in theory, these developmentalists and educators were synthesisers in practice—and thus harbingers of the kind of synthesis that actually came about after World War II.

In the realm of theory, Freud battled with Wilhelm Reich, who earned Freud's criticism when he left the democratic socialist camp and became a communist, and because he propounded an instinctual drive theory that was much too crudely biological for Freud. *Civilization and Its Discontents* (1930a) is the book of their quarrel. In it, Freud emphasised the dangers posed to humans living together by their inborn aggressive instinct, which is rooted in the death instinctual drive (*Todestriebe*), which he thought Reich ignored. In a particularly Hobbesian passage, Freud (1930a, p. 111) wrote: "... men are not gentle creatures, who want to be loved, who at most defend themselves if they are attacked; they are, on the contrary, creatures among whose instinctual endowments is to be reckoned a powerful share of aggressiveness."

In *Civilization and Its Discontents*, Freud makes it clear that aggression is the most dangerous instinctual drive, which must be strongly contained. Meanwhile, confusingly, the sexual instinct and the ego instincts of survival, together called the "life instincts" (Eros), have become more Aristotelian than they were in the "Three Essays on the Theory of Sexuality" (1905d): they have become more given to sociability.[1] Eros binds humans into groups and groups into larger and larger formations in the Aristotelian manner. Freud even wondered if Eros might directly cure, by love, the disruptions of aggression, rooted in Thanatos. But he ended his text on a sceptical and ambivalent note:

> ... civilization is a process in the service of Eros, whose purpose is to combine single human individuals, and after that families, then races, peoples and nations, into one great unity, the unity of mankind. Why this has to happen, we do not know; the work of Eros is precisely this. These collections of men are to be libidinally bound to one another. Necessity alone, the advantages of work in common, will not hold them together. But man's natural aggressive instinct, the hostility of each against all and all against each, opposes this programme of civilization. (Freud, 1930a, p. 122)

Any socialist Freudian reading this passage in 1930 would have perceived it as a conundrum. Although Freud had been speculating about the Eros/Thanatos contrast for nearly a decade, he had never said what he wrote in this passage: that civilisation is *in the service* of Eros; it is Eros's therapy for taming aggression. In all Freud's earlier socio-political works, the "programme of civilization" had ruled over libido, repressing it, reining it in, and inducing neurosis with its control. Now Eros and its programme of civilisation must try to cure aggression—or, perhaps it would be better to say *control* aggression.

Despite this ambivalent passage, Freud was so convinced of the power of aggression that he found all theorists—not just Wilhelm Reich—who believed in innate sociability to be as hopelessly naïve and as idealistic as Rousseau. Indeed, concerning the naïve followers of Marx, with their "idealistic mis-conception of human nature" (Freud, 1930a, p. 143), Freud wrote:

> According to them, man is wholly good and is well-disposed to his neighbor; but the institution of private property has corrupted his nature. The ownership of private wealth gives the individual power, and with it the temptation to ill-treat his neighbor; while the man who is excluded from possession is bound to rebel in hostility against his oppressor .... [A]bolishing private property [would only] deprive the human love of aggression of one of its instruments, certainly a strong one, though certainly not the

strongest; but [it would] in no way alter the differences in power and influence which are misused by aggressiveness, nor [would it] alter anything in its nature. Aggressiveness is not created by property ... (p. 113)

So, a social therapy that eliminated private property would do no good, Freud thought, because aggression only uses—or misuses—property. Property does not create aggression. Even before civilisation, among "primitive" people with little property, aggression reigned, as it reigns among children in a nursery. Freud (1930a, p. 113) implied that aggression is somehow more fundamental than Eros or the life instincts: "[It] forms the basis of every relation of affection and love among people (with the single exception, perhaps, of the mother's relation to her male child)." (This last remark would, I think, be recognised by most readers then and now as an instance of wishful thinking and as clear evidence that people—even the pioneer theorist of unconscious wishes, Sigmund Freud—theorise according to their wishes.)

When Freud offered his redefinition of Eros as a constructive, binding force in *Civilization and Its Discontents*, the sexual liberationists could claim that Freud had come back to their camp and was once again their therapist, their visionary. But, of course, to make Freud once again a therapeutic Aristotelian theorist of inborn Eros-driven or life-instinctual sociability, it was necessary to jettison Freud's theory of the death drive, Thanatos. So, just before and then again after World War II, Reich railed against the death drive theory while he developed his own fundamentalist sexual-instinctualist drive theory and attributed aggression to sexual repression (1933). Fenichel (1953) wrote a sophisticated, meticulous critique of the death instinct. Erich Fromm, in *The Sane Society* (1955), and later Herbert Marcuse, in *Eros and Civilization* (1955), each in his own way rejected the death drive. It can even be said generally that any Freudian who wanted—or who now wants—to be a socialist must dispense with the death instinct in its Freudian formulation. You cannot assume that human beings can be liberated from repressive social arrangements and their self-defeating, hubristic ways, while you assume at the same time that there must be a strong state to control the "hostility of each against all and all against each" (this was Freud's rendering of *homo homini lupus*, man is to man a wolf, the aphorism dear to Hobbes). But, on the other hand, if you do not think aggression is drive-based in the Freudian way, you need to work out a different understanding of it.

When these debates among Freudians and between Freudians and Marxists continued after World War II, they took different forms, and there were variants in different national and regional contexts. But, in general, it can be said of Western Europe that postwar socialism was centrally concerned with national social support—the so-called "welfare state"—and with the security that might come from a united, federated Europe, beyond the nation state. The focus was on therapeutically supporting sociability and on building larger unities; in other words, making treaties to weigh against the tendency of societies to self-defeat. Socialism—especially in Western Europe—became more about therapy than about control and total economic planning, especially as the totalitarian nature of the Stalinist Soviet Union became better known. In the immediate postwar period, the effort to redefine aggression focused on prejudices considered as social diseases (or as hubristic immoderation in Aristotle's terms).

There was an especially stark contrast between this situation in Western Europe and that in the United States, where what little socialist theorising had existed in the prewar period, particularly during the New Deal, disappeared as the Cold War escalated. The émigré socialist analysts from Europe had to go underground when they arrived in the United States, and the generation of their trainees became (with a few exceptions) studiously nonpolitical and uninterested in social theory, which, when it existed, was neutrally called "applied analysis".[2] The most important postwar developments in US psychoanalysis originated among the European émigré analysts. But because they had no domestic *political* audience, for political influence they had to rely on psychoanalytic colleagues who had remained in Europe, where psychoanalysts were far freer to establish alliances with socialists. Because many of these colleagues had relocated to Great Britain, it was there that psychoanalysis, particularly child analysis, was most vigorous, and most influential among socialists.

The postwar moment was, of course, ripe for this collaboration because the British Labour Party unexpectedly defeated Churchill and swept into power in 1945 with a programme for comprehensive social security, as well as a vision of an extensive nationalisation of industries—a vision not shared on the Continent. The result was the most planned postwar economy outside the Soviet sphere of influence. The cooperation between psychoanalysts and the Labour Party took place mostly in the domain of the National Health Service (NHS), which had been outlined to the British people over the BBC during the war in the 1942 Beveridge Report. The promise of this report was one of the main reasons why the Labour Party fared so well with the British electorate. The NHS was also the part of the postwar socialist vision that lasted longest and was most important—far outlasting the ineffectual nationalisation initiative.

Not just in Great Britain, of course, but across Europe, psychoanalysis and socialism had postwar resurgences. Both developed in countries that had been—unlike the United States—materially devastated. Entire civilian populations (not just soldiers) were psychically traumatised by the war, which claimed an estimated fifty-five million lives worldwide, and by the Holocaust, in which six million Jews and Romani and also large numbers of socialists and communists died in camps. Psychoanalysts and socialists alike had to respond to the needs of traumatised populations; both were, so to speak, trauma-focused and trauma-driven.[3] Most psychoanalysts shifted to emphasising environmental influences on people—especially children—internalising, and responsive psychic splitting. People and their unconscious minds came to be viewed less as influenced by instinctual drives (including aggression) and more as influenced by their environments and their object relations—particularly by their experiences of loss, separation, exile, abandonment, grief, and shame and guilt feelings about all of these experiences. Group analysis flourished. Only Melanie Klein and her followers in the British Psychoanalytical Society retained Freud's theory of Thanatos in its prewar form, and this allegiance prevented them from having any political influence until they modified it and became "modern Kleinians" (as many South American Kleinians were all along).[4]

Socialist theorists, activists, and elected representatives to postwar governments, who came to be known collectively as "social democrats", emphasised working through state programmes to provide healing and healthy developmental contexts, particularly for children and their mothers (and especially war widows). The "welfare states" they sponsored were designed to serve development from the cradle forward, especially in terms of services that families alone could not provide. This therapeutic emphasis had never been central to Marxism in its prewar versions, from democratic socialism to Leninism and Stalinism.

For their therapeutic purpose, the social democrats needed a theory of development, a theory of basic human needs, and psychoanalysis had such a theory, especially for children. The British Labour government commissioned reports on children's needs from, for example, John Bowlby, and took heed of the wartime residential nursery work done by Anna Freud's group at Hampstead. By the 1950s, the theory was being articulated as a theory for the human life course by Erik Erikson. *Childhood and Society* (1950) was better known in Great Britain in the 1950s than it was in the United States, where Erikson was frequently criticised for his socialist European past and questioned by the House Un-American Activities Committee. So the "Marx-Freud synthesis" of the immediate postwar period was a practical synthesis especially focused on child development: not a matter of grand theory but of pragmatic theory. Europe's reconstruction was deeply linked to psychoanalysis's reconstructions of disrupted, traumatised childhoods and adult lives.

I do not have the space to tell the complicated story of how different social democratic variations grew in postwar Europe, in Japan, as well as in the states that emerged in collapsed European colonial empires or that struggled in the shadow of the Soviet Union. Nor can I tell the story of how European émigrés were crucial in fostering South American social democracies after the war, particularly in the states that later succumbed to horrific US-backed anti-socialist military dictatorships in the 1970s (e.g., Argentina, Chile, Uruguay), when so many analysts were persecuted. But I do want to emphasise that postwar social democrats around the world neither embraced revolutionary violence (as many communists did) nor subscribed to the Hobbesian notion that normal aggression needs strong state control. Most took their stand as pragmatists and reformers, but many were drawn to Mahatma Gandhi's philosophical commitment to nonviolent action, which had been so effective in the Indian independence movement (at least until Gandhi was assassinated in 1948). Gandhi's theory of human nature involved renouncing any conception of inborn human aggression (i.e., anything like the Freudian death instinct).[5]

Nowhere in Western Europe did practising psychoanalysts participate in or theorise about social democratic states in terms of their economic and political principles, but they did, as I implied before, try to meet in their therapeutic terms the acute need amongst Europeans to rebuild, restore, find security, and deal with a massive—indeed, an unprecedented—social-political trauma. Insofar as the social democratic states were states supplying necessary services, psychoanalysts were at their most influential as health and education theorists, operating out of what they had learned in the course of the war concerning the basic human developmental needs that must be met by families, communities, and states. In turn, psychoanalytic therapeutic work and research was subsidised and promoted by the social democracies as it never had been before the war (except for brief periods in Budapest and Berlin). The postwar British Labour government gave psychoanalysis perhaps its most important public moment when it sponsored BBC broadcasts of parenting talks—published later as *The Child, the Family, and the Outside World* (1964)—by D. W. Winnicott, who had worked as a paediatrician for evacuation services during the war.

Eventually, the psychoanalysis-socialism synthesis was articulated in a basic shared principle, which is, by this time, known around the world. That principle is that in the first years of a human being's life, a foundation is laid for good physical and mental health or the lack thereof—and the remainder of life is either supported by a good foundation or undermined by a poor one. (Technically, the principle is known in psychoanalysis by the name Erik Erikson gave to it: "the epigenetic principle".) This general principle now guides all national and international policy that is or aspires to be progressive. For example, in the 1990s, the World Health Organization prioritised maternal and child health on this principle, aligning itself with the way the principle was written into the 1959 UN Declaration on the Rights of the Child and the 1989 Convention designed to implement the Declaration.[6]

However, the postwar social democracies were at their best and most therapeutic when their leaders thought not only in terms of what children and adults need for healthy development but in terms of the root causes—not just the symptoms—for conditions that do not favour healthy development. They looked to the causal interactions among inequality and poverty, violence, and war. Dozens of psychoanalysts wrote books on the causes of war that were well known among progressive activists, especially those who became involved in the Campaign for Nuclear Disarmament in Great Britain.[7] They were at their most therapeutic when they were also concerned with—to use Aristotle's analytical term—*hubris* and the human proclivity towards prejudice and defeating the natural aspiration of people to combine into larger and large unities. "What is the origin of prejudice?" largely replaced "What is the origin of aggression?" as the key question of what might be called "misdevelopment".

For this dimension of their therapeutic work, directed at conditions that do not foster healthy development, psychoanalysts supplied many ideas, including ideas directly relevant to child-care institutions. For example, René Spitz (1965), a protégé of Sándor Ferenczi, examined how child misdevelopment happens in hospitals that do not meet a child's basic needs for love and nurturing. Hospitals can become "psychotoxic", producing "hospitalism". Eventually, theorising about social trauma and its psychological effects came from these ideas (and connected up with a prewar vein of theorising about traumatic war neuroses and about child abuse). But no general theory concerning prejudices and aggression—the motivations for inflicting traumas—developed, although the old death instinct theory continued to be vigorously criticised and various frustration theories of aggression were advanced.

Postwar social democrats such as Jean Monnet, who were dedicated to a future united Europe, addressed themselves to this matter of misdevelopment without the benefit of psychoanalytic theory. They imagined a world beyond fascisms and nationalisms; beyond exclusionary ideologies and prejudices. They shared this vision with those who drafted the Charter of the United Nations in 1946, and the Universal Declaration of Human Rights in 1948. Since the end of World War II, the number of federations and international organisations, governmental and NGO, working in the Aristotelian mode to guide human beings into larger and larger entities has grown exponentially. How to overcome the boundaries of developmental differences and prejudices is a constant topic. The most direct psychoanalytic contributions to this trend and this topic were made when the UN Convention on the Rights of the Child was drafted between 1959 and 1989. The Convention's international drafting group included several psychoanalytically trained developmentalists, but no theorists of prejudice.[8]

Those who worked pragmatically for a psychoanalysis-socialism synthesis after the war did not look to the prewar Marxist Freudians or Freudian Marxists for their theoretical orientation. Indeed, quite the opposite. They looked to two elements of the Freudian tradition that the prewar synthesisers had begun to develop but had not, ultimately, established theoretically. The postwar Freudians took these elements up practically, and worked on them theoretically; but—in my opinion—there are further theoretical steps to take.

Let me consider these two elements of theory by returning to Freud's instinctual-drive theory. In his later years, starting with *Beyond the*

Pleasure Principle (1920g), Freud (as I noted before) subsumed the sexual instincts and the ego instincts under the combinatory term "life instincts". But he gave no attention to developing this concept; he just behaved as though "life instincts" was another term for libido—particularly by using the term Eros as a synonym. What are the elided ego instincts? Before 1920, in his first instinct theory, Freud viewed hunger (first satisfied in the oral stage) as the paradigmatic ego instinct and spoke of individual and species survival and security (i.e., life maintenance) as the goals of the ego instincts.[9] In his "Three Essays", he had associated the "functions of vital importance" or ego instincts with what he called "the affectionate current" of human desire, as contrasted to "the sexual current" (1905d, p. 200). This implies that affection, love, and attachment are essential to an individual's survival, to preventing failure to thrive, and to growing in relatedness to others.

But Freud did not explore the affectionate current or the ego instincts generally as he became preoccupied with Thanatos. Only a few prewar analysts were concerned with the ego instincts. The most important investigation was in the Budapest School with Imre Hermann's (1936) work on clinging and Michael Balint's (1968) elaboration of it. There was a step in the same direction with Ian Suttie's (1935) attention to a child's need for tenderness (see Young-Bruehl, 2004), a step suggested by Ferenczi in his last papers.[10] Rudolph Loewenstein wrote suggestively in 1940 on the "vital and somatic instincts", but the American publishers of his *Selected Papers* (1982) did not include the paper in their volume! European psychoanalysis did not arrive at the importance of clinging or needing tenderness until John Bowlby got there under the term "attachment"—his translation of Hermann's clinging instinct, and Winnicott under the concept of "using an object". (Object relations theorists such as Ronald Fairbairn wrote about relationality, but did so by distancing themselves from Freud's drive theory.) Thus, it took a long time to establish the idea that there is a basic human drive for attachment and security, for relationship (which is also obvious among the mammals, which are by no means "wild animals"). As linguists, neurolinguists, and evolutionary psychologists have moved in recent years in the direction of hypothesising that there is an innate drive for language and symbolic communication (i.e., an innate "universal grammar"), "the language instinct" has begun to be explored as though it were what the Budapest School theorists called an "ego instinct".[11]

Bowlby and Winnicott were truly Aristotelian, as Ferenczi, Hermann, Balint, and Suttie had been (and as Sullivan was in the United States). They were not arguing—in the way Freud thought naïve—that "Humans are born *good* and desirous of community," which is a moral (and even moralistic) proposition; their claim was "Humans are born for and into relationships, without which they cannot live, they fail to thrive." Unfortunately, it was not until the 1970s that this European strand of thought connected with the most influential psychoanalytic work on the ego instincts in postwar social democratic Japan. There, Takeo Doi explicitly took his bearings from Freud's (and Darwin's) concept of the ego instincts, arguing in *The Anatomy of Dependence* (1971) that human beings have an innate drive for sociability—called *amae* in Japanese—that can, when frustrated, become perverted into prejudices and aggression against other humans and, on the national level, perverted into militarism. Doi felt that most Freudians—he excepted Balint's book *The Basic Fault* (1968)—completely ignored or underestimated human dependency needs in early childhood. Thus, they could not focus on the central human task of continuing to get these dependency needs fulfilled while becoming more independent in adulthood. This is the task of community-making in which the childhood dependency needs can be met and adult dependency needs can be allowed.[12]

But, even though they lacked a concept such as ego instincts, those analysts who emphasised attachment or relational needs were certainly aware of their centrality in the early mother-child dyad, and aware that if they are not satisfied there or in another relationship, pathology (or misdevelopment) ensues. And it became apparent during the postwar period that the pathology that ensues is not just the *neurotic* pathology that ensues when the sexual drive is unsatisfied or distorted, but what is now known, thanks to Anna Freud's postwar work, as "developmental pathology".[13] Developmental pathology is most frequently caused by adverse external, environmental conditions—in the family or in society—affecting one or more of what Anna Freud called "the developmental lines".

It is a short trip from this elaboration of the ego instincts (without the name "ego instincts") to the idea that human beings cannot live well or happily in their families or communities or political arrangements unless these do not thwart their ego instincts; and to the idea that this simple truth should be the basis for social psychoanalysis and its synthesis with socialism. A social democratic society should, before all else, support the ego-instinctual drive, for a healthy child is the parent of the future as well as of the future's children. Included in that goal is a healthy sexual development—the old Freudian Left ideal—because a healthy sexual development will not occur for an unhealthy, neglected, or abused, or generally not well-parented, educated, or provisioned child who is not prepared for democratic political life.

The ego-instinctual element of Freudian theory has, thus, slowly received an articulation in theory, even if not one with a drive theory or with a reworking of Freud's first drive theory. The second element, which is key to thinking about misdevelopment or developmental pathology on the social level, has been much less explored. That second element, which the prewar political Freudians hoped would be the foundation for social psychoanalysis, was Freud's characterology.

Freud himself never elaborated his characterology, but kept making gestures in his late work, including *Civilization and Its Discontents*. In the short essay, "Libidinal Types" (1931a), he outlined a three-part characterology consisting of hysterical, obsessional, and narcissistic types (*Idealtypen*), which are normal but which over the life course can become distorted and misdeveloped (or we might say now "disordered"). The political Freudians all went this way, wanting to be able to arrive at what they called social or societal character types as well. Their launch was Reich's *Character Analysis* (1931) a kind of *summa* of the ideas that he developed while offering seminars in Vienna between 1924 and 1930 on his therapeutic technique, which was called "the analysis of character".

Characteristically, Reich, who was himself extremely narcissistic, came to interpret his own technique narcissistically, and made it into a kind of strong state, planned economy of a technique, full of instruction. But, more generally, not just Reich but the other leftist Freudians were held back from really developing their character theory—as Freud himself had been—by their view of character distortions as distortions only of the sexual drive, to the neglect of the ego-instinctual drive.[14] The Japanese psychoanalyst Takeo Doi was an exception: after the war, he developed a characterology and a theory of social character by focusing on modes of frustration of the ego-instinctual drive for affection and security, *amae*.[15]

However, the analysis of character in its early-Reich formulation (to which Berta Bornstein and Anna Freud also contributed) was crucial within psychoanalysis to the later development of defence analysis into analysis of social defences. After World War II, social defences, the key ingredients of social pathology and character diseases, went under the name prejudices.

Among the most important postwar explorations of social defences or prejudices were the volumes in the Studies in Prejudice series, including Ernest Simmel's inaugural edited volume, *Anti-Semitism: A Social Disease* (1948). In 1951, the Frankfurt School Marxists in exile produced the best-known volume in the series, *The Authoritarian Personality*, by Theodore Adorno et al. These works convinced postwar pragmatic socialists that they needed to focus their attention not just on class conflict and class struggle, but on all forms of social and political exclusion and production of inequality—on all forms of prejudice considered as a social disease. Social democracy came to mean, in this sense, maximally inclusionary democracy, and the European social democrats designed programmes for bringing excluded peoples into citizenship—and into the welfare states. (Later, terms such as "multiculturalism" came into play to point to the ideal of maximal inclusion.)

It is a short trip from this line of thought to the idea that some societies and political arrangements promote some kinds of character development whereas others promote others. And to the corollary idea that societies are shaped by the clustering in them of characters of one sort or another (as Freud (1921c) had thought obsessionals and narcissists cluster in armies or hierarchical churches). Societies do as the dominating or preponderating kinds of characters in them do, and the dominant influence the next generation's character-formation. There are characters who are undeveloped, immature, distorted, or in some way developmentally pathological and they come to be so in societal environments, just as they help make societal environments unhealthy when they have the power to do so. A societal diagnostic sense is key to societal reform, or, at least, to working towards a mature society that supports healthy characters of different sorts and does not foster character disorders or social diseases that are, basically, aggressively exclusionary. Societal disease identification is to social theory what epidemiology is to preventative public health—except that identifying social diseases and their causes is much more complicated than finding a microbe.

Postwar social democratic societies needed a clear sense of which human needs are basic, how those basic needs develop, and how society could and should be responsive to them; and they got that sense from psychoanalysis—at least practically. But they also needed a theory of prejudice in order to understand how to focus democratic socialism on equality and maximal inclusion of once-excluded groups, on human rights, and on political structures moving beyond nation states and exclusionary sovereignty. It would have been helpful if they had obtained this, too, from psychoanalysis, but it was not available in the needed form, which I am suggesting could be characterologically oriented.[16] When the social democratic states came under attack from within, from groups of their own citizens, in the late 1970s and 1980s, this need became glaringly obvious.

Let me turn now to what happened to postwar European social democracies in the 1970s and 1980s, when, as I have suggested, they came under attack from within. This is a complicated story, so I will be stressing only particular parts of it as I look at the unravelling of the guiding but incompletely theorised postwar psychoanalysis-socialism synthesis—for it is that part of the story, in my opinion, that present psychoanalysts need to address more completely. Let me begin by looking at the main factor that kept the ego-instinctual drive from being theorised and the main factor that kept the theory of prejudices from being in place when it was acutely needed, as it was in the 1980s and as it still is today.

During the late 1960s, feminists came forward to criticise forcefully psychoanalysis for its theory of female psychology and development—a much-needed criticism, launched among socialists by Simone de Beauvoir right after the war. Many socialist feminists wanted to jettison Freudian theory altogether, which they considered a monument of Victorian sexism. On the other hand, there were feminists who wanted to reform psychoanalysis rather than reject it, and many of them were inspired by the prewar "Freud-Marx synthesis" with its emphasis on sexual liberation[17]—and not so much by the postwar work on child development or on prejudices. For the 1960s Women's Liberation Movement, the 1920s sexual liberation theorists, and the 1920s critics of Freudian female psychology like Karen Horney and Clara Thompson, were key. Only later did it become clear how the feminist critique of the patriarchal family had left unexplored the question of what kinds of childrearing arrangements would be best for children—girls and boys.

As the Women's Liberation Movement grew and became influential outside the European-American world, one feature that had not been addressed at all in the 1920s became especially prominent: more and more women realised that their own sexual development had been shaped by experiences of sexual violence or childhood sexual abuse. Many came to believe that the commonness of sexual abuse had been known by the early psychoanalysts (i.e., Freud and his followers), but denied or attributed only to unconscious fantasy. A second surge of feminist criticism developed in the 1980s and launched what are known now as "the Freud Wars".[18] As these wars went on, feminists made important contributions to trauma theory, but Freud's theory of the instinctual drives largely disappeared, being judged by many to be part of the reason he so misunderstood or misconstrued the ubiquity of sexual trauma among women. The whole of Freud's work on instinctual drives—sexual, ego-instinctual, or aggressive—receded from view. Eventually, this recession became characteristic of psychoanalytic theory in general while it responded to the feminist critique. The ego-instinctual drives were not explored. They were forgotten; attention to object relations grew whereas instinctual drive theory in general shrank—as though the two dimensions of theory were detachable or irreconcilable.

Many feminist theorists also turned their attention away from the postwar studies on prejudice and the characterological investigations that underpinned those studies, because Freudian characterology was deemed too embedded in Freud's instinctual drive theory. Prejudice against women—called "sexism" after 1965—received enormous attention from feminists, much of it referencing Simone de Beauvoir's *The Second Sex* (1949). However, the various feminist psychoanalytic theories of sexism focused not on types of sexist character or social character, but on the psychodynamics by which all men in patriarchal societies denigrate women in similar ways. In recent years, because feminists have had to devote considerable attention to the waves of backlashes against women from religious and political fundamentalisms, there has been more pointing out of sexism in action and mounting of efforts to combat it than theorising about it—certainly than theorising about it with a characterological framework. (The major exception to this generalisation is the wealth of theorising about how various prejudices intermingle—sexism, racism, homophobia—but in this important work definitions of those prejudices are often presumed in advance and the role of character in them is not a topic.)

On the socialism side of the psychoanalysis-socialism synthesis, the European-American world of the late 1960s was a period of anti-government protests precipitated by opposition to the United States' war in Vietnam. In Western Europe, a generation of young socialists led anti-war demonstrations, which soon turned into demonstrations against a particular feature of their own European welfare states. This was that the states were not prepared for the changed demographic of the so-called Baby Boom generation and the large portion of it that was prepared for university work because of the social democratic emphasis on universal public education. Universities in Great Britain and on the continent were turning away—because of a lack of space, faculties, and scholarship—most of those who wanted a university education. Many of the protesters identified not with the socialisms of the welfare states in which they had grown up and that seemed to be failing them but with the socialisms of the non-European developing world—such as Vietnam, Mao's China, and Castro's Cuba. Their psychoanalytic theorist was Franz Fanon. Embraced for his analysis of prejudice in *Black Skin, White Masks* (1952), which reduced all prejudices to racism, Fanon was embraced even more for his support of revolutionary violence in *The Wretched of the Earth* (1961).

The violence-minded young socialists did not prevail. As student revolts moved into the Eastern European colonies of the Soviet Union, which were stirring with labour movements such as the Polish Solidarity movement, debates about whether violent tactics were justified were resolved in the direction of Gandhian nonviolence for workers and students. After the fall of the Berlin Wall in 1989 and the collapse of the Soviet Union in 1991, the revolutions in Eastern Europe were "velvet revolutions", that is, they were nonviolent revolutions to establish social democracies of the sort that had emerged and flourished in Western Europe between 1945 and the 1980s. Today, in Russia and the countries of Eastern Europe, there are psychoanalytic societies and many NGOs working to improve conditions for healthy childhood development (and, importantly, to prevent child abuse, including sexual abuse) in the manner of the social democracies in the immediate postwar period.

But, in Western Europe, the rebels of the 1960s and 1970s did not turn to psychoanalysis or to the psychoanalytic emphasis on a healthy early childhood or to preventing prejudice in order to ground (or reground) the policies of social democracy. Instead, they became caught up in either defensively trying to stop the gradual decline of the social democracies or in contributing to that decline themselves, as the "New Labour" members of the Labour Party did in the UK when they abandoned the ideals of social democracy and turned away from the European Union. Many of the exceptions to these trends have become activists in the European Green Parties, which are constructively social democratic, environmentalist, and support the European Union.

The specific context in which the internal crisis of the Western European social democracies began was the recession of 1973, the so-called "oil recession", which was the first truly global recession since the 1930s, and which became a spur to the reactive phenomenon known by the early 1980s as "globalisation". The rise of transnational corporations, transnational banking, and speculative financial markets was a reaction to a global recession. Simultaneously, the financial sustainability of the European welfare states came into question and an alluring theory of "free market" capitalism was taken up by national leaders opposed to the welfare state—chiefly, Margaret Thatcher in the UK. US President Ronald Reagan was a critic of "welfarism" and a proponent of the privatisation of service industries, and his policies were buttressed by neoconservative "free market" economic theorists (based at the University of Chicago) for whom social democracy was anathema. By the mid-1990s, propelled by the collapse of the Soviet Union, US conservatives were asserting the world triumph of capitalism. The Western European social democracies influenced by this so-called "Washington Consensus" lurched away from their founding principles of social welfare and international federation. Even the paradigmatic social democracy, Sweden, went under conservative leadership several times in the 1990s and suffered the consequences for years, even after it turned back to social democracy—only to lurch away again during the current economic crisis.

In sum, during the last two decades, even before the acute economic crisis of the last two years, European social democracies have been riven with controversies and shifts to the centre and the right. The goal of European union has stayed in view, but it has come under enormous countervailing pressure by subscribers to strong-state nationalism and by people who welcome the idea of states controlled by *economic* elites—elites willing to make the state work for the benefit of capitalist enterprise by privatising and deregulating. But the most influential trend undermining the European social democracies, as everyone can now see, is their internal conflicts over how to deal with the huge swells of immigration from countries in which the gaps between the rich and the poor have become chasms as a consequence of the "Washington Consensus". The surge of economic refugees—and of political refugees, as well—has strained the social welfare provisions of the social democracies, but, even more, it has stirred up tremendous prejudice and impulse to exclude. There is a direct correlation between the rise of rightist national parties dedicated to prejudice against those deemed non-national—immigrants, non-Christians, non-Whites—and the globalising form of "free market" capitalism. So the relative lack in the social democracies of a fully articulated theory of prejudice is an urgent matter.

All the European social democracies now contain political parties with explicitly anti-immigrant platforms similar in their formulations to the racist and anti-Semitic platform of the Nazi Party in 1933. Germany has a growing extreme right-wing party, as do Austria, Holland, and France. Even a relatively homogenous society like Sweden now has the misnamed rightist Sweden Democrats, which is not just conservative but explicitly anti-immigrant and anti-Muslim. In Israel, founded as a social democratic state in 1948, with a radical psychoanalytic-educational *kibbutz* system, the current far-right parties have exclusionary anti-immigration platforms.

In the face of this worldwide convulsion, psychoanalysis has been almost entirely on the defensive. The effect of the shift towards strong states governed by *economic* elites—not political elites in the old Hobbesian sense, but a wealthy class buoyed up by the growth of transnational corporations and international speculative banking—on psychoanalysis has been a loss of public standing, research capacities, and patients as other forms of psychiatry and psychopharmacology that are more profitable and less concerned with human development have flourished. Health care, specifically, has become increasingly a matter of economic decisions influenced by economic elites in the pharmaceutical industries and in the private and state insurance industries.[19]

The most active research that is still psychoanalytic is in the area of neuroscience, but this has been for the most part resolutely apolitical, that is, it is not concerned descriptively or preventatively with the social contexts in which children develop in a healthy way, even though it is appealed to by educationalists committed to early childhood education and preschools. Psychoanalytic neuroscience possesses a principle that is directly related to the epigenetic principle that grounds concern for early childhood development: it is called "neuroplasticity", which means that the brain is not an organ that is "hard-wired" like a machine, but an organ that is always changing at the neuronal level, and can be influenced therapeutically far more than was previously thought. But this principle has not yet been explored for its political or therapeutic-political importance. And it is not yet being used to protect children from being psychopharmacologically treated for conditions that are the result of being raised in poor environments and familial and social trauma.

In the realm of Studies in Prejudice, psychoanalytic work has been done since the 1970s on the roots of violence and trauma that has extended to encompass "intergenerational transmission of trauma", which is now understood to be crucial to intergenerational transmission of prejudice. But earlier characterological investigations of prejudices are not being drawn upon and developed to explore the worldwide surge of prejudice accompanying the vast movements of population and the internal deteriorations of social democracies. In my book, *The Anatomy of Prejudices* (1996), I mapped the lines of theory development that I think are needed, beginning with the claim that prejudices are not all alike in their origin or structure, although they share common features such as the projection or externalisation onto a target group of parts of the prejudiced person's self or a prejudiced group's self-image.

There seem to me to be three basic forms of prejudice, correlating to the basic Freudian character types: narcissistic, obsessional, and hysterical, each with a particular defensive function. Relating the forms of prejudice to the characters and motivations of prejudiced persons, not to the characteristics or alleged characteristics of their target groups, can make it clear that, for example, narcissists can be prejudiced against women, as sexist narcissists certainly are, but also against other groups, like adolescents or children, who are not as the narcissist wishes them to be. Narcissistic prejudice denies "the other" any independent identity—or, in the case of children, development towards independence. Obsessionals can be prejudiced against Jews, but also against other groups (e.g., Muslims) perceived to be part of a conspiracy infiltrating and spreading evil and corruption or terror within the fortress of the obsessional's pure society—operating like germs or pollutants. Obsessional prejudice is eliminative towards "the other".

The hysteric's prejudices protect him or her primarily against groups perceived as primitively sexual and both alluring and envy-inspiring. Emphasising the function and purpose of prejudices for prejudiced persons is, to my mind, the key to prevention. When people do not need their prejudices to inflate themselves or armour themselves because of their feeling of vulnerability to infiltrators, or keep themselves from forbidden (e.g., incestuous or same-group) desires, they are less inclined to satisfy their needs with aggression, oppression, and violence. There are "developmental lines" of prejudice development that can instruct us about reducing *needs for* prejudices. Such need-reduction should be a part of all national public health and education initiatives.[20]

Basically, psychoanalysis has not gone fully forward on the two fronts where it did its most important work in the postwar period; it has been on the defensive, as the social democracies it supported have been. And it is, it seems to me, on these two fronts—the elaboration of ego-instinctual needs and ideas of how to meet them, and the characterologically grounded theory of prejudice development and how to use it for prejudice prevention—that psychoanalysis and socialism both need to focus. This is crucial to their continued work for the therapeutic politics that was their shared postwar vision and that was their deep connection to the vision of therapeutic politics that has continually struggled for inclusion in the Western tradition.

Notes

1. The *Standard Edition* often uses "instinct" where Freud used *Trieb* (drive), for example, *Todestrieb, Sexualtrieb, Ichtrieb, Lebenstrieb*. The drives are not instincts as the word is commonly used in English, that is, immutable hereditary patterns of behaviour shared by virtually all members of a species. Drives are inborn but vary from person to person in terms of their pressure for action, their aims, and their objects.
2. See Russell Jacoby (1983) and Paul Robinson (1969).
3. As were the psychoanalytic groups in the Southern Cone of South America, which had many European émigré members. As their period of one-party military dictatorships began in the 1970s, the South Americans frequently compared (and contrasted) their "social traumas" with those inside the Third Reich between 1933 and 1945. Before then, the "Marx-Freud synthesis" among South Americans was more related to the prewar European synthesis. The career of the Viennese-trained Marie Langer (1989) in her Argentinian exile and then in her second exile in Mexico is like a microcosm of this two-part developmental line. (See Balan, 1991; Hollander, 2010.)
4. Lacan also retained the death drive thesis, and it was adopted by those in Paris who tried to synthesise not Freud and Marx but Lacan and Althusser—a story I cannot take up here.

5. Gandhi's therapy for human *hubris* and self-defeat was more ascetic than was acceptable to most of his followers, who engaged in socialist-oriented nonviolent political action, like Martin Luther King, Jr. or Nelson Mandela. Erik Erikson took up the matter of Gandhi's asceticism in *Gandhi's Truth* (1969).

6. The epigenetic principle guided the drafting group of the US 1971 Comprehensive Child Development Act, which included psychoanalytically trained paediatricians; but that unusual postwar "Good Society" legislative effort of a social democratic sort was vetoed by Richard Nixon after narrowly passing in both houses of Congress. Dr Benjamin Spock was able to be more influential with *The Common Sense Book of Infant and Baby Care* (1946), which has been read by an estimated fifty million people and has gone through ten editions since.

7. Among the most consulted were Edward Glover (1946), James Strachey (1957), and particularly Roger Money-Kyrle (1951), who was employed by the British government to interview Germans about their war experiences as they were being considered for positions in the postwar German government. In the United States, see Sullivan (1950).

8. No concept of prejudice against children emerged in the otherwise excellent Convention, so it is not guided by a prejudice concept, as the Convention on the Rights of Women is by "sexism". See Young-Bruehl (2009) on "childism".

9. In his paper on psychogenic disturbances of vision, Freud (1910i) made a first summary statement about the nonsexual "great needs" or the ego instincts aimed at self-preservation of the individual, and how they interact with—and can conflict with—the sexual instinct. As an example: "The mouth serves for kissing as well as for eating and communication by speech; the eyes perceive not only alterations in the external world that are important for the preservation of life, but also characteristics of objects that lead to their being chosen as objects of love–their charms …" (p. 214). See Young-Bruehl, "The Hidden History of the Ego Instincts" (2003a).

10. In the United States, the Budapest School's emphasis on inborn sociability appeared in the work of Harry Stack Sullivan, who was trained by Ferenczi's American trainee Clara Thompson, a training analyst in the Baltimore group. (See Sullivan (1947) on two basic needs, for satisfaction and for security (the latter the ego-instinctual need) in *Conceptions of Psychiatry* (p. 95).) Hans Loewald was analysed in Baltimore by Lewis Hill, and always credited his training experience—his "Budapest connection"—for his own concern with the mother-child dyad, which became important theoretically (not in terms of social policy) in the United States in the 1970s.

11. Steven Pinker's *The Language Instinct* (2007) gives a good overview of the developments based on Chomskian linguistics and the controversies.

12. When American analysts (such as Spitz's trainee Robert Emde and Alan Roland, who developed a psychoanalysis concerned with cultural differences) read Takeo Doi in the 1980s, they did not follow his idea that *amae* is an ego instinct. For a synopsis of Doi's work, see Young-Bruehl (2003b) and Young-Bruehl and Bethelard (1999); and Doi's collected papers (2005).

13. On the concept of developmental lines, see Anna Freud throughout Volume 8 of her *Writings* (1981).

14. Erich Fromm, one of the most important postwar characterologists, set his various characterologies on different bases; the one most concerned with thwarting of the ego instincts was in *Man For Himself* (1947, p. 248), where he rejected the death instinct and wrote: "If life's tendency to grow, to be lived, is thwarted, the energy thus blocked undergoes a process of change and is transformed into life-destructive energy. Destructiveness is the outcome of unlived life … ."

15. Doi's characterology in *The Anatomy of Dependence* (1971) also consists of three types: hysterics, people who are *yakekuso ni naru*, losing control and making histrionic or masochistic demands; obsessionals who are *toraware*, caught up in their anxieties or self-preoccupied; and narcissists, who are *wagamama*, spoiled, overindulged, unable to leave their mothers—unlike the Freudian narcissists, who are much more likely to be wounded and unloved. See Young-Bruehl and Bethelard (1999, p. 135ff).

16. As I noted before, there was important psychoanalytic literature on the origins of war, but it did not focus on group prejudices as obstacles to unity among groups. The development of the Studies in Prejudice "social disease" line of analysis was virtually stopped in its tracks by the summary of it offered in Gordon Allport's *The Nature of Prejudice* (1954), which both misrepresented the psychoanalytic contribution to prejudice study then existing (leaving out its characterological orientation) as well as disconnecting the whole topic of prejudice from any Marxist or socialist analysis. The book was an American Cold War product, which had tremendous influence around the English-speaking world and among the United States' anti-Soviet allies.

17. Especially Juliet Mitchell; see her *Psychoanalysis and Feminism* (1974).

18. The Freud Wars were launched by Jeffrey Masson's polemical *The Assault on Truth: Freud's Suppression of the Seduction Theory* (1984), which was tremendously influential among US and European feminists, particularly those concerned with violence against women. Among European

analysts, the Swiss Alice Miller, in a series of books (e.g., Miller, 1984) read widely in the United States, including by Masson, accused Freud of "assaulting the truth" of child maltreatment.

19. It is fascinating to observe that in the South American countries, where military dictatorships directly attacked psychoanalysts as subversives, psychoanalysis is now once again flourishing as it did in the immediate postwar period, when the South American social democracies were struggling to be born and to fight US control. I think this is because the postwar "Marx-Freud synthesis" was so practical, so oriented towards psychoanalytic work in public clinics and hospitals and the development of public health services (serving the poor)—many of them models for the Cubans, as the Cuban public health system, although always underfunded, became a model for other South American countries. Psychoanalysis was not exclusively for elites, and it was embedded in public consciousness. (See Hollander, 2010.)

20. This argument is made more fully in Young-Bruehl (2012).

References

Adorno, T. W., Frenkel-Brunswick, E., Levinson, D., & Sanford, R. N. (1951). *The Authoritarian Personality*. New York: Harper.

Aichhorn, A. (1925). *Wayward Youth*. New York: Meridian, 1955.

Allport, G. (1954). *The Nature of Prejudice*. Reading, MA: Addison-Wesley.

Balan, J. (1991). *Cuentame tu vida: Una biografia collective del psicoanalisis argentine*. Buenos Aires: Planeta Espejo de la Argentina.

Balint, M. (1968). *The Basic Fault: Therapeutic Aspects of Regression*. London: Tavistock.

De Beauvoir, S. (1949). *The Second Sex*. C. Borde & S. Malovany-Chevalier (Trans.). New York: Vintage, 2010.

Doi, T. (1971). *The Anatomy of Dependence*. New York: Kodansha International, 1973.

Doi, T. (2005). *Understanding Amae: the Japanese Concept of Need-Love*. Folkestone, UK: Global Oriental.

Erikson, E. (1950). *Childhood and Society*. New York: W. W. Norton.

Erikson, E. (1969). *Gandhi's Truth*. New York: W. W. Norton.

Fanon, F. (1952). *Black Skins, White Marks*. R. Philcox (Trans.). New York: Grove Press, 2008.

Fanon, F. (1961). *The Wretched of the Earth*. R. Philcox (Trans.). New York: Grove Press, 2004.

Fenichel, O. (1953). A critique of the death instinct. In: *The Collected Papers of Otto Fenichel*, Vol. 1 (pp. 363–373). New York: W. W. Norton.

Freud, A. (1981). *The Writings of Anna Freud, Vol. 8*. New York: International Universities Press.

Freud, S. (1908d). "Civilized" sexual morality and modern nervous illness. In: *S. E. 9*: 177–204. London: Hogarth, 1958.

Freud, S. (1905d). Three essays on the theory of sexuality. In: *S. E. 7*: 125–248. London: Hogarth, 1958.

Freud, S. (1910i). The psychoanalytic view of psychogenic disturbance of vision. In: *S. E. 11*: 209–218. London: Hogarth, 1958.

Freud, S. (1920 g). *Beyond the Pleasure Principle*. In: *S. E. 18*: 1–64. London: Hogarth, 1958.

Freud, S. (1921c). *Group Psychology and the Analysis of the Ego*. In: *S. E. 18*: 67–134. London: Hogarth, 1958.

Freud, S. (1930a). *Civilization and Its Discontents*. In: *S. E. 21*: 57–146. London: Hogarth, 1958.

Freud, S. (1931a). Libidinal types. In: *S. E. 21*: 215–222. London: Hogarth, 1958.

Fromm, E. (1947). *Man for Himself*. Greenwich, CT: Fawcett Premier.

Fromm, E. (1955). *The Sane Society*. Greenwich, CT: Fawcett Premier.

Glover, E. (1946). *War, Sadism, and Pacifism. Further Essays on Group Psychology and War*. London: Allen & Unwin.

Hermann, I. (1936). Clinging-going-in-search: A contrasting pair of instincts and their relation to sadism and masochism. *Psychoanalytic Quarterly*, 45 (1976): 5–36.

Hollander, N. C. (2010). *Uprooted Minds: Surviving the Politics of Terror in the Americas*. Relational Perspectives Book Series, No. 47. New York: Routledge.

Jacoby, R. (1983). *The Repression of Psychoanalysis: Otto Fenichel and the Political Freudians*. New York: Basic.

Langer, M. (1989). *From Vienna to Managua*. M. Hooks (Trans.). London: Free Association.

Loewenstein, R. M. (1940). The vital and somatic instincts. *International Journal of Psychoanalysis*, 21: 377–400.

Loewenstein, R. M. (1982). *Practice and Precept in Psychoanalytic Technique: Selected Papers of Rudolph Loewenstein*. Introduction by Jacob A. Arlow. New Haven, CT: Yale University Press.

Marcuse, H. (1955). *Eros and Civilization*. New York: Vintage, 1962.

Masson, J. (1984). *The Assault on Truth: Freud's Suppression of the Seduction Theory*. New York: HarperCollins.

Miller, A. (1981). *Thou Shalt Not Be Aware: Society's Betrayal of the Child*. New York: New American Library, 1984.

Mitchell, J. (1974). *Psychoanalysis and Feminism*. New York: Pantheon.

Money-Kyrle, R. E. (1951). *Psychoanalysis and Politics*. London: Duckworth.

Pinker, S. (2007). *The Language Instinct* (3rd edn.). New York: HarperCollins.

Robinson, P. (1969). *The Freudian Left*. New York: Harper & Row.

Reich, W. (1931). *Character Analysis* (Enlarged edn.). New York: Simon & Schuster, 1972.

Reich, W. (1933). *The Mass Psychology of Fascism*. New York: Farrar, Straus & Giroux, 1970.

Simmel, E. (Ed.) (1948). *Anti-Semitism: A Social Disease*. New York: International Universities Press.

Spitz, R. (1965). *The First Year of Life: A Psychoanalytic Study of Normal and Deviant Development of Object Relations*. New York: International Universities Press.

Spock, B. (1946). *The Common Sense Book of Infant and Baby Care*. New York: Dutton.

Strachey, A. (1957). *The Unconscious Motives of War*. London: Allen & Unwin.

Sullivan, H. S. (1947). *Conceptions of Modern Psychiatry*. Washington, DC: White Psychiatric Foundation.

Sullivan, H. S. (1950). Tensions interpersonal and international. In: H. Cantril (Ed.), *Tensions that Cause War*. Urbana, IL: University of Illinois Press.

Suttie, I. (1935). *The Origin of Love and Hate*. New York: Matrix House, 1966.

Winnicott, D. W. (1964). *The Child, the Family, and the Outside World*. London: Penguin.

Young-Bruehl, E. (1996). *The Anatomy of Prejudices*. Cambridge, MA: Harvard University Press.

Young-Bruehl, E. (2003a). The hidden history of the ego instincts. In: *Where Do We Fall when We Fall in Love?* (pp. 45–74). New York: Other.

Young-Bruehl, E. (2003b). *Amae* in ancient Greece. In: *Where Do We Fall when We Fall in Love?* (pp. 311–328). New York: Other.

Young-Bruehl, E. (2004). The taboo on tenderness. In: M. Bergmann (Ed.), *Understanding Dissidence and Controversy in the History of Psychoanalysis* (pp. 229–248). New York: Other.

Young-Bruehl, E. (2009). Childism: Prejudice against children. *Contemporary Psychoanalysis*, 45(2): 251–265.

Young-Bruehl, E. (2012). *Childism: Confronting Prejudice against Children*. New Haven, CT: Yale University Press.

Young-Bruehl, E., & Bethelard, F. (1999). *Cherishment*. New York: Free Press.

CHAPTER FIVE

A brief history of prejudice studies

Introduction

To study prejudice scientifically requires first of all, of course, some sense of it as a phenomenon and one in need of study. In the European tradition, we have evidence from the pre-Socratic Greek philosophers of awareness that people are religiously prejudiced because they make their gods in their own images and judge themselves superior to other peoples with other gods, other beliefs. As Xenophanes, forerunner of Parmenides, said around 500 BC: "The Ethiopians say that their gods are snub-nosed and black, the Thracians that theirs have light blue eyes and red hair." But this awareness, like later echoes of it in the Mediterranean world influenced by the Greeks, was in the service of an aspiration to a kind of philosophical monotheism—a doctrine of Being—that all superior men should embrace. Although none of the pre-Socratic Greeks ever worshipped a transcendent God, or developed a religion from a transcendent God's revelations, as did the Hebrews led by Abraham, the Christians, and the Muslims, they did criticise people for not being monotheists like themselves and for persisting in their particular customs and beliefs, their pre-judgments (*praejudicum* is the Latin word for prejudice). But criticising other people's prejudices because they do not conform to one's own superior and purportedly universal vision is not studying them in the scientific sense. Among the Europeans this step came only with the Enlightenment.

Studying prejudices requires the consciousness that all peoples have prejudices, that any group will develop customs and ways of thinking that lead the group members to form prejudgments (and often to be unable to make the next step and see their own prejudgments). This capacity for judgment is apparent in Montaigne's remarkable essay "Of Cannibals", written during the period in the 1500s when Catholics and Protestants were slaughtering each other in France. Considering several visitors to France from the New World, dressed in their tribal costumes, he refused to see them as inferior to the Europeans because they had practised cannibalism: "I think there is more barbarity in … tearing by tortures and the rack a body still full of feeling, than in roasting him and eating him after he is dead." All peoples, Montaigne understood, think their own religions, governments, and manners are perfect, so a student of this phenomenon must take his own formation into account and try to seek knowledge unencumbered, separating church and science. Knowledge was conceived as the opposite of prejudice; or, to say the same thing, prejudice was conceived as ignorance and religiously supported superstition. So in 1790, Mary Wollstonecraft could assert that only when English women were educated and could act as true and full citizens would their country be filled with knowledge and light.

Confronted with more of what we now call "cultural diversity" than any scientists before them as the planet Earth began its evolution into a cosmopolis of interconnected suburbs, Enlightenment scientists tried to make order out of the plethora. Unfortunately, the open-mindedness of Montaigne was difficult to maintain, even though Kant gave it a secure footing by describing judgment, *Urteilskraft*, as "enlarged mentality", and one regressive quasi-religious way to explain the diversity of peoples proved particularly appealing. That was to assume that the different types of people were different species, and that each had come forth in a separate creation. From Adam, the white people were descended. This assumption ruled out the idea that there had been historically a single type and all other types were lesser versions of it, deteriorations, or hybrids which would cast in doubt the wisdom of God's creation. So the Scottish philosopher David Hume could, for example, opine: "I am apt to suspect the negroes and in general all the other species of men (for there are four or five different kinds) to be naturally inferior to the whites" (1753). Others had different ideas about the types—the great botanist Carl Linnaeus said there were four regular types, plus two exceptional types: wild children (*enfants sauvages*) raised by animals, and monstrous men. One of Linnaeus's followers, the German Johann Friedrich Blumenbach, a student of human skulls, rejected the idea of separate creations and solved the problem of attributing to God a programme of evolution by positing a single white *Urrasse* (hypothetical original race) from which other races had evolved under climatological influence, while, at the same time attributing to the inferior races the possibility of evolving into whites, particularly by intermarrying. The *Urrasse*, Blumenbach suggested (1775), revealing quite an aesthetic prejudice, had flourished in the Caucasus Mountains of Georgia, where he found the most beautiful people in the world, the Caucasians, still living.

Most classifications of peoples generated in the seventeenth, eighteenth, and nineteenth centuries were mixtures, like this one, of careful empirical study and prejudice—often little better, ultimately, than science in the service of prejudice. Similarly, in the domains of legislation or political categorisation, strange mixtures of Enlightenment, universalism, and prejudice intermingled. Thomas Jefferson, so associated with the ringing words of the American Declaration of Independence— "We hold these truths to be self-evident, that all men are created equal"—was also a man who believed that the Africans were an inferior race. Jefferson's view reflected the fact that one hundred years earlier in Virginia black people had been legislatively classified as slaves. Legislation subsequent to the Declaration—and on the books until 1952— continued this idea of blacks as slaves by admitting into citizenship only immigrants to America who qualified as "free white persons". The implication was that only free white persons were independent enough to think and vote as citizens; a non-white person, owned or dominated by another, would be too easily influenced—as women were held to be by their husbands and as people without property were held to be because of their susceptibility to being bought. The self-evident truth that Jefferson held was that all free white men are created equal.

Studying prejudice as a phenomenon requires more than the knowledge that all people have prejudices, for the knowledge that all people have prejudices does not necessarily make it possible to acknowledge or explore one's own prejudices. The basic condition of human narcissism makes this form of self-knowledge ultimately impossible, although people of outstanding self-critical ability, like Montaigne, are inspirational: no one can see himself or herself objectively or out of the context of his or her own group and its prejudices, which are assimilated as much unconsciously as consciously. The key requirement for studying prejudice as a phenomenon is that the people who are classified be able to confront the classifiers and question them, protest; that the people who have been the victims of prejudice point out the prejudices of even those who are trying to study prejudice and not just to continue the Enlightenment project of classification. In American history, the 1845 autobiography, *Narrative of the Life of Frederick Douglass, an American Slave* is the emblematic story of a black slave who learned to read and write, who acquired the forbidden education, and was able to use it to reject his classification, to inspire the abolitionist movement (and the suffragette movement as well).

In the second half of the twentieth century, scientific study of prejudice could begin because there had been a long preparatory period—from the French Revolution forward—of political movements organising around a shared sense of victimhood or oppression and identifying the ideological components of their oppression. In America, after the Second World War, in the wake of the Holocaust, study of prejudice took on a new urgency and flourished in university departments of many sorts, from anthropology to zoology, and in the non-university clinical precincts of psychoanalysis. But, still, the development of prejudice study first focused narrowly on anti-Semitism. Then it moved to racism with the emergence of the civil rights movement (successor to the abolitionist movement), then to sexism with the women's liberation movement (successor to the suffragette movement), and then to homophobia with the gay liberation movement, which identified and named a prejudice with a long history but until 1972 had no name. Although this postwar period was also marked by study of the abuse and neglect of children, and the creation of a field, child abuse and neglect (CAN), there was no children's movement, as children do not organise or write, so there is no name for prejudice against them—no "childism", it might be called—and no statements from them of what they have suffered, but only a literature from adult survivors of child abuse and neglect.

Dialogue or confrontation between perpetrators and victims does not, of course, guarantee that study of prejudice will be, or become, as prejudice-free as possible, but it does, at least, prevent the results of such study from congealing or going unquestioned and thus becoming foundational for new ideologies and new practices of prejudice. This means that when the president of Harvard University makes an obviously sexist assessment of the problem of women's representation in the ranks of scientists, a huge protest greets him.

In this chapter, I want to track in quick sketches the history of American studies of anti-Semitism, white racism, sexism, and homophobia in the postwar era, showing as I go how crucial to these studies were the voices of Jews, blacks, women, and gays, and bringing this story up to the present era of prejudice channelled through fear of terrorism.

Overgeneralisations and questions to ask about them

Although the natural and social scientists and historians who studied prejudice after the Second World War could see that it has taken very different forms in different historical epochs and in different cultural contexts, they shared the Enlightenment desire to make a grand map, a universal analysis, a classification assuming a single principle or a single key to the mystery of prejudice, which was equated with the mystery of why people cannot live in peace, avoiding wars of the colossal destructiveness they had just witnessed. No matter what academic discipline they worked in, these students of prejudice came again and again to the same conclusion. Relentlessly, compulsively, they announced that all prejudices are alike and that all people who are prejudiced are alike, sharing the characteristic that their prejudice against one group entails prejudice against all other groups as well. Intolerance is a general condition: it is a melting pot which so dissolves all differences among prejudiced people and their prejudices that all differences among victim groups dissolve, too. It is not surprising, of course, that this melting pot conclusion was questioned by multiculturalists and members of victim groups, who insisted that each victim group has its irreducible specificity, its unique victimhood, sometimes its superlative—our suffering is the worst, this prejudice is the least acknowledged, this other one the most ubiquitous or radical. A theoretically inchoate surge of opposition stressed victim group difference in face of the sameness conclusion. But this opposition frequently dissolved, too, because it did not go beyond victim group differences to focus on prejudiced people or their prejudices; the multiculturalists fell back on the argument that even if all prejudiced people are alike and do hate all out-groups, they can still select out a special target because of something perceived to be in the target.

Psychoanalysis and Marxism, in the collaboration arranged by the Frankfurt School in exile, contributed the first big impetus to the way postwar studies in prejudices have repeated themselves. There is, so the authors of *The Authoritarian Personality* (Adorno, Frenkel-Brunswick, Levinson, & Sanford, 1951) argued, a single "prejudiced personality"—a rigid, conventional, puritanical, unintrospective, shallow, obsessional type—whose breeding ground is not the class struggle per se but the falsely enlightened bourgeois family under capitalism. It is not anti-Semites specifically, but rationalistic authoritarian "ethnocentrists" who hate Jews and all other groups who represent nature, primitivism, hedonism. Gordon Allport, in his classic *The Nature of Prejudice* (1954), popularised this synthetic Freudian-Marxian conclusion by calling all prejudices "ethnocentrism", in-group hatred of all out-groups. Jean-Paul Sartre, too, supported the synthesis in *Anti-Semite and Jew* (1946) by presenting the anti-Semite as a petit bourgeois snob who might just as well have displaced his hatred onto blacks or women—any "pretext", any scapegoat, any out-group.

Neither psychoanalysis nor Marxism, singly or together, ever again flourished in America as they flourished in the late 1940s—behaviourist, radical "anti-psychiatries", and anti-Communism dealt them stunning, distorting blows. So all later American studies in prejudice tended to be strictly empirical and either psychological or sociological, but not both, not synthetic, so the important idea that prejudice is a function of a character type (with a character defence or armour), which a given society will promote or discourage, was not pursued. But the basic conclusion that prejudice is singular and all are prejudiced alike, reached during the time when anti-Semitism was the galvanising topic, continued on as the mainstay of American studies of racism in the civil rights era, of sexism in the 1970s and, most recently, of homophobia. As these prejudices came, one by one, to the fore in American social history and theory, analogies were forged: racism, an ethnocentrism like anti-Semitism, leads to ghettoisation and genocide; sexism, an ethnocentrism like racism, is enslavement of a sex-group as racism is of a race-group; homophobia, an ethnocentrism like sexism, targets gay men who have a woman or femininity in them. In recent years, as prejudice against recent immigrants in Europe and America has grown, and as ethnic or ethnic nationalist groups have battled in Europe and throughout the formerly colonial world, the sameness-of-prejudice conclusion has been transferred without emendation.

This analogising tradition is especially strong among Americans and as applied to American prejudice phenomena, but it is common everywhere. I heard a variant of it in a 1994 lecture by the Slovenian social critic Salvoj Zizek, whose psychoanalytic orientation is more to Lacan than Freud. He argued that all prejudiced people are prejudiced alike in having an out-group that is somehow a phantom, somehow uncanny. An "unfathomable traumatic element" is displayed by the hated out-group, and this fantasmatic element directs our attention, Zizek says, to the Freudian castration complex, for it is like the maternal phallus, which gives rise to an unbearable anxiety because it is nowhere to be found. In this, the fantasmatic element is quite different from the Name-of-the-Father, which is everywhere to be found. The Name-of-the-Father omnipresent fiction does, however, get what Zizek calls "holes of repression" in it, out of which the fantasmatic elements arise. Always, Zizek argues, when symbolic or fictional systems become fissured, phantoms or apparitions like "the Jew" arise to haunt those ethnocentrists who have depended on the system: "The Nazi harmonious *Volkgemeinschaft* returned in the guise of their paranoiac obsession with the Jewish plot," for instance.

As he drew this background/foreground distinction, this duality of "symbolic fiction and spectral apparition", Zizek himself became anxious and hoped that he had not become lost in "speculative murky waters that have nothing whatsoever to do with concrete social struggles", and I think he had every real reason to be afraid. He did lose something concrete—any sense for the concrete differences among prejudiced people and their situations or among different victim groups' histories. He lost the possibility of making any kind of analysis of the history of the Jews except as they are experienced apparitionally by their enemies. As Sartre put it in *Anti-Semite and Jew*, if the Jew did not exist, the anti-Semite would have to invent him, for all ethnocentrists need an out-group, a pretext, a scapegoat, a target, when their symbolic systems inevitably break down. But Zizek also lost any sense that castration anxiety associated with fantasy fixation on the maternal phallus might be the psychological precondition neither for ethnocentric prejudice in general nor for anti-Semitism in particular, which seems so obviously indebted to anal fixations, but for a specific kind of prejudice—sexism—that grows out of anxiety about sexual difference.

Zizek was trying to find a general conceptualisation for a general prejudice: ethnocentrism. His was a very sophisticated general conceptualisation. Among journalistic commentators on his homeland, then a battleground, the tendency takes simpler forms. The tragedy of the former Yugoslavia was routinely interpreted as an outbreak of ethnocentrism or ethnocentric nationalism, and the language of clashing ethnocentrisms used for the former Yugoslavia was even exported to situations, like South Africa, where it was hopelessly inappropriate and where it served the purpose of a crude biologism or sociobiologism that says all people "naturally" form groups that hate out-groups and then "naturally" desire both to cleanse themselves of members of those out-groups and to triumph over the out-groups, to homogenise and establish winning, impermeable borders. In almost any newspaper you picked up in the 1990s, you could read something to the effect that nationalism was on the rise in the late twentieth century, particularly as a result of the collapse of the mid-century superpower system. This cliché is, I think, part of the larger problem of how discussion of prejudice has become channelled into the overgeneralised ideas that all prejudiced people are prejudiced alike and that anyone prejudiced against one out-group is also an ethnocentrist *tout court*.

As I proceed to look at the history of postwar prejudice studies in this essay, I would like to sketch for you a way to deconstruct these overgeneralisations and to supply a theoretical alternative constructed along psychoanalytic lines that has not been explored by victim groups concerned with their own particular victimisation. Let me restate my complaint about the overgeneralisation in the form of three broad questions that I will, then, take up in what follows:

> Are all prejudiced people alike and prejudiced alike?
> Are people who are prejudiced against one group prejudiced against all, and all alike?
> Are victim groups alike in their victimisation—that is, are they all affected alike by being victims?—even if not in their group characteristics?

Character types and their social settings

The idea, advanced by the Frankfurt School, that there is only one prejudiced personality, is, I would like to suggest, profoundly unpsychoanalytic. In Freud's theory, the differences among people of different character types and types of psychopathology are everywhere stressed: each type has different characteristic developmental lines and defence mechanisms, different compromise formations or symptoms. There is overlap at the level of symptoms, but a hysteric is not an obsessional, and although both of these types may have narcissistic features neither resembles psychically a narcissistic character. All three may present with—for example—depressive features or sadomasochism, but their depressions and their sadomasochism will not stem from the same psychodynamics. If prejudices are, as I am going to assume they are here, like defence mechanisms—one might call them social defence mechanisms—then it would be impossible to think that all people have them alike.

There is not a single prejudiced personality, but, I would like to suggest, three ideal types (*Idealtypen* in Max Weber's sense) with variations and mixtures. As I will sketch them briefly here, these types are constructed from the simplest version of the Freudian characterological theory, which was, in turn, constructed from a nosology that assumed three basic disorder categories—hysterical, obsessional, and narcissistic.

First, there is a characterologically obsessional type, often with paranoid features, who is marked most saliently by rigidity, moralistic conventionality (reflecting either a very severe or a very faulty superego), and tight-fisted focus on money; by conformity, being unable to keep from splitting affects off from intellectual operations, and a kind of cold rationality or hyper-rationality. This type appeared in the Frankfurt School postwar research as "the authoritarian personality", the only prejudiced type for two reasons. First, this type is the one whose intellectual style is to generalise, who sweeps all groups into his or her prejudice because all groups seem connected in a vast conspiratorial system, a plot, usually one controlled by a scheming wily leadership group, like the Jewish people, or like the Soviet communist agents then (in the early 1950s) held to be taking over the American State Department. Second, this type flourishes in families and institutions (especially the military) that promote money discipline, order for order's sake, the Protestant ethic or "Prussian" values, sexual suppression, enviousness, and affectless intellectualism—just the kinds of milieus that were flourishing when the Authoritarian Personality researchers designed their questionnaires. The sociologist William Whyte described the type in *The Organization Man* (1956), while cultural psychoanalysts like Eric

Fromm spoke of the rigidly conformist "marketing character" and Karen Horney of "the neurotic character in our time".

A second type of prejudiced personality is characterologically hysterical and most recognisable by the way in which he or she splits up or dissociates into opposing "selves"—a good, chaste self and a bad, lascivious self, a real self and an impostor self, a conventional self and a renegade. Such a person can be an upstanding citizen by day and a Ku Klux Klansman by night; hypocrisy is so much his way of life that he will disavow or dissociate from his other half's activities. Instead of, or in addition to, the bodily symptoms (conversion symptoms) that are typical of the "classic" hysterics known to Freud, prejudiced hysterical people have their bodily symptoms on the bodies of others—they make others ill, keep them down in sickening conditions, beat them, and focus all kinds of violence upon their genitals, from castration to rape.

This type flourishes in milieus where the family life is double or two tier, where a family of slaves or domestic servants or colonials is woven into the primary family, so there are two mothers, two fathers, two sibling groups, and the hysterical character can assign one part of himself to each family. His lower and darker self goes to the low (in class terms) and/or dark people (in race terms), either for love or for venting of aggression or both, while his lighter and higher self idealises the light and high people. Incestuous desires and rivalries can be acted out with a parent or sibling who is not the biological parent or sibling. So the prejudices of such characters are endlessly sexualised. Their victims are imagined as archaic, primitive "natives" of grotesque sexual appetite— the id personified—whose intellectual abilities are inferior. This is the racism of Virginia in the seventeenth century (and onwards), which is very different from the race thinking of a Johann Friedrich Blumenbach, for whom black people were more spectral and whose central passion was obsession with order (particularly aesthetic order) and intellectual achievement (which he thought blacks capable of by intermarriage, a possibility the hysterical reject).

A third type is characterologically narcissistic and its male members are identifiable by their grandiosity, their complex phallocentrism— they worship both their own phalluses and the phalluses they magically attribute to their female victims; they lack empathy or ability to see things from another's perspective, and they radiate expectation that they should be privileged, lucky, indulged.[1]

I think it is helpful to distinguish body narcissists, who emphasise that everyone has or should have a body like their own, from more developmentally complex mental narcissists, who, having recognised that not all bodies are alike, having registered the fact of sexual difference, insist that the "other", the not-us, is mentally inferior, culturally deficient.[2]

But most mental narcissists retain their earlier bodily narcissism, so that their images of the "other" are layered, contradictory. Their other is both the same and different—both saintly and whorish, pure and impure, spiritually adept and mindless, beautiful and dangerous, desirable and terrifying, and so forth. The victims of sexism are compelled to battle their own confusion when they are elevated and despised in the same act, the same sentence, the same institutions.

Among psychoanalytically influenced feminists, the sexism of males has usually been attributed to their need to disidentify with their mothers and be taken up into male peer groups. Men disparage the femininity that they must reject in themselves, and this necessity also explains, then, their homophobia in the sense that they reject all forms of femininity in males. But I think that this prevailing feminist psychoanalytic understanding of sexism is partial because it does not rest on an interpretation of narcissism, and thus it has also not been linked to social investigations of what kind of institutions and societies promote narcissism. The rule of thumb here is, I think, the smaller and more insulated and intra-generationally eroticised, focused on reproduction, and prolonging of childhood that families are—the more nuclear—the more they support elaborate narcissistic entitlements and the more complexly, layeredly, contradictorily sexist they are. The central feature of their complex sexism is male control over every controllable facet of reproduction, which means that men reproduce themselves in every way but the actual bearing and birthing of children. More extended families or clans in more agricultural settings do, of course, repress women, often very violently and in bodily forms like genital mutilation, but the primary reason for this repression is to secure claims of paternity and ownership of the children who are future labourers, not to become, as much as possible, the reproducers. Awe over female reproductiveness gives way in complex industrialising cultures to envy and the characteristic of the envious—that they attack what they cannot be or have.

Types of victims, patterns of change

I have been sketching three types of characters and their characteristic prejudices, and I would like now to track back over the terrain of these distinctions by sketching these types' characteristic victim groups. Each type both finds its appropriate victim group, paying attention to real qualities in the people, and constructs or imagines the group, fictionalises it. In the history of postwar prejudice studies, the victim groups have been the ones to detail their own characteristics as they have felt them being imposed upon them, projected onto them.

Obsessional characters react with particular intensity and violence to groups that they perceive as penetrating the fortresses of defences they have erected to keep their acquisitive (especially their anal, hoarding) desires in control. Their enemies come in from the outside, as immigrants or refugees, and penetrate—the metaphors are usually of anal rape—right into the commercial bowels that the obsessional considers crucial to the workings of the society. The strangers become what sociologists call "middleman minorities". By the obsessional's definitions, they become spies, secret agents, infiltrators, propagandists, for the vast network of their relatives and co-conspirators residing in their place of origin and in their new homes. Animosity against such people simmers among obsessionals, but it turns deadly under specific conditions: an economic depression or an ongoing economic deterioration wipes out the savings and the security, the sense of future, of classes that have pulled up with huge effort or spent great amounts of prestige on staying in power, while war conditions have destroyed many of the rules and regulations that have checked aggression. In this condition, the condition of Germany after the First World War, someone must be blamed and eliminated to restore law and order. The blameworthy group is accused of taking over the government, so that obsessional prejudice becomes anti-state, ultimately supranationalist. Genocide is the logical punishment—it is the purgative "final solution" to a threat that threatens with its survivability, its remnant.

In Eastern Europe and the Balkans in the 1990s, this kind of obsessional prejudice was of the greatest importance, as the rigid and conformist social conditions of postwar communism fostered obsessiveness there as pervasively as the Nazi-created social conditions did in prewar Germany and Austria. In the context of the former GDR, to illustrate, it was clear that much of the pre-unification skinhead and neo-Nazi violence directed against punks and, most vehemently, against *Gastarbeiter* ("guest workers", i.e., foreign workers) was focused on the economic competition, disorder, and dirtiness these groups represented, but it was also being directed at the GDR government, which was held responsible for bringing in the guest workers from Warsaw Pact neighbours and socialist states in the third world and then—so the obsessional rumours went—indulging them, allegedly creating employment competition. In the usual anal obsessional language, many East Germans complained "The state blows sugar right up those foreigners' arseholes." When the communist government collapsed, skinhead and neo-Nazi violence was directed at all who could be construed as polluters but also at representatives of the communist system (including the police): "Turks out!" and "Jews out!" and "Ruskies up against the wall!" graffiti were jumbled on many a building. The anti-state rhetoric was of conspiracies and betrayal and expansionist extolling of *Lebensraum* and "Greater Germany" that had also become the anti-state rallying cry in the West German rightist parties.

When the word "nationalism" was used to explain the violence that rocked most of the Eastern European and Balkan states after 1989, the anti-state, in the sense of anti-political, nature of the most important groups was missed. Groups like the Croatian Democratic Community, the Movement for a Democratic Slovakia, the Movement for Rumania, the Hungarian Democratic Forum, like the "people's front" organisations in the former Soviet Union, were not understood as beyond party politics; they wanted an end to party politics, and they wanted a supranational entity, not one stopping at any existing state borders. Their rhetoric was often isolationist and anti-modernist, so it sounded familiarly nationalist, but "greater"—as in Greater Germany, Greater Serbia—was their essential adjective. When they did come into parliamentary politics, they behaved as though their opponent parties had no status whatsoever, because the opponents did not represent the national soul and expansionary destiny. Not vying in elections, but silencing and purging were the tactics; not debating, but demonising the enemy. The enemies within were also routinely linked to "the West", viewed as standing ready to pounce on the defenceless peoples of Eastern Europe. And, of course, behind the supranational "West" there was inevitably a Jewish financial conspiracy. In the Romanian weekly magazine *Europa*, the International Monetary Fund, billed as a Jewish conspiracy directed from Israel, was said to have the single goal of transforming "the Romanian people into cesspool cleaners, dog catchers, refuse collectors, and porters serving individuals who are foreigners to the nation and to the country" (Hockenos, 1993, p. 282).

The anti-state, anti-political rhetoric of the obsessional prejudices—so obvious in America in the pronouncements of the Christian Coalition and its leader the Rev. Pat Robertson—is one of the key features distinguishing the obsessional prejudices from the hysterical. Hysterical characters need victims that they can humiliate, so they do not try to eliminate them from an expansionary supranational movement; they are not "ethnic cleansers". Rather, they appropriate existing political means to split up the victim group so that the victims cannot breed normally or gather their resources for rebellion. They rape and impregnate the victim group women, they beat and castrate the victim group men; they treat both women and men as rivals who need to be bested in every domain, especially any domain that involves intelligence, which the victims are said to lack as they are people of the body, the appetites. Discrimination against these victims grows worse whenever they threaten to move up in the world, out of their place in the hierarchy that the hysterical think is natural. Moving up is most critically represented by marrying up, so miscegenation is the cardinal sin in the sexualised world of the hysterically prejudiced. The apparatus of the state is coveted by the hysterically prejudiced for institutionalising their prejudices; they are not anti-state but against states' rights in political orientation—they like their politics very local and very familial. (The current Republican Party in America is split between old-fashioned states' rights advocates who are opposed to big government and a more obsessional group that is supranationalist, wanting to impose democracy by means of crony corporate capitalism on the whole world, regardless of the cost.)

In America, racism has been fostered by a long tradition of two-tier families, in the contexts of slavery and then domestic servitude, in the South and in the North, to the point where an entrenched image of the African Americans as a servant group is pervasive, across classes. Much of the anti-immigrant fervour that is so widespread in America now is hysterical and modelled on the traditional racism: the point of its legislative forms is to humiliate the victims and break up their families (even to attack the health and safety of their children as the California initiatives against illegal immigrants did). In colonial settings, similarly, the two-tier family fosters what the sociologist Pierre van den Berghe (1967) called "paternalistic racism".[3]

The situation in Europe now is, of course, a complex of the legacy of colonialism and the presence of large immigrant populations from the former colonies. Some of these immigrants are, as I noted, greeted with obsessional prejudice, particularly clannish middleman minority groups like the Roma or the Turks, but some are greeted with racism, particularly those who are people of colour and from the Third World. Miscegenation that in any way admits the lower into the higher group is, as always, the central racist focus. So, for example, many of the Mozambican and Vietnamese female guest workers in the former East Germany had to sign contracts forbidding them to bear children during their residences; pregnant Cuban women were shipped home (Hockenos, op. cit., p. 36). Men of colour were usually beaten up, in more or less symbolic acts of castration, while elimination tactics like fire-bombing buildings were directed at the Turks, who are the most "Jewish" group in terms of their clan organisations and business success.

Racism and sexism are obviously very closely linked, in the sense that racism is gendered—it falls differently on its male and female victims as it takes different forms in its male and female perpetrators. Racism, as Frantz Fanon wrote in *Black Skin, White Masks* (1952), exists "on the genital level". But it seems to me that the sexism that is directed by the men of one group at the women of another, construed as lower, should be called sexist-racism (or sexist-classism) to distinguish it from that sexism which is directed at women of a sexist's own group. Narcissistic characters, I think, focus first on women of their own group, women whom they model on their own mothers. But other women, who are darker, lower, can become carriers of the images first constructed for in-group women—particularly the bodily narcissistic images of phallic women. In both Europe and America, dark-skinned women are phallicised; even when they are construed as "mammy" figures, hypermothers, they are said to be matriarchal, male-dominating, often castrating, dangerous. Rape is a way to keep them in their place, but also to assign their half-breed children to a lower status. The obsessionally prejudiced, by contrast, forbid all sexual relations with the polluting people they hate.[4]

There are, of course, many people in whom the traits of the various character types mingle, as there are social circumstances that promote more than one kind of prejudice. But it does seem to me that most people have a main prejudice, as they have a prevailing trait or characterological pattern. On the other side, many groups will be primarily suited to be targets of one type of prejudice, but there are some groups that can serve a plurality of prejudices. Children and adolescents, homosexuals, and immigrants or foreigners, for example, are three kinds of groups that include a number of subgroups anyway, and can be construed as cunning infiltrators like Jews, as primitively sexual like blacks, or as lacking the phallus as (or like) women. They can be blamed and envied, put in their places, or controlled in their reproductive sexuality. The main reason why study of homophobia is still so preliminary, so riven with clichés, and so overburdened with the whole history of social scientific bias about prejudice, is that homophobia is usually construed as a single prejudice—when we ought to be, at the least, speaking of "the homophobias", and not just because prejudices against male and female homosexuals take different forms. Prejudice against foreigners comes, similarly, in multiple varieties, including not only the three main character-based types I have been noting, but also perhaps a simpler, less character-specific form that resembles the "stranger anxiety" of childhood and deserves the vague title "ethnocentrism" or its older equivalent, "xenophobia".

The victims speak

In America after the 1960s, when confrontations over the Vietnam War temporarily obscured much of the ongoing prejudice, the tendency of victim groups to assume along with social scientists that all victim groups are victimised alike broke down. When blacks and Jews both thought of themselves as victims of racism, they fought a common enemy—racists. Now, to many blacks the Jews are whites—and very commercially successful whites, who can serve as targets of black economic rage (particularly that cultivated in very obsessional milieus like the puritanical communities of the Nation of Islam). To many Jews, the blacks are an unsuccessful and often unintelligent group perpetuating their own social pathology. When white feminists coined the word "sexism" on the model of the word "racism", and thought of themselves as an enslaved or patronised sex-group, they could not hear the protests of black feminists who reminded them that black women experience both sexism and racism and do not think the two prejudices are the same. Now the camps of white and black feminists have to struggle to find their shared ground.

It is common knowledge now among victims that different victim groups have different experiences and agendas, and people who belong to more than one victim group have multifaceted experiences, often depending on which of their identities is to the fore in any given moment or milieu. But it is clear, I think, that the price for this necessary deconstruction of the social scientific sameness conclusion has been break-ups of social and political coalitions. When all victims were construed as alike and alike in their experiences of victimisation, it was certainly much easier for them to imagine themselves a united front. This problem is particularly acute as immigration increases around the globe, because different groups within and around the waves of immigration will have different experiences—although all may suffer alike from anti-immigrant legislation, to which prejudiced people can subscribe for a great variety of psychic and social reasons, each in the service of his or her own type of prejudice.

The situation of global immigration has become much more complex in the last decade because of the rise in various parts of the world of religious fundamentalisms, which foster obsessiveness and are by definition prejudiced against all out-groups and capable of having an impact, particularly by means of terrorism, way beyond their geographical locations. The very real threat of terrorist international conspiracies and infiltration brings out the obsessional defences of any society and favours the rise to political prominence of obsessional types. In America, we have seen Muslim "middleman minority" groups suspected of being terrorists and legislation being concocted to defend against them in the classic obsessional manner, but, even more ominously, we have seen the legacy of the Enlightenment separation of church and state that our democracy presupposes—and that is crucial to the study of prejudice—eroded. Separation of mosque and state has not existed since the great period of Islamic tolerance for the cultures existing in the Iberian Peninsula in the eighth century, when conquering Muslim armies crossed the Straits of Gibraltar.[5]

To my way of thinking, the chief reason for the rise of religious fundamentalisms at the end of the twentieth century was the dramatic increase in immigration globally, particularly as the Cold War ended with the collapse of the Soviet Union, which brought new political and economic conditions to most parts of the world. Like eighteenth-century overseas shipping capitalism, and nineteenth-century industrialising railroad capitalism, late twentieth-century banking and electronics driven capitalism connects the peoples of the world, brings them into proximity. Familiarity breeds at once understanding and contempt—which is a word that encompasses fear and rivalry and desire for control. Whether familiarity can breed understanding in the established communities depends crucially on whether the people who immigrate to them can be heard, whether their protests when they encounter prejudice—as they inevitably do—can become part of the established community's self-reflection, as the New World visitors to the Old World were in the works of Montaigne.

Most of the communities of the very diverse Muslim world are not recipients of immigrants (except for temporary workers in the oil industries and refugee groups like the Palestinians), although some, like Afghanistan, have been militarily occupied. They are more closed, and most wish to preserve themselves from the influence of "the West". More secular regimes, like Saddam Hussein's in Iraq, have been expansionist and despised for that by more traditional religious Muslims. The one internationally, not nationally, based organisation with super-nationalist goals is al-Qaeda, whose members follow the late Osama bin Laden in his extreme Wahhabist form of Islam, which has none of the legacy of toleration from the Koran or from the periods of Muslim rule in the Iberian Peninsula. Bin Laden invoked a new caliphate and world triumph over all infidels—a kind of crusade. There is no discussion to be had with a totalitarian on the rise, who has no motive to avoid violence, but it would be sheer prejudice to assume that all Muslims are of this sort and that no alliances can be made with those who are less prejudiced towards non-Muslims (or towards groups, like women, within their own communities). What we are witnessing now is not, as is so often alleged, a "clash of civilisations", but a plurality of clashes among groups in "the West" (among ethnic groups, or between fundamentalists and liberals, for example), among groups in "the Muslim world" (among ethnic groups, as well as between westernised secularists and traditionalists), and between the extremists from both camps.

Theorists of prejudice have, so far, not been able to compass all the different sorts of prejudices that make the contemporary global situation so dauntingly complex. I hope to see more work in the direction of an adequately complex theoretical framing of the different experiences of victim groups in their communities and victim groups immigrating into new communities and—on this basis—a sense for what shared experiential ground there is and what political bonds can be made on it, as part of the emerging, growing international human rights movement. Psychoanalysis can provide this project with the basic insight that prejudices are mechanisms of defence—one might, as I suggested, call them social mechanisms of defence. Each type has a developmental history and a social developmental history, but all can be grasped—interpreted—by the same kind of analytical techniques. In the context of individual psychoanalysis, one would speak of defence analysis; that is, analysis proceeding from the surface to the depths, proceeding through analysis of resistances and transference. In social terms, what the surface consists of is all of the speech and action of discrimination and oppression, including violent oppression. These surface phenomena display the characteristic forms of the prejudices:

1. the charge of international secret infiltration (=anal penetration) and conspiracy central to obsessional prejudice;
2. the charge of primitive (=rapacious phallic or devouring vaginal) sexuality rising-from-below that is central to hysterical prejudice;
3 the charge of bodily lack and threatening mental difference that is central to narcissistic prejudice;
4. and the charge, which I will just note in passing, of fearful and alluring gender identity transgression that is central to homophobia as homophobia serves all the different prejudices.

But all the prejudices do have in common that they are mechanisms of defence, which means that all victims have as their enemies people who have turned a mechanism of defence into a way of life, who are—it might be said—monomanically defended. The one cause for optimism that follows from this characterisation is that the various prejudices can be described and targeted by therapists, by educators, by culture critics and social policy makers, by thoughtful political leaders. They are not so diffusely structured, psychically or socially, that they defy description or ameliorating approach; they each have a character and can be understood characterologically.

Acknowledgements

My thanks to the editors of *The Journal for the Psychoanalysis of Culture and Society* for allowing me to use here parts of an earlier essay they published (Fall, 1997); this, in turn, is a kind of synopsis of my book *The Anatomy of Prejudices* (Cambridge, MA: Harvard University Press, 1996). Thanks also to Marc Aronson for reminding me of many of the nineteenth-century examples used in the first several pages of this brief history.

Notes

1. I am going to discuss male sexism here, but female sexism certainly exists in the muted forms that patriarchal social conditions permit. Women do not generally have the expectation that all beings are phallic; rather, they imagine all beings are like themselves and their omnipotent mothers. Their disillusionment may lead to penis envy—as Freud assumed, universalising—but it can have many other outcomes, among them denigration of the phallus and alliance with other women, extended mother-bonding. But the variability of female developmental lines away from omnipotence seems to me to contrast sharply with the invariability of the male story.

2. In terms of their visions of human sexuality, male bodily narcissists imagine that all people have the male genital. Females have an interior or inverted phallus—that is what their genitals consist of. Mental narcissists recognise that there are two different sexes, with different genitalia, but they believe that there is only one kind of mind, the masculine; women are mindless. There are, accordingly, two types of in-group sexism, that which attributes all sexuality and reproduction to male organs—the male sperm is, for example, a little man who is harboured for nine months in the female's inverted phallus—and that which acknowledges female reproductiveness and ova but wants that reproductiveness under male domination. On these sexual theories, cf. Thomas Lacquer, *Making Sex* (1992).

3. Van den Berghe was one of the first to distinguish racism from the vaguer, more diffuse "ethnocentrism" and to insist on the two-tier family plantation conditions underlying paternalistic racism, which, in turn, configures diversely in industrialising conditions, as it transforms into that "competitive racism" which adds "uppity" to the basic catalogue of reproaches against the victims.

4. One measure of the complexity of the situation in the former Yugoslavia is that the Muslims, who were "Jews" to their Serbian oppressors—that is, they are construed as an interloper mercantile and culturally conspiratorial group with clan connections across the Middle East—have been displaced and sent to concentration camps on the Nazi model, but their women have also been subject to programmatic rape, something that is usually a feature of hysterical but not of obsessional prejudices. What may be reflected here is a difference in psychic and sociocultural formation between the rural Serb army soldiers—the rapists—and the more urban, more educated ideologues who envisioned and engineered the "ethnic cleansing" campaign against the Muslims, focusing their attention on the cosmopolitan Muslim culture of Sarajevo.

References

Adorno, T. W., Frenkel-Brunswick, E., Levinson, D., & Sanford, R. N. (1951). *The Authoritarian Personality.* New York: Harper.

Allport, G. W. (1954). *The Nature of Prejudice.* Reading, MA: Addison-Wesley.

Blumenbach, J. F. (1775). *On the Natural Variety of Mankind.* Doctoral dissertation, Universität Göttingen, Germany.

Douglass, F. (1845). *Narrative of the Life of Frederick Douglass, an American Slave.*

Fanon, F. (1952). *Black Skins, White Marks.* R. Philcox (Trans.). New York: Grove Press, 2008.

Hockenos, P. (1993). *Free To Hate: The Rise of the Right in Post-Communist Eastern Europe.* New York: Routledge.

Hume, D. (1753). Of national character (footnote). In: *The Philosophical Works of David Hume, Volume III* (p. 228). Bristol, UK: Thoemmes Press, 1996.

Lacquer, T. (1992). *Making Sex.* Cambridge, MA: Harvard University Press.

Sartre, J.-P. (1946). *Anti-Semite and Jew.* New York: Schocken, 1965.

Van den Berghe, P. (1967). *Race and Racism.* New York: John Wiley.

Whyte, W. H. Jr. (1956). *The Organization Man.* New York: Simon & Schuster.

CHAPTER SIX

Reflections on women and psychoanalysis

Introduction

I wanted to prepare a historical and clinical text that would bring us to the present tense of "Women and Psychoanalysis", let us reflect on how we—we in the field of psychoanalysis—have come a long way on this topic, and where we might be going. So I thought about writing a brief history—a "multibiography"—of women psychoanalysts, our foremothers, and comparing their situations with ours. Then I thought about writing a brief history of women in psychoanalysis—of women as patients—focusing on how women patients now are understood and treated. With these possibilities, I wanted to avoid writing a history of changing views in psychoanalysis of female psychology, as that has been done many times, for many purposes. Not one of you is in need of such a treatise, for you have all taken whole courses on this "changing views" theme at your training institutes, and many of you teach such courses. In fact, one of the key features of the present moment of "Women and Psychoanalysis" is that we are all well aware of the history of changing views in psychoanalysis of female psychology; we are thoroughly historicised.

Reflecting on our historical consciousness, I decided to walk a path in relation to it that is—to use a fancy term—metahistorical. We are in a moment in the history of the conjunction of "women and psychoanalysis" when it is important to share with each other not just the history of theories but our questions about how and why the history of theories has been constructed as it has. And to work metatheoretically, asking psychoanalytic questions about what kinds of theoretical strategies have shaped the history—doing what I once, on another occasion, called "psychotheoretical critique" (Young-Bruehl, 1999). Our collective self-consciousness about the history of women and psychoanalysis should by now be helping us not to be condemned to repeat that history, in our theorising or in our consulting rooms.

Getting myself oriented, I made a list of characteristics of the present moment of "women and psychoanalysis". At the top of it I wrote, a little facetiously: "The most famous question that the conjunction 'women and psychoanalysis' brings to mind is Freud's 'What do women want?' and this question is no longer being asked; it could no longer, for example, be the focus of a seminar as it was so famously for Jacques Lacan in 1972–3." Why not? First, because it presumes that there is a Woman doing the wanting who is or represents all women, as it presumes that there is one reference for the what that She wants. But ours is—thank goodness—an era of suspicion as far as such general concepts go, or as far as any essentialist definition of Woman goes. Correlatively, in research terms, ours is an era in which much psychoanalytic interest is focused on phenomena that call the categories Woman and Man, masculinity and femininity, directly into question as *categories* of sex and gender: for example, the phenomena of intersexuality, transsexualism, and gender identity disorders.

From other angles, too, the categories Man and Woman have come into question. Historians working in the relatively new sub-discipline, the history of sexuality, have shown the many ways in which even physiological and anatomical differences between the sexes, once thought to be matters of objective knowledge, are always interpreted. A single great dichotomy of types of interpretations has appeared. Sometimes the biological "facts" have been interpreted as indicating that males and females are sexually very different and at other times as indicating that they are very much the same. Biology is no more without prejudices or prejudgments than psychology or psychoanalysis.

One of the most remarkable of the new histories of sexuality, Thomas Lacquer's *Making Sex* (1990), for example, begins by showing how the basic picture of human sexuality that arose in Europe with the ancient Greek Hippocratic physicians featured the idea that men and women have similar desires and similar sexual organs, in the sense that their genitals—penis and testicles—are structurally just the same. For centuries, physicians accepted as fact the idea that these genitals, apparent on the exterior of a man's body, are to be found on the inside of a woman's. By the mid-nineteenth century, however, this sexist conviction, this product of narcissistic inability to tolerate difference, which now seems so bizarre, had given way and its opposite prevailed: scientists believed that there are fundamental differences between the male and female sexes, and, further, that the sexes are different in every conceivable aspect of body and soul, in every moral and physical aspect. A theory of radical dimorphism replaced the "one sex" everyone-has-a-phallus-model, and, in terms of relations between the sexes, a theory of radical incommensurability reigned. This nineteenth-century emphasis on difference was a very important development for opening the way to exploring female sexuality, and also female psychology as not phallic and not a subset of male psychology. In this crucible, psychoanalysis was born.

But the way has proven a very hard one to go, and it has—as I will note later—its own distortions and difficulties. Breaking away from thinking of women in male terms allowed Freud's question "What do women want?" to be posed, but, as generations of feminists have pointed out, the question has remained all set to be sexist in its own way. It can so easily presume that what men want is already known and normative, which means that whatever women want is going to be something peculiar or deviant or lesser. The answer will turn out to be that women want something men already *have*—like a penis—or men already *are*—like in power. And the desires and needs—two sorts of wants—common to men and women in their conditioned existences will go unexplored.

So "What do women want?" is out of favour now among the heirs of Freud. And those for whom it is out of favour—I include myself and most of you, I will assume—are struggling to avoid all the pitfalls that come with thinking of Woman categorically, definitionally. What we do, rather, is think of all the fundamental psychoanalytically discovered ingredients of identity generally (and the subsets of sexual and gender identity particularly) *in the plural*. We exist in the moment of the pluralisation of psychoanalytic concepts. The concept "developmental line", for example, has become: plural and overlapping and interactive lines of development leading to maturity as a quilt of traits, not a static condition. Or, to take another example, we think not of identification and introjection, but of plural identifications and introjections. A girl child—or a boy child—identifies with female figures and male figures, and with the femininity of masculine figures and the masculinity of feminine figures, and, over the course of her development, we expect that there will be shifting and changing in her identificatory mélange. We think—to take another example—of "object choice" not so much in end-result type categories—say, heterosexual, homosexual, bisexual—but in processes. We do not think of there being bedrock in identities, much less a single bedrock. And, in the clinical situation, we think of a diagnosis as a working description of a great variety of interacting psychic tendencies and mechanisms, more like a simulation of a journey than like a map. Our psychodynamic formulations are more dynamic than formulaic. We do not think of "the transference" as an entity but as an interactive field of forces and figures, kaleidoscopic; not the analyst's authority, but the mutuality of analyst and analysand and the analysand's experience of dependency are crucial to cure.

Nonetheless, accurate as this characterisation of what we do may be, it is still, in many respects, ahead of our metapsychology or of our ability to understand what we are doing, as it is ahead of contemporary inquiry into human sexuality from biology or psychology. And I think you can see this by noting that in our literature as well as in the literatures of biology and empirical psychology the question "How do men and women differ?"—the question that really lies behind "What do women want?"—is still being asked without the benefit of historical reflection. So is "How are men and women similar?"—although this variant is less common. These questions ought to be suspicious, too, for the same post-modern reasons that knocked off "What do women want?" in the ways that I have been sketching. But, interestingly, they linger. I will take the persistence of "How do men and women differ?" as my lead-in to the further reflections on the present tense of "women and psychoanalysis" that I want to offer.

The question "How do men and women differ?"

If you look back over the one hundred years of psychoanalysis's history, I think you can observe a pattern that is very instructive. Every time psychoanalysis has asserted differences between the sexes very strongly, while asserting at the same time that men are superior in their difference, there has been a reaction, led, not surprisingly, by women, who have not appreciated being judged inferior, regardless of the scientific pretence of the judgment. There have been, basically, two kinds of reaction.

First, it has been asserted against patriarchal, sexist psychoanalysis that, yes, there are differences between men and women, but those do not indicate any inferiority of women; in fact, the differences point to a superiority, which men envy. Most frequently, the difference focused upon is that women are capable of motherhood, and the assertion is made that this is their destiny: anatomy is destiny. Arguments of this sort I will call "reversals" after the defence mechanism that Anna Freud was the first to describe in detail. Generally in the history of psychoanalysis, reversal arguments have been polemical and polarising, becoming beacons for camps and schools of analysts and thus living long lives because complexly institutionalised.

The second way that the sexist psychoanalytic emphasis on differences and male superiority has been combated is by means of theories about an underlying similarity between the sexes that is of much greater significance than any differences or alleged differences. This underlying similarity may be said to be hidden by the historical circumstances of patriarchal culture, which create differences and set hierarchies in place. In the future, when circumstances change, the similarity will become manifest. Or, in a variant on this argument, the similarity may be specifically named as "undifferentiation", and a claim be made that there is a period of undifferentiation in human development when boy and girl infants are the same in every significant psychological way. This psychological sameness is, then, held to be more significant than either inborn biological differences or the kinds of psychological differentiations that come about after the period of undifferentiation.

While the first strategy I noted resembles "reversal", this one can resemble to one degree or another "disavowal", for it can involve setting aside or denying differences that are experienced as traumatic. As perceiving the absence of the penis in women or the presence of the penis in men can be traumatic, so can conceiving sexual difference in theory—and for some people the theoretical plane may actually echo an earlier traumatic experience of perceiving. But it is also apparent, looking over the history of psychoanalysis, that sameness arguments, when they involve little disavowal, when they acknowledge differences but try to keep them in sameness perspective, are less polemical and distorting than reversals. (Similarly, one might note that a disavowal taken to a great degree prepares the way for a mere perversion, but a reversal taken to a great degree opens up psychosis.)

Sigmund Freud, the most powerful articulator in all of psychoanalysis of differences between the sexes, both anatomical and psychological, also supplied the paradigms for the two forms of sameness argument. Both men and women, he said, are bisexual, both physiologically and anatomically, and in terms of their object choices. They only become monosexual in object choice, if they ever do, over the course of their development, as they repress some choices and follow others or an other. If the historical circumstances promoting the cessation of bisexuality of object choice and "polymorphous perversity" of modes of sexual pleasure-seeking were not in place, men and women might remain more similar than different. "Civilised morality" promotes constriction. And, under conditions of constriction, Freud argued, women remain more bisexual in object choice than men because nothing prompts them to resolve their Oedipus complexes as definitively. This assertion of eventual difference with which Freud concluded his argument about bisexual sameness has, of course, been greeted with reversals: yes, such arguments go, women are more bisexual than men and that is truly wonderful and indicative of their superiority in being able to relate to both sexes intimately.

Freud also supplied the paradigmatic sameness as a developmental stage argument. He made the claim, after 1914, that all human beings begin their development in a state he called "primary narcissism", and only slowly leave it. Men leave it much more clearly than women do, so they become capable of object love while women remain predominantly narcissistic lovers, being pulled towards object love and beyond their narcissism—most manifest in their attention to their own bodies—only by their children, especially their sons. Of course, this assertion of eventual difference between men and women has been greeted with many reversals in which the narcissism of men is asserted and the object-related nature of female desire and the caring quality of women extolled as superior.

As I will indicate in a moment, I think it was really a very unfortunate turn of theoretical events for psychoanalysis that the way Freud explored the possibility that there is a period of pre-differentiation in human development was exclusively through the notion of primary narcissism. This turn effectively kept out of consideration for two generations any other kind of period of pre-differentiation. It is one of the key features of our current moment that the notion of primary narcissism, so long problematic, no longer blocks the view psychoanalytic infant researchers take towards object relations or attachments in the first year of life.

But let me return to my overview of the theoretical territory. Because the responses to Freud's sexist emphasis on difference were so few and so stereotyped, they did not really have much reform effect. It has been the experience of many persecuted groups that neither responding to the prejudices directed against them with reversals—by asserting that the differences between groups have been wrongly evaluated and the oppressed are really the superior group—nor responding with humanistic pleas for the realisation that all human beings are really more similar than different, have much effect on the prejudiced group or on the various internalisations of their prejudices that some in the victim groups have suffered. Neither "reverse racism" nor appeals to the common humanity of blacks and whites have had much effect on the everyday, ordinary white racism, for example. These responses meet with the same fate that interpretations meet with in the clinical situation when work on the resistances has not preceded them, when the way has not been properly prepared for their reception. Prejudices are resistances, or, as I have elsewhere argued, they are social mechanisms of defence, and they only yield to defence analysis—that is, analysis directed by the questions "Why do you need this prejudice? What does it do for you? What does it defend against?"

But this matter of reversals and disavowals in psychoanalytic theory has another dimension, too. Over the history of psychoanalysis, as critics of Freud have offered various kinds of reversals and disavowals, it has become more and more obvious that the way in which Freud's own assertions of difference and sameness were structured had great implications for the way his critics structured their counter-arguments and found themselves unable, eventually, to break through the prejudice or shift away from its terms. I would like to linger over two key movements in Freud's thought (and thus in the thought of his critics) when alternative ways of thinking almost surfaced. My plan is to show how these might-have-been possibilities have finally appeared, or reappeared, in the present moment, and this will give us a way to judge whether an exit from the impasse I am describing is really at hand.

Nosological similarity becomes the nosological difference

The first moment I want to consider is the one that I take to be paradigmatic for psychoanalytic psychopathology. It is a story of how preoccupation with sexual difference pushed diagnostic-theoretical thinking into channels that were much more narrow than they needed to be.

When Freud set out on the road that led, eventually, to psychoanalysis, he was, as you know, studying hysteria. The road had begun in Paris, in Jean-Martin Charcot's Salpêtrière clinic, where the great French neurologist was defying conventional neurological wisdom by working clinically and by taking an interest in hysteria, a disease most researchers then thought incurable, inevitably degenerative. Freud followed Charcot in claiming that the conventional wisdom on hysteria as a hereditary degenerative disease was wrong, and he also agreed that it was to be found in men, not only in women. The disease named after the female womb, *hysteros*, is not a mark of sexual difference. Men and women are similar as hysterics.

Freud was making a very important and clinically accurate sameness argument against an existing prejudicial difference argument. Then, as he developed his own approach to hysteria, and distinguished it from Charcot's, he took the sameness approach further, placing more and more emphasis on the aetiological factor, which he identified as early sexual experience. He also broadened his study to encompass the role of early sexual experience in obsessional neurosis, which he had the distinction of identifying as a distinct psychoneurosis. "I was obliged to begin my work with a nosological innovation," Freud explained. "I found reason to set alongside hysteria the obsessional neurosis as a self-sufficient and independent disorder, although the majority of the authorities place obsessions among the syndromes constituting mental degeneracy or confuse them with neurasthenia" (1896a, p. 146).

The isolation of obsessional neurosis was exhilarating in and of itself to Freud, but also because it gave such support to his theory of the traumatic origins of hysteria, the so-called "seduction theory" postulating that a childhood sexual experience was causal in all hysterias. He noted:

> The obsessional neurosis arises from a specific cause very analogous to that of hysteria. Here too we find a precocious sexual event, occurring before puberty, the memory of which becomes active during or after that period ... There is only one difference which seems capital. At the basis of the aetiology of hysteria we found an event of passive sexuality, an experience submitted to with indifference or with a small degree of annoyance or fright. In obsessional neurosis, it is a question on the other hand of an event which has given pleasure, of an act of aggression inspired by desire (in the case of a boy) or of a participation in sexual relations accompanied by enjoyment (in the case of a little girl). The obsessional ideas ... are nothing other than reproaches addressed by the subject to himself on account of his anticipated sexual enjoyment, but reproaches distorted by an unconscious psychical work of transformation and substitution. (Ibid., p. 155)

Although Freud was quite clear that both males and females can be hysterics and obsessional neurotics, when he read his monocausal understanding of the two psychoneuroses through a supposed biological differentiation—activity and passivity—he moved in the direction of a differentiating generalisation about men and women. "The importance of the active element in sexual life as a cause of obsessions, and of sexual passivity for the pathogenesis of hysteria, even seems to unveil the reason for the more intimate connection of hysteria with the female sex and the preference of men for obsessional neurosis" (ibid., p. 156). Once he had stepped in this direction, bringing into the foreground the biological difference he unquestioningly assumed between passivity and activity, Freud began to lose the complex view he had of how both sexes become both hysterical and obsessional. Similarly, he lost sight of how hysteria and obsessionality as forms of psychoneurosis intertwine, overlap—as both sexes are bisexual, including in terms of the activity he associated with males only and the passivity he associated with females only. Although Freud alluded to his early insights as late as his case study of the Wolf Man, he did not explore further his idea that there is a hysterical core to every obsessional neurosis and that obsessional symptoms are part of every hysteria, while both conditions share the common ground—common, also, to both sexes—of phobias. Psychoanalysis began to move in the direction of discrete diagnostic syndromes each of which was to have one cause. Later, when that one cause was no longer early sexual experience but fixation at or regression to one libidinal stage, hysteria was said to have passive "oral" origins, and obsessional neurosis active "anal" origins. Psychoanalysis was headed towards a very rigid diagnostic thinking—not as symptom-oriented as the DSM eventually became, but nonetheless, very boxy.

I offer this diagnostic story as an example of what has happened time and again in psychoanalytic theory when an unexamined biological assumption about sex difference has been brought forward in such a way as to undermine a clinically perceived similarity. In psychopathology, hysteria and obsessional neurosis came to be seen only in their differences. And that is one of the main reasons, I think, why, by the late 1930s, when analysts were noting that they saw very few hysterics (that is, hysterics of the fin de siècle symptomology) in their clinics, a pathology called "borderline" was outlined, covering the clinical phenomenon of severe hysteria with aggressive obsessional features. "Borderline" was—like the fin de siècle hysteria—thought to be much more common in women than in men (the DSM claims twice as common). Then, again, in the late 1970s, another form of severe hysteria with obsessional features appeared in epidemic proportions and was thought to be "for women only": anorexia nervosa. It took many years for the realisation to spread through the clinical community that males suffer from anorexia, and, further, that both women and men can conduct their anorexia in the medium of obsessions, like obsessional exercising or body culture, and, further, that cultural conditions influence the way an illness develops.

One-cause thinking in combination with sex-stereotyping led psychoanalysis away from the realisation that the psychoneuroses are culturally shaped—hysteria more than obsessional neurosis, but both to some degree—but even more generally it led psychoanalysis away from developing any broad-based, multidimensional, flexible, descriptive character typology. This meant that there never appeared any Freudian characterology drawing on the whole range of Freud's developmental lines rather than just on the libidinal stage theory and the unexamined biological notions about activity and passivity. It became unusual for Freudian psychoanalysts to appreciate that similarities and differences in character among people are a broad arena—an arena of plurals—of which similarities and differences in sex and gender are a part, an appreciation that is fundamental to contemporary Jungian multi-type analysis, as it had been to the whole characterological tradition in Europe from the Hippocratic physicians forward.

A second key example of difference theory dominating

I have been sketching how psychoanalysis was tilted towards diagnostic particularism as Freud focused on sexual difference and how this contributed to closing off clinical exploration of the psychoneuroses in their intermixtures, exploration of the psychoneuroses in cultural context, and study of character. The present moment is a moment for the return of all these repressions. But I want to turn my attention now to a second moment in the history of psychoanalysis and a second type of theory construction.

As I indicated before, and as is well known, Freud eventually abandoned his so-called "seduction hypothesis", having become convinced that it could not completely explain the origin of the psychoneuroses—that is, neither of hysteria nor of obsessional neurosis, and neither in women nor in men; and seduction especially could not, being less than universal, explain the universal presence of psychoneurotic traits. Recently, this abandonment of the seduction hypothesis has been the focus of much controversy fostered by polemicists or reversalists concerned only with seduction of women and only with hysteria. The critics have claimed that Freud disavowed the ubiquity of seduction of women in his patients' milieus. But Freud was looking for a single, truly universal cause of both the two psychoneuroses, in men and in women, and of all the psychoneurotic symptoms common to everyone. So he turned his attention to the language of dreams, which all of us do have in common. *The Interpretation of Dreams* (1900a) was the book in which he hoped to show the universality of a sexual experience of another sort than seduction, that is, the experience of the incest taboo, the experience of desiring familial figures and having to renounce that desire. Later, *Totem and Taboo* (1912–13) was the text in which Freud made his claim about the universality of the Oedipus complex across the history of the species—his ultimate sameness argument, as big as Darwinism.

In *The Interpretation of Dreams*, as in "Three Essays on the Theory of Sexuality" (1905d), Freud stressed the similarity of males and females in their Oedipal object relations—both love the opposite sex parent and develop a rivalry with the same sex one. His drive to find a single sexual aetiology and to universalise it made him maintain that girls take as their *first* love object their fathers while boys take their mothers—the Oedipus complexes of the two sexes, that is, are structured similarly. And the similarity was kept clearer, too, by another disavowal: Freud noted but minimised parental desire for the child, parental seductiveness; that is, he did not conceptualise the Oedipus complex as an interactive formation. Among the early Freudians, emphasis on the interactive Oedipus complex came from Sandor Ferenczi and his Budapest colleagues. Among social psychologists and anthropologists, it was the Hungarian-trained George Devereux who pioneered the study of the interactive Oedipus complex.

Later, having given more attention to the period that came to be called pre-Oedipal (or, in libido theory terms, the oral stage), and under pressure to rethink his views on female psychology, Freud, of course, changed his mind and said that both girls and boys take their mother as their first love object. Initially, that is, there is a period of undifferentiation or pre-differentiation. This position, which is by now accepted in one form or another by analysts of the most diverse views, had as its consequence, Freud thought, that he had to show how differences arose—which really meant showing how women ever moved towards heterosexuality, leaving their mother bond. Or, as he put the matter in later terms, how they moved from their negative (same sex) to their positive (opposite sex) Oedipal bond. Freud had to identify, he felt, a determinative mark or point of differentiation, and for that he turned to a staple in his clinical observation, penis envy, to which he gave greater determinative weight than he had ever given it before. The girl turns towards her father having discovered that she lacks the penis, unconsciously wanting his, and wanting a baby who unconsciously is a penis.

As has often been noted, this makes female heterosexuality, which Freud often identified as the "normal" type of outcome from the initial bisexuality, into an achievement that comes about only from frustration and a sense of lack. Reversalists protested and put together all kinds of arguments about how heterosexuality is the inborn, biologically determined direction of female sexuality, as is motherhood. In the 1920s and early 1930s Karen Horney was the leading reversal theorist, but others—Ernest Jones, Melanie Klein—came forth, each with her or his own version of the reversal. The crux of the debate was really about whether an event turns the woman's sexual instinctual drive to men and to motherhood or whether this happens naturally unless an event interrupts, deflects this drive.

Interestingly, before these debates of the 1920s, Freud had pointed to another experience of frustration, not sexual instinctual, as the truly universal experience of frustration for children, and also as the *earliest* experience of frustration. Very clearly in his "Three Essays on the Theory of Sexuality", Freud had cited children's experiences of not being cared for—including nursed—as much or as well, or as securely or constantly, as they need and wish, as crucial for them. He was indicating not experiences of unpleasure, in erotic or libidinal terms, but of what he usually called helplessness (sometimes he spoke of dependency) in the relationship he called anaclitic. Much more than animals' babies, a human baby is completely dependent on its carer's care, and feels any lapse of that care—no matter the intention—as loss of love. Anxiety over loss of love in this sense, Freud would note in his (1926d) *Inhibitions, Symptoms and Anxiety*, is the elemental anxiety—and it is common to males and females.

Why did these experiences—and a child's reactions to them—not come to be thought of as determinative for a child's developing object relations? Because in his work of the 1920s, when he was operating with an instinct theory organised around Eros and Thanatos, Freud had only one instinct to interpret in object relational terms—the sexual instinct. To be able to credit as determinative for future object relations the infant's or the child's experiences of deprivations of care, he would have needed to think in terms of an instinctual object other than the sexual instinctual object. Similarly, Melanie Klein, the great theorist of the importance of weaning in a child's psychic life, was only able to view weaning as loss of an erotic object. Freud had, in fact, once had such an object in his theoretical scheme. Between 1910 and 1914, he had spoken of the sexual instincts and the ego instincts or self-preservative instincts—the instincts of hunger as contrasted with sex—as the two fundamental instincts. The ego instincts, he had said then, are the ones that draw an infant to its mother's nurturing breast, preparing the way for a later sexual instinctual investment in her breast and in her. Males and females are similarly drawn, by implication.

I am dwelling on this undeveloped avenue in Freud's work because I want to note in a moment how it has opened within recent psychoanalysis and is coming to transform it deeply. The avenue was, in fact, developed in the 1920s by the group that surrounded Sandor Ferenczi in Budapest, while Freud himself was going where the dual instinct theory and his strong emphasis on sexual difference led him. But the Hungarian work, although it was, of course, known in the psychoanalytic community, was marginalised as Ferenczi himself was marginalised in the years before his death in 1932 and thereafter. What Ferenczi called "primary object love" was the ego instinctual love Freud had started to explore in the period between 1910 and 1914—as I will show later. But for the moment, let me put the question, "Why did Freud move away from his consideration of a love that is equally determinative for both sexes and towards his emphasis on sexual differentiation?"

How sexual difference came to dominate over similarity in Freud's late thinking

In the history of psychoanalysis, the first woman to play a major role was Lou Andreas-Salomé, who arrived in Vienna in 1908, as her wonderful journal relates, just as Freud was quarrelling with Alfred Adler. He was charmed that she chose him rather than Adler as her teacher, but she was not ever a "passive" student.

During the period from 1910 to 1914, while Freud was writing about the sexual instincts and the ego instincts, stressing that the ego instincts are from the start oriented towards objects—towards the mother's breast—and that they set down pathways in which the sexual instincts *later* flow, Lou Andreas-Salomé was with him. But as Freud began to think of the primal state of undifferentiation as a narcissistic state, dominated by a sexual instinctual drive directed at the ego, not by an ego instinctual drive directed towards the mother's breast or towards the first carer, Lou objected. She thought Freud was pathologising the primal sexually undifferentiated state, making it the origin of the "narcissistic neuroses", while in her estimation it had a positive influence on all later development. It symbolises Woman, she held, and the bond of mother and child. Wanting to regress to it, she held, is a sign of health—and, she stressed, drawing on her interest in artistic creativity, and anticipating later descriptions of "regression in the service of the ego", regression can be a sign of creative power. Such a regression could signal, to use a term later employed by Ferenczi's student Michael Balint, a "new beginning". For the present moment in psychoanalysis, the main theorist of creative regression and new beginnings has been D. W. Winnicott.

Frau Lou also disagreed with the way Freud in his anthropological speculations of the time—in *Totem and Taboo*—associated the undifferentiated beginnings with a primal patriarchy, while she thought in terms of a primary matriarchy, a reign of mothers, which, she reminded Freud, had been written about by contemporary anthropologists. In their correspondence, neither Freud nor Frau Lou pursued further Freud's reasoning for the position he took in his famous 1914 essay "On Narcissism". The correspondence in which Freud's shift is chronicled, however, is the one with Carl Jung, for it seems very clear that it was Jung's move in the direction of a concept of undifferentiated beginnings, with more and more stress on the earliest mother-child bond, that provoked Freud's thoughts on narcissism. Objecting to what he viewed as Jung's abandonment of the libido theory and his substitution of a non-sexualised primary energy for libido, Freud insisted on having the primary state defined as sexual, libidinous. To do this, he pushed his own concept of the ego instincts to the side—eventually so far to the side that he subsumed the ego instincts completely in his later theory of Eros. Then, as Freud put more and more emphasis on his libido theory, he brought the differences in libidinal development between the sexes to the fore.

In the "On Narcissism" essay, which should be read, I think, as Freud's great good riddance to Jung, Freud was on the path that later led him to emphasise female difference as centrally a matter of wounded narcissism. As I noted a moment ago, he stressed that girls envy the male penis, and after 1914 he described their sense of lack in terms of wounded narcissism. The one of his followers who did most to buttress the emphasis on female wounded narcissism was Karl Abraham, whose 1920 essay Freud never ceased to praise. In the strongest possible terms, Abraham presented penis envy as (to use Freud's later term) "bedrock" in the psychology of women. And Abraham also drew overtly the conclusion that Freud and many others of the early Freudians accepted: penis envy is of a piece with the feminist desire for sexual and every other form of equality. Feminism and "the masculinity complex" became two descriptions of the same phenomenon. This development was of great consequence, for it meant that thereafter any clinical or political protest against Freud's and Abraham's difference theories, whether in the mode of reversal or in the mode of disavowal, could be dismissed as a form of penis envy or wounded narcissism. With this strategy, psychoanalysis, once a politically progressive mode of thought, began to metamorphose into a reactionary mode of thought.

A slow change opens into the present

It is no exaggeration to say that from the 1920s to the mid-1930s all the protests against the view that Freud ended up advocating, which excluded any sense that all humans originally seek loving care, with their erotic or sexual lives following in the paths of this earliest seeking and its fulfilment or lack of fulfilment, were reversal protests. Lou Andreas-Salomé's critique was lost, and, as I have stated, the work of the Budapest School was marginalised. It is also the case that even after the 1930s, whenever Freud's journey towards his final view was repeated, as it was very self-consciously by Jacques Lacan in the early 1970s, for example, the resulting protests took very similar reversal forms. Among the Lacanian trainees who questioned their master's views, many varieties of reversal were articulated, but they all had and have in common the idea of motherhood as the natural destiny of women and of women as essentially different from men, different in their sexuality as in their *écriture féminine*.

After the1930s the alternative path of critique emerged, one which I described as asserting that an underlying sameness is gong to be revealed in the future as the situation of women is reformed. Karen Horney, who had been the great reversalist of the 1920s, shifted to this view and in the mid-1930s warned women that it was a trap for them to concern themselves with what is feminine and what is masculine, with sex differences. A true understanding of the sex differences that are apparent in any given time and place, she said, will only come when women have developed their potentialities as human beings. As she made very clear in *New Ways in Psychoanalysis* (1939), Horney had become convinced, helped along by the interpersonal psychology of Harry Stack Sullivan and the anthropological work of Margaret Mead, that most personality traits and behaviours and types of pathology attributed to sex differences with roots in biology are, in fact, products of culture, and, specifically, products of parental transmission of cultural values. Femininity, is, as we now say, a social construct.

Horney's culturalist view had little impact within psychoanalysis itself before World War II, but by the late 1960s American feminists who put achievement of equality in all domains at the centre of their political work converged upon all kinds of psychoanalytically buttressed emphases on sexual difference. Difference became the enemy. And it became especially important for radical feminists to try to separate—as Freud once had in his own way—biology and social identity or social role, sex and gender. A full-scale attack was mounted upon prescriptivism about "natural" female roles and domesticity, even to the point of Shulamith Firestone's famous suggestion—taking Simone de Beauvoir's position in *The Second Sex* (1949) to the max—that in a brave new technological future, women should be freed from biological motherhood, which had always been the anchor of patriarchy. Radical feminists in one way or another argued that anatomy is not destiny and that the humanity men and women have in common, not their differences, should be the focus of all political vision.

In terms of human sexuality, the debates of the day focused on the female genitals and the question of whether the clitoris or the vagina should be designated the defining sexual site. The emphasis, that in the 1920s Karen Horney and other psychoanalysts who had stressed motherhood as the essentially female destiny had put upon the vagina and upon the Freudian claim that a mature woman is one whose sexual pleasure has been transferred successfully from her clitoris to her vagina in puberty, was challenged by sex researchers like Masters and Johnson as well as by the psychoanalyst Mary Jane Sherfy, who was famous for arguing that women are capable of multiple orgasms. The "clitoral woman", the woman whose masculinity complex doomed her to unsuccess as a woman, to lesbianism, or to feminism, began to disappear from the psychoanalytic nosologies where she had resided since the 1920s.

Both within psychoanalysis itself and from feminism, the intense attention trained on female sexuality and specifically on the nature of female orgasm in the late 1960s and early 1970s was eventually criticised. From within feminism came a form of reversal. Those of the so-called "cultural feminist" schools insisted upon the differences between men and women, emphasising the value of virtues alleged to be specifically female, particularly those involved in establishing caring and concerned relationships and specifically female cultural achievements. Investigation of differences between the sexes was, once again, given impetus, and female superiority was argued in many ways. But, at the same time, among psychoanalysts, there was pressure to reassess not just female sexuality but the whole range of questions that contests over female psychology had raised. Robert Stoller was particularly forceful in expressing the obvious, that orgasmic response as it was debated by Sherfy and others is no measure of a total personality, while psychoanalytically oriented feminists, led by Juliet Mitchell, began to reassess the history of psychoanalytic theory about female sexuality. Much of this 1970s struggle was just polemical, but it did—stirring things up—make possible the admission into psychoanalytic theory of a strand of work that had been building in child analysis, distinguishing itself from both the camps of those adhering to Freud's late views and those in dissent. As has always been the case in psychoanalysis, it was from the margins that a challenge arose to both orthodox Freudianism and the critical stances that have arisen to try to reverse or disavow that orthodoxy.

A new beginning

The story of the rise in modern psychoanalysis of the tradition called object relations has been told in quite a number of recent studies. What I want to emphasise about this story, in the context of considering the psychoanalytic concern with differences and similarities between males and females, men and women, is that there came about, from its origins in the Budapest School and through the work of D. W. Winnicott, a renewal of concern, now at the very centre of psychoanalytic infant research, with development prior to differentiation along sexual lines and with objects other than sexual objects. Slowly, into consideration came Imre Hermann's remarkable work on clinging, which was mediated through John Bowlby's work on attachment; Michael Balint's work on "primary object love", which took off from Ferenczi; Alice Balint's work on the first year of life and the development of it by René Spitz; Margaret Mahler's work on separation and individuation; and Ferenczi's own controversial explorations of psychoanalytic techniques that might reveal or even re-create the mother-child dyad.

These revenants deserve a paper to themselves, but here I am just going to suggest that when the majority of the Hungarian group moved to London, they had great influence on the British Middle Group. In Winnicott's work, the fundamental developmental line is not the libidinal line marked oral-anal-phallic-genital (although he certainly acknowledged this line), but one that goes: absolute dependence or helplessness, relative dependence, towards independence. His notion of the infant's mother is twofold: she is "object mother", the object of excited sexual desire, but she is earlier—from before her child's birth—"environment mother", source of care, provisions, safety, place of holding, rest, and eventually ego integration. She is the mother without whom the self cannot be preserved. Winnicott is the great theorist in psychoanalysis of dependence and of the way in which we all come to our humanity by a process of being supported in our helplessness—our helplessness that never entirely ceases, that is carried over into our maturity, and that is always there to be regressed into, as Lou Andreas-Salomé had said.

Into current theory and treatment has come Winnicott's basic idea that out of our reactions to and memories of our dependence and the support we got (or did not get) in it, we become able (or not) to support ourselves and eventually show concern for others. But we are still assimilating the significance of this basic idea for the construction of "female psychology"—about which Winnicott did not write specifically, because his concern was with sameness far more than difference—as we are still assimilating to our understanding of sexism, in psychology and more generally. With his focus on dependency and development, Winnicott was the first to encompass a crucial ingredient of sexism, one just as important as the ingredient that stems from narcissism or inability to tolerate signs of sexual difference, the ingredient that is so apparent in the images of genital sameness that Lacquer studied in *Making Sex* (1990). As Winnicott expressed his insight in a 1950 talk called "Some thoughts on the meaning of the word 'democracy'" (1965, p. 262):

> In psychoanalytical and allied work it is found that all individu-
> als (men and women) have in reserve a certain fear of WOMAN
> .... The root of the fear of WOMAN is known. It is related to the
> fact that in the early history of every individual who develops well,
> and who is sane, and who has been able to find himself, there is a
> debt to a woman—the woman who was devoted to that individual
> as an infant, and whose devotion was absolutely essential for that
> individual's healthy development. The original dependence is not
> remembered, and therefore the debt is not acknowledged, except
> in so far as the fear of WOMAN represents the first stage of this
> acknowledgement.

Winnicott implied that the main reason why it has taken psychoanaly-sis so long to come to an appreciation of dependency and of the deter-minative role of dependency experiences in human psychic life is that fear of dependency—fear of Woman—makes it impossible for us to remember our dependency, to re-feel those feelings. Lifting the amnesia that surrounds Woman, along with the amnesia about original and paradigmatic sexual desires that Freud pointed to, is not just crucial to psychoanalytic therapy but crucial for psychoanalytic theory of development, including theory of sexual and gender identity.

This conclusion could be put in other words by saying that the key similarity between men and women is that the figure of dependency, called Woman (although in some people's stories, the figure may be male), is the original and paradigmatic object of both love and fear for both women and men. In light of this conclusion, the question of difference becomes: in what ways (the plural is crucial) do women and men of all sorts—all developmental courses, all characters, all pathologies—grow from the original (and historically influenced) condition of dependency and what roles do sexual differences (also historically influenced and interpreted) play in those ways of development and become influenced, in turn, by those ways of development?

I have put this conclusion in these terms in order to highlight how the topic of "women and psychoanalysis" has shifted on its axis since the turn of the last century. The conjunction "women and psychoanalysis" now points beyond all the ways in which psychoanalysis has tried to understand women, the history of theories of female development. That long history of theories, in which "women" stood out as either the unknown or the mistakenly known province, the key challenge to psychoanalysis, the main location of its errors and prejudices, can be seen as covering over the deeper territory that is now being explored in the dynamic and pluralising clinical settings I described earlier and in infant research that is focused on the nature of primary and subsequent dependencies or attachments. It is our challenge now to come to know that deeper territory of Woman in everyone's love and fear, in everyone's primary relatedness. And we as women, and women of many different sorts, have many distinctive experiences that we are bringing to bear on that challenge.

References

Abraham, K. (1920). Manifestations of the female castration complex. In: *Selected Papers of Karl Abraham.* New York: Brunner/Mazel, 1979.
Andreas-Salomé, L. (1964). *The Freud Journal.* New York: Basic.

De Beauvoir, S. (1949). *The Second Sex*. C. Borde & S. Malovany-Chevalier (Trans.). New York: Vintage, 2010.

Devereux, G. (1953). Why Oedipus killed Laius. *International Journal of Psycho analysis, 34*: 132–141.

Freud, S. (1896a). Heredity and the aetiology of the neuroses. *S. E. 3*. London: Hogarth, 1962.

Freud, S. (1900a). *The Interpretation of Dreams. S. E. 4–5*. London: Hogarth.

Freud, S. (1905d). Three essays on the theory of sexuality. *S. E. 7*. London: Hogarth.

Freud, S. (1912–13). *Totem and Taboo. S. E. 13*. London: Hogarth.

Freud, S. (1914c). On narcissism. *S. E. 20*. London: Hogarth.

Freud, S. (1926d). *Inhibitions, Symptoms and Anxiety. S. E. 14*. London: Hogarth.

Horney, K. (1939). *New Ways in Psychoanalysis*. New York: W. W. Norton.

Horney, K. (1967). *Feminine Psychology*. New York: W. W. Norton.

Lacquer, T. (1990). *Making Sex: Body and Gender from the Greeks to Freud*. Cambridge, MA: Harvard University Press.

McGuire, W. (Ed.) (1974). *The Freud/Jung Letters*. Princeton, NJ: Princeton University Press.

Winnicott, D. W. (1965). *The Family and Individual Development*. London: Tavistock.

Young-Bruehl, E. (1998). What theories women want. In: *Subject to Biography*. Cambridge, MA: Harvard University Press.

CHAPTER SEVEN

Sexual diversity in cosmopolitan perspective

The globalisation of sexology and changes in its categories

In the last decade or so, the concept "sexual diversity" has shifted its meaning and compass in the European-American world, where the scientific study of sex—called sexology—began in earnest at the end of the nineteenth century. For most of the twentieth century, lay people and scientists alike subscribed to a model of human sexuality stipulating that human sexuality normally (and normatively) has little diversity in it. There are just two sexes, male and female; two genders, masculine and feminine, with corollary social roles; and two kinds of sexual preference, same-sex and opposite-sex. "Sexual diversity" was roughly equivalent to "sexual pathology" and that meant (above all else) "non-heterosexual preference".

In the wake of the European-American second wave feminist movement and the gay liberation movement, the scientific study of sex became much more sophisticated and much less governed by prejudices against women and against homosexuals, so both the prejudices themselves and this Noah's Ark two-of-everything paradigm of sexuality could shift. Now, among progressive people around the world, homosexuality can be considered an ordinary, non-pathological type of sexuality; in the movement's political terms it is "different but equal". The political situation has changed so dramatically that a 2006 petition entitled "For the Universal Decriminalization of Homosexuality" was launched in the hope of getting the United Nations to favour abrogating the anti-gay laws of the seventy-five countries in the world where homosexuality is still a crime.

In the domain of scientific study of sex, the result of the political shift and the paradigm shift has been that the biological sex binary male and female has become a continuum that includes all kinds of intersex states between the extremes of male and female; the gender binary masculine and feminine has turned into a "social construct" to be studied comparatively and deconstructed by sex activists, so that it, too, has become a continuum stretched between extremes of masculine and feminine gender identity and role; and bisexuality now encompasses heterosexuality and homosexuality as two extremes on its continuum (as Alfred Kinsey had proposed in the 1950s).

In the 1970s and 1980s much of the scientific impetus in the European-American world for the paradigm shift away from binarism and towards thinking in continua came from studies of gender identity and role, which revealed great diversity in womanhood and manhood around the world and across history, and which then helped medical practitioners understand how to design flexible policies for addressing the HIV/AIDS pandemic. Recently, the impetus for the shift has come from the addition of "transpeople" to the list of people to be studied (and people doing the studying), for their experiences disturbed all of the taken-for-granted binaries at once. At the turn of the twenty-first century, sexual minorities were politically grouped as not just LGB but LBGT, lesbian, gay, bisexual, and transgender.

But these very compactly stated scientific and political results, which I will explore further later, were also the consequence of a wave of new information about human sexuality that came to European-American researchers from researchers and political-sexual activists all over the world. As the European-American sexual liberation movements rippled outwards, and then as local and international groups organised to combat the worldwide AIDS epidemic, sexual minorities which had been in hiding and often unnamed, unorganised, sequestered, or persecuted "came out". With their visibility, a wealth of stories and data became available, and that meant, given the existence of new communications technologies, available around the world. To offer just one example, you can go to the internet and find out from a newsgathering site like globalgayz.com that in 2003 Nepal's first ever organisation for sexual minorities was founded, and that the Blue Diamond Society welcomed under its banner and to its AIDS-oriented medical clinics not just gay men, lesbians, and transgender people but sex workers and people who engage in various types of ritual sexual practices from singing contests to transvestitism. Similar progressive political organisations in South Asia and elsewhere try not to be prescriptive about how people define themselves and are often critical of European-American insistence on viewing a practice as defining an identity.

In terms of the amount of persecution suffered by sexual minorities, the globalisation of the reformed scientific attention to prejudice and persecution and of the liberationist political struggle has had mixed results: in some areas, persecution has diminished, in others it has increased and become more public; in some areas, there is greater toler-ance, in others greater backlash. For all kinds of sexual minorities, the recent rise of fundamentalisms in all the world's imperialistic religions, which has been intensified by globalisation even in states with long secularising trends, has been horrible. However, one trend is unambig-uously progressive.

After 1989, when the human rights movement emerged from under the shadow of the Cold War, the struggle for civil rights conducted by the gay liberation movement in America and in most Western Euro-pean countries transformed into a worldwide struggle for human rights conducted by groups sharing experiences of persecution motivated by a wide range of prejudices, not just sexism and homophobia. The con-solidation of the period of civil rights struggle and the commencement of the human rights struggle was signalled in 1990 when the World Health Organization removed homosexuality from its list of mental dis-orders and in 1991 when Amnesty International included persecution on grounds of sexual orientation in its reporting and then extended that inclusion to trans people. The International Gay and Lesbian Human Rights Commission (IGLHRC) was founded (and from the start it included transgender people's human rights in its mandate).

The globalisation of study of prejudices against sexual minorities and sexuality

One of the great achievements of the recent study of sexuality has been to show that prejudice against either women or sexual minorities or both has always gone along with and promoted misinformation about sexuality. For example, when hormones were discovered in the 1920s, it was assumed that males had one kind of hormone (testosterone) and women another (oestrogen), because men and women had to be very distinct beings, and no man should have any admixture of femaleness, which would make him homosexual. The extraordinary complexity of the human hormone system and the presence in all people of every type of hormone was slow to be appreciated—and still is full of mysteries. Misinformation, in turn, contributed to the petrification of the very prejudices that had produced it.

Historical and historiographical study has freed contemporary scientists to look at human sexuality and the stories that have been told about it with much greater objectivity, and it has also provided the foundations for study of prejudice itself. After prejudice against women was clearly identified in the 1960s and given a name—sexism—that designated it as a prejudice, comparable to racism or anti-Semitism, that is, as involving characteristic acts and an ideology (not just the attitude long named misogyny), researchers could raise the question: did this prejudice originate in a particular context or contexts, psychological and sociological? Is it now global or species wide?

Once the question of sexism's origin had been raised and explored, it became obvious that the analogous question should be raised about homophobia, a prejudice which does not exist except in contexts where sexism is endemic, as its forms—and they are plural—are all variants of sexism. Homophobia was named and understood as a prejudice in the 1970s, but to this day there is no word for prejudice against sexual minorities other than homosexuals, either generally or specifically, and it is not yet clearly understood that prejudices against sexual minorities other than homosexuals have been built up on the foundations of homophobias. Hermaphrodites (now more commonly known as intersexuals), for example, have in some times and places been persecuted, but there is no word in any language for such a prejudice. In some societies, trans people—males living as females, or females living as males, who may or may not be anatomically intersexual or homosexual in terms of sexual practices—are held to be a third sex and valued, or at least not stigmatised. But in other societies trans people, particularly males living as females, are assumed (falsely) to be homosexual and are despised.

Sexual minorities persecuted from nameless motivation obviously have in common that they challenge sex-and-gender binarism conventions or stereotypes; they are non-conforming in the matters of either genital appearance or gender role or both, and they may also be non-conforming in the matter of sexual preference (as they are assumed to be). Diverse sexual minorities have become hated in contexts where conformism itself has become valued as the means for group cohesion. And a comparative historical survey can indicate, further, I believe, that the most prejudicial environments are generated when groups that have achieved group cohesion defensively, while fending off persecution and humiliation, then turn aggressive and use their group cohesion for conquest, or some form of imperialism.

To use psychoanalytic terms for this aggressively maintained group cohesion: persecuted groups master their group trauma with conquest over other groups. Prejudice against sexual minorities, including homosexuals, seems strongest in groups that have achieved cohesion defensively through an ideology of active, self-punishing asceticism or body-rejection. In persecuted, defended groups, sexual minorities are accused of being the reason for the group's weakness, or of being a threat to the reproductive strength that might overcome weakness, or of interfering with a vision of how to transcend persecution by asceticism in this world and by focus on life in the next world. As such groups turn aggressive themselves, seeking the this-worldly power they have been denied, they accuse their sexual minorities of being like the outsiders who are to be conquered. The hated sexual minorities are usually said to inhibit or undermine (as a kind of fifth column) the conquest project by not contributing to the regular reproduction that would reinforce the group's imperial strength.

Within some persecuted groups that subscribe to an ascetic ideology, sexual minorities are felt to challenge by their very existence, which calls attention to sexuality and to the body. The most influential example of this sort of ideological asceticism in world history has been the small, persecuted eastern Mediterranean Christian communities of the first century after Christ, in which anticipation of the next life and denigration of life in this world (along with apocalyptic visions of the imminent end of this world) became the norm. At the same moment in the first century, there was an ascetic strain in persecuted Jewish communities, but it was less strong and less other-worldly among the Jews, who emphasised family bonds and regular reproduction to provide for group survival. The third Abrahamic religion, Mohammedanism, the least persecuted in its originary moment, was not body-rejecting or anti-sexual or other-worldly, and it was also, of the three religions, the least intolerant of sexual minorities.

Early in the first century, St Paul, echoing contemporary neo-Platonic and Jewish ascetic writings, railed against both male homosexuality and cross-dressing (or what would now be called male-to-female transgender behaviour). The most consistently despised practice was "sodomy", named (as it was in Jewish and Islamic traditions as well) after the biblical story of Sodom and Gomorrah, which had been interpreted—contemporary scholars would say grossly misinterpreted—as a story of male homosexual activity punished directly by God.

From its imperial inception in AD 313, the Christian empire proclaimed by the Roman Constantine, drawing on its heritage of body-rejection or anti-sexuality or asceticism, and perpetuating that heritage through an ascetic priesthood in its Catholic branch, has been the greatest single source in world history of prejudice against male homosexuals, male-to-female trans people, and male transvestites. Those who came under its expanding sway, as did the Goth or Visgoth peoples who vanquished the Romans, adopted its edicts. As a general rule, it can be said that the more militantly proselytising the Christians have been, the more they have engaged in repression of male deviants—and eventually female as well, although because female homosexuality does not directly threaten patrilineal reproduction it is less politically offensive.

Among the diverse Muslim societies that were suppressed by the Christian crusaders, homosexuality had generally been condemned, with reference both to the Qur'an, where the "people of Lot" are censured, and to the Haditha (sayings attributed to Mohammed). But at the same time the "Greek love" of older men for their beautiful protégés and courtiers was the subject of a revered genre of Arabic love poetry, and homosexuality between males was, in reality, punished only if it had been witnessed or was in some way publicly expressed. Tolerance for private acts was much greater than in the early Christian and Jewish traditions, and this was especially the case through the great seventh and eighth-century period of Muslim rule in the Iberian peninsula, when the Umayyad Muslims subdued the debased Visigothic culture, but then ruled peacefully from their capital in Cordoba, encouraging Muslim, Christian, and Jewish peoples of Andalusia to intermarry freely.

In the modern Muslim world, militant prejudice against homosexuals and other sexual minorities has gone along with militant nationalism, which can be described as the effort of diverse types of Muslims to recover from their humiliating suppression by the Christian states, dating from the period of the Crusades. Among modern capitalistic Christian imperialists, the British, whose educational institutions were single-sex and quite puritanical, excelled at sexual suppression, particularly of their supposedly common practice, sodomy. As in the early Christian communities, an ascetic form of Islam emerged during the rise of persecuting capitalist imperialism as the form most intolerant of sexual minorities, and Wahabbism retains that distinction to this day, when it has grown progressively more imperialistic.

Recently, although the number of Muslim nations in which homosexuality is punishable with death was reduced from seven to five as the Taliban were defeated in Afghanistan and as Saddam Hussein was overthrown in Iraq, Saudi Arabia, the chief seat of Wahabbism, has grown less and less tolerant and Wahabbism has been exported from there into terrorist camps across the Middle East. The 1979 ascetic fundamentalist revolution in Iran brought about an enormous wave of sexual persecution—for homosexuality, but also for adultery—that has also been exemplary for fundamentalists in other Muslim nations where homosexuality is said to be a Western aberration, an import. The importation charge is also made in many African nations, Muslim and non-Muslim, where dictatorial leaders claim that their sexual minorities are products of Western influence and that there are no such things as indigenous African homosexuality or transgenderism.

Christendom's anti-minority prejudices are the world's most potent example of prejudices that began in ascetic social practices turning aggressive and, in the context of developing imperialism, becoming more political—that is, becoming like planks in policy platforms. The contrast is very stark between the Christian Church's anti-sexual minority prejudices and the situations in parts of the world uninfluenced by it (or by Christian influenced Islam). In ancient China, for example, during periods of both Taoist and Confucian religious practice, male homosexuality was common in the courts of the emperors. No anti-homosexual legislation was created in China until Christian missionaries brought along their models, although by far the worst period of persecution was during the nationalist upsurge of the Chinese Cultural

Revolution led by Mao, which was a period of assault upon the corrupting Westernisation of China.

Tolerance for multisexuality in the globalising world

Recent scientific study of sex, more aware of this history of prejudice and reducing the amount of misinformation it has generated, has established that humanity, like all the mammalian species, has evolved as a species in which there is great diversity of sexual constitution and behaviour (with behaviour not in any simple way the consequence of constitution or in any simple way correlated to gender). That is, it became obvious that human sexuality is very diverse in constitution and expression when it was understood that all human beings are mixtures of chromosomal sex (the presence or absence of X and Y chromosomes), hormonal sex (involving a mixture of many types of hormones), gonadal sex (the presence or absence of testes and ovaries), external genitals, and reproductive sexual functions (involving the capacity to produce ova and lactate, or to produce sperm). Hermaphroditism or intersexuality, originally referenced exclusively to the appearance of a person's genitals, is now known to be quite common and to come in varying degrees, involving different configurations of chromosomes, hormones, gonads, and genitals. Approximately seventy intersex syndromes have been described. There are more than two dozen known causes for genital ambiguity alone, and worldwide as many as two per cent to four per cent of newborns have ambiguous genitals, while many more are intersexual in ways that cannot be detected visually.

There are places in the contemporary world where certain intersex conditions are acknowledged without stigmatisation. Similarly, there are societies where transgender people are not stigmatised—indeed, where they are elevated. Among many Native Americans tribes, *nadles* or "Two-Spirit People", constituting a third sex and often entering into same-sex marriages, are honoured with a special status and specific tasks, including skill transmission and wisdom teaching. What is known in sexology as sexual identity is not assumed by many Native Americans to be a developmental product, a conjunction of many factors, biological and psychological, which a person claims as an identity. Rather, sexual role or performance is a product of shamanistic dreaming; it is assigned by a dream and the dreamer chooses to welcome the assignment as a gift, a vocation.

In other traditions as well sexuality is thought to be produced by choice of practice or choice of way of being sexual, not just by inborn make-up. Sexual identity is not a distinct kind of identity, but part of the microcosm that each individual is. In the ancient Taoist sexual theory, all people were thought to be born with a mixture of the cosmic male body spirit yang and the female body spirit ying, which are exchanged by adults in sexual intercourse. Right sexual practice was supposed to preserve a person's unique harmonious body spirit admixture; so men, for example, were cautioned against exclusive homosexual practice because it involved too much yang-yang mixing and would result in not enough ying. Bisexual practice not only served reproduction, but served yang-ying calibration, keeping males female enough for harmony. By contrast, in cultures like the ancient Greek or the modern Melanesian, male characteristics were thought to be enhanced by transmission of semen from an older man to a younger, so homosexual practice was key to initiation rites or rites of manhood that are meant to keep a boy from being too female or too much of the female world of his mother.

Considering these diverse philosophies and practices, it seems to me generally accurate to say that, as defensive asceticism is the taproot of prejudice against sexual diversity, the taproot of tolerance for it or appreciation of it is a sense that sexuality is a manifestation of a body spirit harmony (that is, a bisexual or ambisexual or omnisexual harmony) and that how this harmony is manifested is a matter of choice or practice. To say the same thing psychodynamically, tolerance or appreciation involves not splitting (or, in theoretical terms, not embracing binarism). Not-split persons are ones who have integrated what is felt to be male/masculine and what is felt to be female/feminine in their make-up. (Among Christian fundamentalists today, "conversion therapy" is promoted for treating homosexuals, and what this means is that homosexuals who cannot split off their forbidden desire and turn into heterosexuals must become ascetic to avoid sinning. Splitting is required, instituted, in either solution.)

Combining these two generalisations, it can be said that defensive asceticism is an extreme form of splitting; that is, so drastically are masculine and feminine split (or purified into extremes) that both disappear, both become disembodied. In the Abrahamic monotheistic traditions, worship is focused on a disembodied male deity who may be accompanied by some form of Holy Spirit which retains the last vestiges of a female component without being available for reproduction in a heterosexual manner. Ascetic splitting itself is revered. By contrast, polytheistic traditions generally include in their pantheons at least a few gods who are hermaphroditic or homosexual or transgendered in some form, that is, they represent the diversity characteristic of human families or social groups. Not-splitting is revered. Within polytheistic societies—the Hindu societies of India, for example—the kind of prejudice characteristic of monotheism only appeared under colonial conditions. In Nepal—to go back to an earlier example—the ancient Hindu and Buddhist temple art depicts many sexual practices and behaviours that were forbidden under British rule.

Sexual pathology in a global context

Scientific study of sexual behaviour in the European-American world was for so long dominated by categories of normality and deviance in relation to the binaries male/female, masculine/feminine, and same sex/opposite sex preference, that all kinds of sexual pathology were fitted to that paradigm. Any pathologies which did not fit into the binary paradigm were almost completely unstudied (although not undocumented). The psychological concept of perversion and the sociological category sex offender, for example, were both organised by the assumption that homosexuality is the key perversion and the related assumption that most sex offenders are homosexual. All other perversions were described in relation to homosexuality, and study of sex offenders hardly existed outside forensics, where offenders were understood as homosexual, which meant, for example, that heterosexual sex offenders in domestic situations (wife batterers) or men ordered or permitted to commit rape as part of military campaigns were not identified as sex offenders.

One of the most important consequences of the paradigm shift away from binary thinking and towards thinking in terms of continua of sex, gender, and preference experiences, has been the opportunity the shift has presented to reconsider sex pathology—a reconsideration that is underway around the world. To put this reconsideration in a nutshell: especially after both the phenomenon of sexual abuse of women and the phenomenon of child abuse and neglect became subjects for scientific study in the 1960s, and the links between these phenomena emerged, pathology was no longer thought of so much in terms of sexual diversity or deviancy as in terms of abusiveness. That is, the focus is now on the quality of the relationship existing between persons engaging in sexual behaviours.

To my mind, this refocus should result in a redefinition of sex pathology as sexual behaviour, usually manifesting a specific ideology or prejudice and certainly involving characteristic acts, which is non-relational (or relationship denying). "Non-relational", as I am using it, means that the pathological person cannot treat another involved in his or her act as a person, an equal, or, one would say in political terms, as a human with human rights. The person's practices involve some form of ownership and do not involve consent or respect for the other's wishes. To use a term from the history of marriage, there is nothing companionate in a sex offender's sexual relationships (or non-relationships). By this "non-relationality" definition of perversion, homosexuality is obviously not a perversion, as it does not (any more than do heterosexuality or bisexuality) involve reducing a person to less than a person or denying human rights. A transgender person is just as capable of a respectful, equal relationship as a non-transgender person.

In the world today, even though there has been progress in writing international conventions to articulate and secure human rights generally and the rights of women and children specifically (if not yet of sexual minorities), a documentable increase is occurring in perverse sexual behaviours (thus defined). This is being fuelled by globalising social and technological conditions that foster abuse of women and children, which, although such abuses are as old as patriarchy, now have novel features. For example, most of the world's wars since 1989 have been interstate wars, and in these wars rape and child rape have come to be used instrumentally to disrupt reproduction within an enemy ethnic group contending for control of the state. An estimated 500,000 women and girls were raped during the Rwandan genocide.

The most obvious abuse type with novel features is child pornography, which can now be manufactured easily and inexpensively with digital cameras and disseminated on the internet by individuals, without the kinds of networks and organisations once required. Solicitation of sex with minors and marketing of child prostitution, too, have moved onto the internet, although traffic in women and children for prostitution still requires the smuggling and brothels long familiar to police and border police. The rise in recent years of global trade has been accompanied by an increase in the transportation of women and children around the world for both labour and sex work; unemployment rate increases in both developed and undeveloped countries have also contributed to increases of sexual trafficking, sexual violence, and sexually transmitted disease. Similarly, as the number of war zones (especially intrastate ones) in the world has risen, so have the number of refugees and people without a safe home, and the consequences of this for abuse of women and children are obvious.

For many years, research into sexual abuse of women and children was hampered by lack of agreed-upon definitions and differences in definitions across states and cultures; by lack of mandatory reporting and inconsistency in reporting; and by the prejudice, which I mentioned before, about the perpetrators being deviants in the now outdated terms. Paedophilia was widely assumed to be a subspecies of homosexuality, although it is now obvious in various cultural contexts that the vast majority of paedophiles are heterosexual males who choose their victims, whether male or female, for their non-adult status and the quality of their vulnerability or powerlessness, not just for their male or female sexual characteristics. A paedophile can avoid humiliation in adult relationships—including with adults who do not want to be infantilised—and play out sexual fantasies of various types with little resistance from an uncomprehending child.

Nowhere in the world is there a concept for a prejudice, comparable to sexism, directed against children—no childism; although in the eighteenth century the word "misopaedia" (child hatred) was coined to acknowledge child hatred as comparable to misogyny and misandry. In the "Century of the Child", as the twentieth century was hopefully named by late nineteenth century child protectionists and opponents of child labour, child hatred was to be eliminated. But we who, despite considerable reform and even the emergence of societies characterising themselves as "child-centred", live with the obvious fact that child hatred did not recede, still do not speak of a childist culture when considering a culture that promotes or sanctions any form of child abuse and neglect. We do not speak of groups that are childist, as child pornographers are, or child sex traffickers, or armies recruiting child soldiers.

Hopefully, as sexual minorities whose behaviours are "different but equal" come to consume less and less of the attention of both students of sexuality and people prejudiced against sexuality and sexual variation, the really problematic sexual minority—those whose sexual behaviours are abusive—will be better understood and the human rights of their victims more understandingly and effectively protected.

CHAPTER EIGHT

Women and children first!

Over the past forty-five years, let us say since 1968, there has been a profound change in the way psychoanalysts, in all schools, have imagined women: who they are, what lines of development are typical of them, what they want, how they live. There has been an effort to leave behind the construction of a representative woman, existing outside any context, any environment, in order to imagine "women" as a collective embracing all women in their diversity, in their diverse contexts.

In psychoanalysis there has also been an effort to avoid understanding women on the model of a representative generic man, existing outside any context, any environment. That is, the idea that a woman is a not-man or a man manqué or a deficient, lacking man has been jettisoned. This change has meant that the representative man has begun to disappear, too, although this process is less advanced because thinking in terms of the generic man is still congruent with prevailing patriarchal cultural norms.

Psychoanalysts, like the general public, are still entranced by the question that troubled Freud: "What do women want?" But most realise at the same time that this question, which implies that someone should step forward with a single solution to the mystery, a single key

141

to its locked door, is really designed to introduce a bold answer that will allay the generalised anxiety disorder of all contemporaries, male and female, who assume that the mystery of what women want is the mystery of why the sexes are so continually at war. Although it retains its allure, the question is now known by many to arise from the wish-laden domain of mythmaking.

A brief history of recent psychoanalytic trends

Before I go on to connect this profound change in psychoanalysis with changes in the larger world, I would first like to track the change historically, for it is always illuminating to explore the specific forces and factors that have promoted a change (and inhibited it) and to keep in mind the specific ingredients of change that are still with us and those that were left aside, unexplored, as roads not taken. One of these roads not taken is, it seems to me, especially important for under-standing the revisionary road psychoanalysis did take—and the roads it might take.

Even after Freud's 1933 essay "Femininity", in which he admitted there were many things he did not know about female psychology and which maybe others—the poets perhaps—knew or would come to know, Freudians quite normally wrote books with "female psychol-ogy" in their titles. (Not so many were entitled "male psychology" since that was assumed to be much better-mapped territory.) The important collection of papers called *Female Psychology: Contemporary Psychoana-lytic Views* (Blum, 1977), continued the tradition. But in that collection, as in other books of that time, readers could see that the edifice sur-rounding the answer to Freud's question was collapsing. (Not Freud's own answer, which he had declared inadequate, but the edifice created out of the Freud-inspired speculating and weaving together of psycho-analytic ideas, from the late 1920s reactions to Freud's views up until the early 1970s.) Even though there was still an assumed representa-tive female in this collection of psychoanalytic views—no women of non-heterosexual preference were discussed, no women with histories of trauma, none with minority status based on race or class, and, for that matter, none with any kind of power—this representative female was not considered in the Freudian manner as not-male. Further, the beginnings of a kind of pluralisation were apparent in the questions raised about what constituted normal female development and about whether the concept of normality that had been deployed in Freudian psychoanalysis was inhibiting.

Within a decade, by the 1980s, the traditional psychoanalytic focus on the intrapsychic life and development of Woman had been completely abandoned by many within psychoanalysis and certainly from every disciplinary direction outside psychoanalysis where feminists were trying to appreciate the diversity of women's lives and the multiplicity of types of factors influencing them. Not only had the Freudian "female" and Freudian notions of normal female development almost vanished, but methodological questions about how to consider intrapsychic experience in relation to other people (and their psyches), to environments, to relationships, and to observers were everywhere in evidence, a thousand forms of them blooming. Child psychoanalysis was dominated by various kinds of efforts to illuminate "the interpersonal world of the infant", a phrase that still echoed the old habit of abstraction—the "infant", not "infants"—but actually referenced work that was more contextual and relational.

In many ways, the situation was comparable to the one that Freud had faced in the years when he developed psychoanalysis. He had started off with an utterly traditional nineteenth-century medical and psychiatric notion that each disease has a cause, a pathogen, so he had looked for the single cause of hysteria and found it in "precocious sexual experience" (as he announced in the 1896 paper "The Aetiology of Hysteria"). The same cause lay behind obsessional neurosis, he then announced, which allowed him to think that both neuroses share a single cause, so a general causal theory of neurosis was in view. Because Freud also held to the traditional idea that once a pathogen is isolated, the disease can be cured by eliminating the pathogen (and perhaps its carrier), he went after the "precocious sexual experience" in his patients. His technique was to get the patient to talk about her precocious sexual experience and its perpetrator and then, didactically, to explain to the patient that *this experience* was the cause of subsequent distress. He applied psychoanalytic theory to the wound and awaited an abreaction or a catharsis. When it became apparent to him that neither his assumption of a single cause nor his assumption of a single modality of cure was right, Freud was left confronting a great diversity of phenomena that his over-general assumptions had obscured.

He did not immediately give up the idea of a single cause; he just turned to an alternative one, the Oedipus complex. In *The Interpretation of Dreams* Freud (1900a) tried to show that the Oedipus complex and its childhood wishes lie at the bottom of every dream, no matter how diverse the disguising dreamwork and the manifest content of the dream may be. The same, he argued, is true of hysteria with all its multitude of symptoms and conversion symptoms (and one might add from a contemporary perspective, its historical and cultural specificity of manifestation). Similarly, he turned to a new treatment modality. Instead of applying psychoanalytic theory, he waited until the Oedipus complex began to play out—like a current onset of fever—in what he called "the transference", and then he analysed it there, interpreting (not explaining) the transference, bit by bit, image by image, as he had learned to interpret dreams. Freud had had the insight (which he had struggled towards in the Dora case) that each person's particular way of repeating—indeed, compulsively repeating—her Oedipal scenario, or disguising it in dreams, demands a particular interpretative treatment. By the time he focused his attention on narcissism and studied the war neuroses during the First World War, eventually discovering a narcissistic neurosis to make a trio of neuroses, Freud was thinking in terms of a plurality of unconscious Oedipal scenario types: hysterical, obsessional, and narcissistic. These he came to call character types, thereby connecting his work with a long Greco-Roman tradition of character study—the very tradition that the poets who might understand female psychology had inherited. Freud (1916d) celebrated this new direction in his work with a series of brilliant essays on "Some Character-Types Met with in Psycho-Analytic Work" and later in his reflections on the three basic unconsciously determined but environmentally shaped character types in *Civilization and Its Discontents* (1930a) and "Libidinal Types" (1931a). Despite the continued pull of his hopes for a single cause and single treatment mode, Freud said that each kind of neurosis is "over-determined", that is, it is fed by many springs, and every treatment must steer clear of the kind of single-story suggestibility typical of hypnosis and typical of his own early cathartic and didactic methods. There may be character types, but each person's character is a particular story constructed, as it were, into her or into him as a lived personality.

When psychoanalysts in America and Europe in the late 1970s and early 1980s managed to free themselves to a great degree of the image of "female psychology" and began to confront the diversity of women's experiences, they did not, however, return to take up the unfinished, indeed, still quite unexplored, new direction that Freud had indicated: the direction of plural Oedipal stories and characterology. This new direction could have led to consideration of multiple female psychologies and to the conclusion that there is not one universal Oedipus complex with three characterological variants, but a plurality of Oedipal variants—just as the anthropologist Malinowski had argued in the 1920s against the rigid, obsessional, and narcissistic opposition of Ernest Jones, a Freudian more Freudian than Freud. Instead, the meeting of feminism and psychoanalysis in the late 1970s focused on the project of freeing women from being thought of psychoanalytically as failed men; it emphasised sexual difference and developmental lines specific to women. It also, generally, focused on the importance of the mother (rather than just the father) in pre-Oedipal and Oedipal development of infants and children and on the "reproduction of mothering" (Nancy Chodorow's phrase, 1978) in girls.

It seems to me that if the characterological road had been taken decisively, we would have today a psychoanalysis much more richly concerned with the fate of the ego instincts for relationship seeking and ego preservation and ego-ideal formation in various familial and cultural contexts. The traditional Freudian emphasis on sexuality and aggression would have given way to an emphasis on innate sociability and the ego instinctual drive for relatedness. Instead, drive theory—and especially the ego instincts that disappeared into the life instincts and were contrasted to a truly mythic death instinct in 1920—was pushed aside, criticised as insufficiently attentive to object relations, as it was in the British object relations tradition and in the feminist appropriation of that tradition. The ego instincts, which are about finding and clinging to objects to satisfy hunger and need for care, protection, and love, disappeared and were not heard of again.

Further, if the characterological road had been taken, I think we would be talking about pre-Oedipal mothering and about the Oedipus complex in various forms as parts of what might be called a "family complex". The Oedipus complex would have come to be understood as a part of the family complex that had been taken or mistaken for the whole, synecdochically, and there would be more attention not just to mothering per se, which is universal, but to its many variants. We would be exploring and cataloguing how children internalise, from infancy onward, family and extended family (cultural) relationships of many sorts, not just the parental ones, and how the whole cluster of any child's internalised vertical (adult-child) and lateral (child-child) relationships, developing from infancy forward, becomes the nucleus of that child's character. The clustered types are plural for both women and men, but different for men than for women, first and foremost for the reason that the 1970s feminists had emphasised: namely, girls retain their primary relation to their mother as an identification, while most boys, although not all, struggle for disidentification with the mother. Women are also differently related to and identified with other women and men, and girls and boys in their nuclear and extended families, because they grow up in a patriarchy, that is, they grow up as "the second sex", dominated, not well educated, constricted in many ways, not accustomed to agency but only to obedience or accommodation or self-sacrifice.

There are many theoretical reasons why this pluralistic characterological road was not taken (or retaken) in the 1970s although some parts of it were, of course, investigated. But the most influential reason, I think, was contextual: psychoanalysts of that period found themselves in the middle of an extraordinary social phenomenon that nearly destroyed psychoanalysis. In that moment of extreme crisis, no one was in the mood to follow a path Freud had pointed to, but that had been little explored by him or by his immediate followers. And, perhaps just as important, that crisis left psychoanalysis largely isolated from feminist work which took place outside psychoanalysis during and after the crisis—a point that I will return to.

The seeds for this crisis were sown by the scientific discovery in the 1960s of physical child abuse (the battered child syndrome), which ushered in a period of discovery of childhood sexual abuse in the late 1970s and early 1980s in America and in Europe. The charge was made that this discovery had been slowed or even blocked because Freud had turned away from his discovery of childhood sexual abuse ("precocious sexual experience") and set psychoanalysis on the wrong road of too much emphasis on the Oedipus complex and Oedipal fantasies of sexual seduction. Psychoanalysis was charged with being the great obstacle to the discovery of childhood sexual abuse. The most polemical anti-psychoanalytic book of the period, Masson's (1984) *The Assault on Truth*, actually went further and accused Freud and then all Freudians of duplicitously covering up child sexual abuse in their theories and practices. European and American feminists in great numbers believed this accusation and castigated Freudian psychoanalysis for denying, particularly, father-daughter incest, which child protection services and the emergent international field called "child abuse and neglect" (CAN) were then documenting.

Almost all of institutional psychoanalysis, after some intense resistance to acknowledging the crisis that had arisen, became involved in a collective hand-wringing over Freud's abandonment of the idea that precocious sexual experience was the sole cause of hysteria and obsessional neurosis. The idea that psychoanalysis had taken a fundamentally wrong turn was hardly a spur for reconsidering any features of psychoanalysis's history other than the unhelpful binary that was then set up in a weak effort at reform: attention to intrapsychic life *vs.* attention to trauma.

No sooner had the reformist idea that psychoanalysis had neglected the study of not just sexual abuse, but trauma in general—including the contemporary traumas related to the Vietnam War that psychiatrists studied and added to the *Diagnostic and Statistical Manual* in 1980 under the title "post-traumatic stress syndrome"—been established than psychoanalysis was attacked from another angle by a motley coalition of critics with quite a different agenda. Their agenda can be summarised under the title of Faludi's (1991) best-selling book of the period: *Backlash: The Undeclared War against American Women*.

In the decade of the 1970s during which childhood sexual abuse (along with all kinds of violence against women) figured intensely in the American and European public consciousness, psychoanalysis seemed retrograde and obstructionist to all feminists concerned with exposing sexist abuse. To many feminists, the project of a rapprochement between feminism and psychoanalysis in order to revise the Freudian theory of "female psychology" seemed a waste of time since to them it was part of an obsolete, misogynistic science. In the 1980s, as America took a radical political turn towards conservatism and a backlash developed against the feminist emphasis on violence towards women and against the discovery of childhood sexual abuse, psychoanalysis was also labelled part of the problem by conservatives who wanted to attack feminism itself. So psychoanalysis was a target for both feminists and conservatives—a war on two fronts.

The forces of backlash had three major weapons. They said that many accusations of child sexual abuse were false and based on manipulation of children's memories and fantasies by lawyers and therapists; and they even invented a disease, "false memory syndrome".

Second, they said that many therapists, particularly those specialising in "recovered memories" were using Freudian theory to induce their patients to "recover" from repressed abuses that had never happened. Third, they said that the discoverers of sexual abuse were emphasising abuse in the family and by fathers when the real problem was in community settings like preschools and involved vast conspiracies of paedophiles, including ritual and satanic ritual abusers. Freudian psychoanalysis got implicated in all these charges because it was the theory of childhood fantasy, of repressed memory, and of nuclear family pathology. Ironically, it was tarred by conservatives with the same brush that was used to tar the feminists who had been so critical of Freudianism in the 1970s: Freud and the feminists were anti-traditionalist, anti-moral, and anti-family. Sexual revolution and social degeneracy were the enemies in this socially conservative and religiously fundamentalist backlash.

The backlash in its most extreme form, which was a "moral panic" or "mass hysteria" about predatory paedophiles and satanic ritual abuse, had died down by the mid-1990s, and so-called RMT (recovered memory therapy) was on its way to discredit which meant, fortunately, that it was decoupled from its alleged source in Freudian theory. But during this two-decade-long period of the discovery of childhood sexual abuse and then the backlash against that discovery, from approximately 1980 to 2000, the entire theoretical effort from within psychoanalysis to reconsider women—prompted by the earlier fruitful alliance of psychoanalysis and feminist criticism—was under the shadow of the charges and countercharges that came to be known as the "Freud Wars".

Nonetheless, the progress that had been made in reconsidering female psychologies, noted earlier, did not disappear. And several features of it became consolidated conceptually. First, the helpful concept of "gender" was assimilated into psychoanalysis from various feminist sources and was used to elaborate more fully than had Freud's term, "mental sexual characteristics", all the factors influencing women's (and men's) development that were not biological sexual factors, that is, not chromosomal sex, hormonal sex, or anatomy, and not sexual instinctual drives in their biological aspect. This gender concept aided psychoanalysts in saying there are different ways to become gendered, to come into a particular gender identity. Unfortunately, however, many analysts held on to the idea that there are only two genders: masculine and feminine.

Second, the concept of homophobia was articulated at the same time that the American Psychiatric Association depathologised homosexuality, and this move aided psychoanalysts in saying sex and gender development results in different types of sexual object preference—heterosexual, homosexual, bisexual, and fluctuating—each of which is "normal development" (if that concept is used meaningfully, that is to say, if normal development leads to the ability to sustain a non-perverse, mature relationship with another whole person). It became less customary to take object preference as the essential element of a person's self and sense of self (the part of identity determining the whole of identity). Third, along with attachment theory, the new field of trauma studies and neuroscientific research on the nature of human memory had given psychoanalysts tools to continue the process of exploring how intrapsychic fantasies and structuration relate to external events. Dissociative states and various kinds of fragmentations of identity became central to psychoanalytic theory and therapy and were applied to the study of women.

Fourth, evolutionary theorists, zoologists, and anthropologists, influenced by changing sexual and social mores, looked out upon the animal kingdom, and especially at the animals evolutionarily closest to humans—the chimpanzees and the bonobos—and observed that among these near-kin sexual behaviour serves two different and not very compatible purposes in evolutionary terms. It serves reproduction, and for reproduction heterosexual intercourse is required. But it also serves group and subgroup formation and group maintenance, which looks very different in the two primate groups because they live under different environmental conditions. All-male subgroups are bonded by the members' homoerotic behaviours, as are all-female subgroups; intergenerational subgroups bond with diverse practices, from grooming to masturbation. Members of a group may find that their erotic attention is divided between their subgroup or groups and the heterosexual male-female reproductive dyad. These observations led evolutionists to understand that among humans, too, the sexual drive ending in reproduction coexists with other drives or other interests that are just as normal and essential for life and survival. Among these other drives and interests are the ego instincts that I mentioned before: the sociability and self-preservative instincts.

In the last decade, as the wars and backlashes over feminism and discovery of sexual abuse subsided, psychoanalysts of all schools have faced a need for further synthesis of developments in psychoanalysis—many of which took place in the shadows during the Freud Wars decades—and specifically for synthesis of developments in the domain of female psychologies. Although this need is being faced, I think it is also important to consider what is happening now in a wider context—in the wider world—that has not yet, although I think eventually it might, influenced the current synthesising effort. While psychoanalysts and others in America and Europe concerned with female psychologies were caught up in the huge upheaval that was the discovery of child sexual abuse, a truly monumental shift took place globally. I wonder whether we, as psychoanalysts, can read that shift for its implications about women's developments. What does it tell us about the domain that we are learning to consider, the interface of unconscious factors and environmental ones?

A changing world of women

Historians agree that there have been two major waves of feminism: the one that arose in the late nineteenth century and crested with the achievement of women's suffrage, starting in New Zealand in 1912 and continuing to the United States in 1919; and the one that arose after the Second World War and reached a decade-long crest between the late 1960s and the late 1970s, before the backlash that I described above. The two periods of rethinking the psychology of women in psychoanalysis coincide with these two waves: the first was in psychoanalysis and was led by women psychoanalysts like Karen Horney; the second was between psychoanalysis and second-wave feminism. Further afield, there is now a third wave of feminism growing up almost everywhere in the world, and not led by women in North America and Europe. Before asking what it might mean to psychoanalysis, I will describe it through quick sketches, using highly visible events and developments.

The development of third-wave feminism can be charted most simply by looking at the agendas and achievements of the four UN-sponsored World Conferences on Women—the first in Mexico City in 1975, where the UN Decade for Women commenced, the second in Copenhagen in 1980, the third in Nairobi in 1985, and the fourth in Beijing in 1995. A fifth conference, although long and widely called for to be held in 2015 by, among others, UN Secretary-General Ban

Ki-moon, has not yet been scheduled after a difficult backlash period of some seventeen years. But during the backlash hiatus, the third wave of feminism has continued to gather force, as it has continued to reflect the vision necessary for its emergence—a vision that had begun to be articulated in the Platform for Action that came out of the 1995 Beijing conference. Section 13 of that platform anticipates my description of that vision: "Women's empowerment and their full participation on the basis of equality in all spheres of society, including participation in the decision-making process and access to power, are fundamental for the achievement of equality, development and peace." This statement documents that the women meeting in Beijing assumed that achieving "equality, development and peace" for all humankind, for the species, would now be, primarily, women's work, and women, primarily, would bring it about. The message was that in an unequal, unevenly developed, and unpeaceful world no woman would be well advised to wait for the protective call "Women and children first!" to come from the patriarchy; women and children must be put first by women, for the sake of all. To use evolutionary terms, women are the subgroup needed for survival.

At Beijing, and since then, the world has become densely populated with women's groups of all sorts, from the informal to the formally administrated, UN-registered NGOs (non-governmental organisations). (Half of the women-related NGOs now registered at the UN did not exist in 1995.) Groups, circles, solidarities are known to be the momentum, the drive, of the third wave. There is no fear that the organisations will conflict or overlap or fall into a hierarchical arrangement: the more groups the better, the vision says, as the number is heading towards an envisaged tipping point when how women are in groups will be how people are on the planet, when a momentum will become a species change, a new habituation. The theory of change that subtends third-wave feminism is a theory of tipping points reached as the number of women involved in groups and in change increases exponentially. Third-wave feminism is not concerned with women's liberation as a revolutionary project; it is concerned with women's organisation or mobilisation as an evolutionary project, a change in the species.

All over the world there are action groups like the original suffragette groups; there are consciousness-raising groups like the ones that drove the second-wave women's liberation movement; there are even conversational salons like the proto-feminist Enlightenment salons.

But there are also groups of every other conceivable kind: groups for rural women, for urban professionals, for students, for women subject to particular oppressions (like lesbians) or particular exploitations (like sex workers). There are groups of young women, middle-aged women, older women; groups for economic development, for saving the environment, for women's and children's rights and legal redress, for political action. There are groups like UNIFEM dedicated to networking and non-hierarchical linking of other groups. Feminist publishing houses and newspapers now exist the world over, as do all kinds of means and media for meeting and exchanging stories and information and projects. A women's rights movement has grown into a leading agenda-setting part of the larger human rights movement, and the force behind a less well-articulated children's rights movement. Tremendous progress has been made in organising and in achieving declared goals for women and more generally for humankind and the earth and peace on earth.

While this monumental organising action has been going on, as evidenced in the compact world survey in *The No-Nonsense Guide to Women's Rights* (van der Gaag, 2004), more women than men have been entering the workforce in every region of the world except Africa, and in the workforce they form women's workforce groups. The gap between boys and girls who are being educated has narrowed, and women's illiteracy rates have shrunk in every part of the world, making women more able to organise groups. The average life expectancy of women has increased in developing countries (a sign of improvement in women's health), as the child mortality rate has decreased; and fifty per cent of the world's women have access to modern contraception. This progress owes much to the decision of the World Health Organization to prioritise women's health, prenatal care, and children's health. More women are entering politics, particularly at local levels, and in twenty-five of the world's nations women make up more than twenty-five per cent of those in national government. Rwanda has become the first state in which women constitute more than fifty per cent of its elected representatives. Legislative changes in all regions offer more protection for women's rights, and in many regions liberalisation of marriage laws has become an established trend. In most of the countries of the northern hemisphere, if not yet the southern, women are marrying at later ages, or not at all, after attaining an education.

But the counterforce to these signs of progress is all too obvious; you can see it in the way third-wave women have experienced both success and defeat at the UN. For example, on November 21, 2007 the UN General Assembly's draft resolution on "The Right to Food" was passed with only one negative vote, from the United States. The resolution protests that each year more than six million children die before reaching the age of five from hunger-related illness and that women and girls are disproportionately affected by hunger, food insecurity, and poverty. Girls are twice as likely as boys to die from malnutrition and preventable childhood diseases, and it is estimated that almost twice as many women as men suffer from malnutrition. In these statistics the gender discrimination and inequality that are central to all the world's grave problems stand out clearly—and the worldwide backlash aggravates them. But the resolution itself is testimony to the successful policy strategy of third-wave feminism, a strategy of "gender mainstreaming" that makes clear the role of gender in every grave problem and builds attention to gender into every proposed solution.

During the period since the 1995 Beijing conference, while third-wave feminism was gathering force and while, at the same time, a formidable backlash from threatened patriarchal institutions was resisting it, the gender mainstreaming strategy grew more and more powerful. Its strength came in part from the fact that the opposition of "the patriarchy" had become so obvious and was so obviously given its rationale by the fundamentalisms that developed within all the world's major religions. These fundamentalisms focused on constraining women and indoctrinating and punishing children. The backlash dictated that the plight of women and children not be highlighted, not be prioritised; on the contrary, women and children were to be even more forcefully kept in their place, within what analysts would call "the Oedipal family". To confront the backlash, particularly in its religious ideological forms with all their regressive consequences, third-wave feminists have had to keep continuously rethinking their own images of women and children. This meant, ultimately, rethinking their notions of women's agency, emphasising how women's agency is in and through relations with other women. The idea that the way to address sexism and the centuries-long ignoring of women's rights was to reform patriarchal institutions and hope for male protection abruptly receded. A new emphasis on women's groups and institutions and women as institution-builders came to the fore. In psychological terms, the idea that only women who are male-identified can be active, can be agents, was understood to be a masculine idea, a way of keeping women in their place, a way of criticising women's initiatives.

It is important to say that this was not a move in the direction of separatism, a strategy that had been advocated in the late 1960s and early 1970s in America and Europe, when radical feminists had argued that, because women would always be second class citizens in patriarchal institutions, they should withdraw and build their own institutions—from political parties to health clinics to banks. Separatism was never a strategy that could be useful outside certain specific social strata in America and Europe, and the third-wave strategy that came to the fore in the late 1980s and was articulated in 1995 in Beijing was carefully distinguished from it. No visions of all-women Utopias were offered. Facing the worldwide backlash against women, the majority of the internationally networked feminists shifted to considering how women could exercise their agency and build multitudes of institutions that were both sustainable by women and relatively impervious to backlash. The institutions envisaged were not separate from patriarchal, male-dominated institutions; they were connected to them, but on the condition that they not be under their authority or susceptible to being inhibited by them or being dependent upon them. They were set up to be able to grow into leadership organisations on the theory that progressive change builds upon and depends upon change in women's status and power. In every way, it was grasped that images of women as dependent had been the essence of female vulnerability within all kinds of institutions, starting with families. Agency through relations with other women and sustainability became key concepts. And in the domain of child rearing or preparation of the next generation, development from healthy dependency to agency through relations with other women and sustainability became the ideal, especially for girls.

As I noted before, this shift is evident in the statements issuing from the World Women's Conference in 1995 and in the planning for the next conference. But I think that it also shows up clearly—boldly—in the statements of the women who have been awarded the Nobel Peace Prize since 1990—a twenty-one year period in which the prize has been awarded to eight women when only six had won it during the prize's entire previous existence. I will also add to the list a man, Muhammad Yunus, who won in 2006, along with his mostly female colleagues in the Grameen Bank. Yunus worked with the same third-wave feminist assumptions that the women who have won the prize share.

Yunus's work dates from before the backlash of the 1980s and resulted in an institution, the Grameen Bank, that was impervious to the backlash. A Bangladeshi economist who earned his doctorate in America, Yunus returned to his country after its liberation war in 1971 and became involved in the national poverty reduction programme after the 1974 famine. While he was teaching in Chittagong University, he discovered that the women of a nearby town, Jobra, who made bamboo furniture were inhibited in the amount of bamboo they could purchase by having to pay for it with high-interest loans. Yunus experimented with making the women small loans at low interest and discovered that they could, with this capitalisation, quickly expand their businesses and pull themselves and their families out of poverty. He went on to institute the microcredit business plan by creating the Grameen Bank (the "Village Bank"), and by 2008 the bank was serving almost ten million small borrowers in Bangladesh. It also sponsored a system of solidarity groups in which the members support each other to secure the loans and make sure that all members are able to pay them back. That is, the women form a group that shares the borrowing risk. The Grameen Bank itself has diversified into units supporting all kinds of ventures, and the model of microfinancing has spread all around the world, including to the United States.

Since its inception, ninety-four per cent of the Grameen Bank's loans have gone to women, because Yunus believed that women, who suffer disproportionately from poverty, are more likely than men to use their earnings to support their families and raise and educate their children as well as possible.[1] He realised that in poor women's lives the female solidarity groups were key to the borrowers' sense of belonging and their efforts for a better future. They did not expect support from their husbands and they certainly did not get it from the Muslim clergy who had, in the 1980s, told women who borrowed from the Grameen Bank that they would be denied a Muslim burial.

Wangari Maathai, who, like Yunus, was born in 1940 and educated in the US, founded the Green Belt Movement in her native Kenya in 1977 and came to be known as "The Tree Mother of Africa". In her environmental work, which eventually brought her to found the Mazingira Green Party in Kenya, and to work internationally to unite green parties and "Young Greens" groups, Wangari Maathai always stressed that women were the primary keepers of the environment. The Green Belt Movement employed women as tree planters and farmers, providing many with a route out of poverty, and then trained them for political environmental work, turning the cause of environmental activism into a much more general support of women working and taking the initiative. Maathai herself paid a direct price for her vision when her husband divorced her, arguing successfully in a Kenyan court that he deserved the divorce because his wife was too difficult to control, too strong. When she protested the judge's concurrence with this complaint, she ended up jailed for contempt. But the movement she inspired and led continued, and she has recently held environmental portfolios in the national government.

To cite one more example: Shirin Ebadi, who, in 2003, was the first Muslim woman to win the Nobel Peace Prize, was directly affected by the fundamentalist backlash when she, the first woman to preside over a legislative court in Iran, was demoted to a secretarial position after the 1979 fundamentalist takeover. Unable to practise as a lawyer, she turned her attention to writing about issues that could strengthen the legal status of women and children and to leading campaigns that directly contributed to the large female vote in 1997 that spearheaded the election of the reformer Mohammed Khatami. During the years that followed, she defended people attacked by conservatives within the still theocratic government, and she established two NGOs, the Society for Protecting the Rights of the Child that sponsored legislation against physical abuse of children and the Defenders of Human Rights Center. Both organisations have trained women activists and established links with international organisations that sustain them with funds and pro-tection against attacks from the regime, a strategy that, Ebadi hopes, will make it possible for dissidents to stay in Iran and not join the Iranians in exile. In her autobiography *Iran Awakening*, Ebadi (2006) summarises her approach to legal and political activism:

> In the last 23 years, from the day I was stripped of my judgeship to the years of doing battle in the revolutionary courts of Tehran, I had repeated one refrain: an interpretation of Islam that is in harmony with equality and democracy is an authentic expression of faith. It is not religion that binds women, but the selective dictates of those who wish them cloistered. That belief, along with the conviction that change in Iran must come peacefully and from within, has underpinned my work. (p. 204)

It is in the spirit of third-wave feminism that the recent female Nobel laureates have themselves formed a group, the Nobel Women's

Initiative, and that among the activities they sponsor and participate in is the "Global Call to Action" made by PeaceJam, a group that is working on one of the most far-reaching—indeed, global—visions of a youth movement ever put forward. PeaceJam organises working relations between the Nobel laureates and young people from all over the world aimed at initiating "one billion acts of peace", aimed at reaching a tipping point into peace.

Third-wave feminism and psychoanalysis

Within the International Psychoanalytical Association (IPA), although its membership includes many analysts who would identify themselves as feminists, there is no, or very little, interaction with third-wave feminism. And the key strategic elements of third-wave feminism—the emphasis on women's institutions and women as institution-builders, and on proliferating and networking women's groups of all sorts and sizes as the momentum of change—are not part of the IPA's own institutions. (Nancy Chodorow has made a historical and sociological study of this fact, which is not countermanded by the existence in the IPA of a Committee on Women and Psychoanalysis, COWAP.) Similarly, the third-wave women's experiences are not part of the theorising about women that appears in its journal or in the regional journals like that of the American Psychoanalytic Association. Third-wave feminism has not had anything like the influence that second-wave feminism had upon psychoanalysis. Neither psychoanalysis as a cluster of institutions nor as a theory, not even as a revised and pluralised theory of female developmental types, has been affected by third-wave feminism.

Interestingly, and not surprisingly, the same could not be said of Jungian psychoanalysis (or analytic psychology), which has its basis in Jung's celebratory ideas about the feminine principle, which begins from ideas about how women and men differ (although, of course, the feminine principle can be manifest in both sexes). In the Jungian camp, a very active group, or cluster of groups, going under the name "Millionth Circle" has formed. It is led, or perhaps inspired, by Jean Shinoda Bolen, a medical doctor in San Francisco and a best-selling author, whose first use of Jungian archetypes to talk about women was published in 1984: *Goddesses in Everywoman: Powerful Archetypes in Women's Lives*. This book used seven goddesses of ancient Greek religion to represent different female types:

> These powerful patterns—or archetypes—are responsible for
> major differences among women. For example, some women need
> monogamy, marriage or children to feel fulfilled . . . Such women
> differ markedly from another type of woman who values her inde-
> pendence as she focuses on achieving goals that are important to
> her, or from still another type who seeks emotional intensity and
> new experiences and consequently moves from one relationship or
> one creative effort to the next. Yet another type of woman seeks
> solitude. (p. 1)

Jungian psychoanalysis is, basically, a characterology. It travelled on the
Freudian characterological road not taken, and so it was well suited
to meet the needs of third-wave feminism, and to learn from it, particularly about the power potentialities in each character type. Jungian
feminism is about agency, and Jungian feminist therapists share Bolen's
(1984) belief that, as she has said, "Women seek the help of a therapist
in order to learn how to be better protagonists or heroines in their own
stories." To use historiographical terms, this therapy is about learning
what story (in part told to you by others) you tell yourself and about
learning to tell it differently, turning to other women as your hearers
and helpers so that at a certain tipping point you become different.

But psychoanalysis does not have to reach for mystical notions of the
feminine principle and of inborn archetypes to connect with third-wave
feminism or to understand in psychodynamic terms the powerfulness of
its theory and practice and what that theory and practice have to teach
about how women can be powerful—or how they can be powerful in
ways other than those in which the patriarchal narratives, including
the original Freudian one, have imagined them to be. In recent years,
Freudian-trained psychoanalysts have made a start by turning to the
topic of what inhibits women from power or from being powerful. For
example, COWAP was one of the sponsors of a February 2000 international conference at Emory University entitled "Women and Power—
Psychoanalytic Perspectives on Women in Relationships, Groups, and
Hierarchies". The presentations were very illuminating about internal
factors—I would call them ingredients or traits of character—inhibiting women. They touched on the following list of factors offered by
Nancy Chodorow (2002, p. 18): Oedipal guilt; anxiety about separation,
loss, or castration; being "wrecked by success" or by spoiling and self-
spoiling powers of envy; grandiose narcissistic fantasies that lead to
fears of humiliation; conflict about aggression; self-punitive superegos;

survivor guilt; and "many other unconscious and conscious fantasies, all of these put together differently by different individuals". But the question, where do powerful women get their power?, was hard to ask in this context of concern with inhibitions developed in and fostered by sexist societies. Within third-wave feminist groups, the answer to the question is simple: from other women who, as is so clear in the Grameen Bank example, share the risk of investing in a better future, and a better story for women and children.

Conclusion

In closing, I want to offer a way to translate this simple, powerful "Sisterhood is powerful" declaration into psychoanalytic terms. What is it that women can give each other in groups? The experience of *power*, which can be simply defined in terms that are both psychoanalytic and political as acting together with equals. If a women's group is non-hierarchical and non-prescriptive, truly a group of equals, it operates like a therapeutic situation, that is, it is aimed at constantly revising the story (with many variants) of necessary submission and accommodation and self-sacrifice that women everywhere learn to tell themselves. The revision process requires safety and trust for increasing openness or revelation of self, revelation of who you are. As a forum, the group operates as an expression of shared experience or healthy narcissistic transference. It allows all its members the experience of being understood, to experience from other members the sense that: "I have also been through something similar, though, not the same, as what you are talking about." The group can build on experiences of similarity and communality, not upon difference since the differences among women are differences of character type, not of sexually based mastery or rulership rooted in child-parent psychodynamics. Ruling over is the opposite of acting together.

A women's group can aim at action that reflects the biologically given female capacity for reproduction, which is family-group generation capacity and more generally a capacity for nurturance and generativity. The group aims to establish this capacity in the world outside the home, augmenting the family circle by connecting it to other circles as its members act together. Power makes power. This is why third-wave theorising places such stress on increasing participation and on tipping points of power. Men can have the experience of acting together as equals, but they cannot by virtue of their biology have the further experience of gestating future generations, future circles, of that acting-together experience. Thus their groups are always degenerating into groups of rulers and ruled, fathers and sons beset by succession crises or questions about how the group will be sustainable as the king grows old. The women's group is inherently future-oriented, that is, it is for the women in it and for their children and grandchildren and the children they take responsibility for. They are not tied to the past or, as men are, to the status quo of patriarchal privilege, because their experience of the past is that it enchains them and they know that ultimately they have nothing to lose but their chains. This orientation to the future and to sustainability means that the group is not distracted from power augmentation and extension by a resort to violence or by the illusion, typically masculine, that using violence brings power. As Gandhi understood, women's groups are inherently nonviolent, and it is this that gives them the possibility of containing and channelling women's aggression rather than turning violent or self-destructive.[2] The model or group-ideal (like a collective ego-ideal) of a women's power group is a female sibling group in which everyone grows up to be equal in opportunity and reward. It is not dominated by either fathers or mothers, in reality or internally, who view themselves as rulers or critics or dispensers of rewards. The mothers invoked in third-wave feminist visions, the ancestral mothers, are idealised mothers, wished for mothers: generative towards the group members as the group members wish to be towards each other and their children. Not all women's groups, of course, live up to the possibilities that I have described—but they do have these possibilities!

Notes

1. At about the same time that Yunus set up the Grameen Bank, Allan Rosenfeld, then head of the World Health Organization, shifted the worldwide strategy of that body towards prioritising women's health, prenatal care, and early childhood interventions on the theory that a child who gets off to a healthy start in life has a much better chance of growing up healthy and able to sustain development, and that healthy women would be the best promoters of this understanding.
2. Gandhi said, "If nonviolence is the law of our being, the future is with woman." See Usha Thakkar's essay on Gandhi's views on women, www.gandhi-manibhavan.org/activities/essay_breakingshackles.html.

References

Blum, H. (Ed.) (1977). *Female Psychology: Contemporary Psychoanalytic Views*. New York: International Universities Press.

Bolen, J. S. (1984). *Goddesses in Everywoman: Powerful Archetypes in Women's Lives*. New York: HarperCollins.

Chodorow, N. J. (1978). *The Reproduction of Mothering: Psychoanalysis and the Sociology of Gender*. Berkeley, CA: University of California Press.

Chodorow, N. J. (2002). Glass ceilings, sticky floors, etc. In: B. Seelig, R. Paul & C. Levy. (Eds.), *Constructing and Deconstructing Women's Power*. London: Karnac.

Ebadi, S. (2006). *Iran Awakening*. New York: Random House.

Faludi, S. (1991). *Backlash: The Undeclared War against American Women*. New York: Crown.

Freud, S. (1896c). The aetiology of hysteria. *S. E. 3*. London: Hogarth.

Freud, S. (1900a). *The Interpretation of Dreams. S. E. 4–5*. London: Hogarth.

Freud, S. (1916d). Some character-types met with in psycho-analytic work. *S. E. 14*. London: Hogarth.

Freud, S. (1930a). *Civilization and Its Discontents. S. E. 21*. London: Hogarth.

Freud, S. (1931a). Libidinal types. *S. E., 21*. London: Hogarth.

Freud, S. (1933 [1932]). Lecture XXXIII Femininity. *New Introductory Lectures on Psycho-Analysis* (pp. 112–135). *S. E. 22*. London: Hogarth.

Masson, J. M. (1984). *The Assault on Truth: Freud's Suppression of the Seduction Theory*. New York: Harper Perennial.

Platform for Action, section 13 (1995). World Conference on Women, Beijing, at www.un.org/womenwatch/daw/beijing/platform/declar.htm.

Thakkar, U. (n.d.). Breaking the shackles: Gandhi's views on women, at www.gandhi-manibhavan.org/activities/essay_breakingshackles.htm.

van der Gaag, N. (2004). *The No Nonsense Guide to Women's Rights*. Toronto: New Internationalist Publications.

CHAPTER NINE

Psychobiography and character study: a reflection

Biography as a relational scene

The other day, a patient of mine, who is a psychoanalyst, came in and told me, excitedly, apprehensively, that she had just come from a session with a patient of hers who was furious with me. Her patient had been reading my biography of Anna Freud, and had concluded that I had wilfully concealed Anna Freud's lesbianism. "What do you think?" my patient demanded of me. "Is she right?" When I questioned her question, my patient and I went off in the direction of her attitude towards me at the moment, which was suspicion and fear for the fate of her usual idealisation of me: maybe, she was thinking, I was homophobic and I would reject her for her own lesbianism. The question of Anna Freud's alleged lesbianism receded from our work while we focused on the homophobia my patient feared in me, but my biography remained there, suspended in the matrix of our talk, having an episode in the life it has had since its first appearance back in 1988. Every biography could be a subject of biography. And a biography's life is, also, part of the afterlife of its subject—part of the subject's public self, or publicly created self.

163

This little exchange can stand for or represent a central feature of contemporary psychoanalytic biography. Each sophisticated reader of such a biography assumes that the biography is the biographer's construct, not an objectively truthful image to be judged by standards of verisimilitude. In this postmodernist time, readers assume that the biographical portrait is a product of the complex interrelation of the biographer and all the sources—the "data"—that are available for constructing the portrait. The portrait, then, will contain all the biographer's assumptions, peculiarities of imagination and style, biases, methodological convictions and ideological convictions, and some of the biographer's unconscious mind as well; that is, the biographical subject is a construction or a projection. There is no independent "self" of the subject, but there is the biographer's concept of the subject's self, as well as the biographer's conception of "the self". When the biography goes out to the readers who have this understanding of the biographer's art (or artifice), the subject as presented in it enters into the matrix of each reader's assumptions about the book and also each reader's receptivity to the subject and once again—many times again—there is mediation, construction.

I take all of this complexity for granted now. It is the intellectual zeitgeist. But I did not take it for granted when I wrote my first biography, of Hannah Arendt, between the years 1976 and 1982. Like the student of classical Greek literature and philosophy that I then was, I thought from within the classical biographical tradition, where lives are for public instruction. To edify readers, classical biographies told the manner in which a person had lived, manifesting his or her character. The subject's way of life was exemplary—usually exemplary of moral or political good, but sometimes of evil or of the ill fortune brought on by bad character.

When I was writing Hannah Arendt's biography, I worked on the basis of this tradition, and it certainly seemed appropriate to her, as someone educated in the Greco-Roman tradition, someone whose life had been caught up in political affairs—war, immigration, political struggle—and as someone whose writing was committed to the *res publica*. Also, it seemed appropriate to her as the author of *Rahel Varnhagen: The Life of a Jewess*—Arendt's first book (1957)—and as the author of the many biographical vignettes in *The Origins of Totalitarianism* and essays in *Men in Dark Times*, all of which were intended as exemplary, instructional lives.[1] I thought of biography as edifying character study, but I also thought of it as a type of intellectual history, concerned with my subject's ideas and how those ideas informed her words and deeds and thus had an influence over others.

Working in this classical way, I hardly gave a thought to Hannah Arendt's unconscious mind, although I certainly tried to tell the story of her childhood with as much regard as the sources permitted for her relationship to her father, who died of paretic syphilis when she was a child, and to her mother, a social democratic admirer of Rosa Luxemburg, who was the key shaping influence upon Arendt's earliest political concerns. But by the time I set out in the winter of 1984–5 to write my biography of Anna Freud, the intellectual climate had shifted into the hypervigilance of postmodernism that I mentioned before and my own conception of biography had become organised around Freudian ideas about the unconscious mind and its determination of conscious life. This does not mean, however, that I abandoned the classical mode of writing an edifying exemplary life. But I wanted to combine this mode with the new one and to make a methodologically complex (perhaps I should say hybrid) portrait of a person who had, I think, a remarkable relationship both to her own mind and with others' minds in a shared mental life, a world of psychoanalytic ideas and experiences. Putting this shift in my conception differently, I could say that I was still focused upon character, but that my understanding of character had changed: I looked now at the development of my subject's character and at how her ego's typical ways and means were rooted in her unconscious life. And, to repeat, I took it for granted that my understanding of character was determined by my own unconscious mind and that I was bringing that determination to the portrait I was constructing—and that my readers would do the same.

To put this matter yet another way: with this shift in conception, I had to accept that the task I was undertaking, a psychoanalytic biography, entailed not just the difficulties of accuracy or historical correctness and thoroughness built into the classical exemplary life or intellectual historical biography, but, ultimately, an impossibility: portraying the unconscious mind is an impossibility. The psychoanalytic biographer can set out looking and listening for the unconscious as an analyst does—assuming that the unconscious can be glimpsed in dreams, parapraxes, symptoms—but what the biographer finds cannot, ultimately, be interpreted, because the subject is not available as a free associator or as a person having a transference to the biographer. The psychoanalytic means of interpretation—free association and transference—are missing. In a psychoanalytic treatment, you and your patient can, working together, slowly, over the course of time, raise to consciousness the patient's unconscious memories, fantasies, desires, aspirations—and perhaps some of your own, too. But this is a "live" interactive process, with a therapeutic aim; it is not an interpretation of documents, not a piece of interpretive writing. (Even in psychoanalytic case writing, the problems of representation that are not present in the therapeutic work itself come flooding in.)

So, of course, the person who is presented in a psychoanalytic biography is—much more obviously than a person presented in the classical exemplary life—an imagined person, an imaginary person. That is, the biographer's imagining process is more evident because there is an explicit focus on the unconscious mind and an explicit effort to do the impossible, to read through documents and into interviews and correspondences for the unconscious layers. The psychoanalytic biography is explicitly a relational scene, whether the biographer chooses to appear in the book in the first person singular, "I", as the imagining, interpreting presence, or not, and whether the biographer's inevitable "countertransference" to the subject and in the relational scene appears as such or not.

A psychoanalytic biography has something of the quality that Kierkegaard once captured perfectly when writing about irony: he said that an instance of irony is like a portrait of an elf wearing the magic cap that makes him invisible.

The absence of a subject who is free associating and transferring is one of the key factors that distinguishes psychoanalytic biography writing from psychoanalysis, of course, but it is also important to recognise the many ways in which this factor interplays with a second key factor: namely, that a biography writer is free associating about and countertransferring onto not only the subject, but the reader—the reader who is present all during the researching and writing, not just when the book is available on publication. In a psychoanalytic consulting room, there is no reader, no audience, in this sense, although both analyst and analysand may very well be performing for audiences in their own imaginations.

Both the biographies I have written have been first biographies, and in both instances this meant that my readers were—in my mind, and then in fact—having a particular kind of discovery experience: they were finding out things about Hannah Arendt or Anna Freud that they had not known and could not know from any other source than my discoveries, and they were having to weigh that information against their preconceptions, which were usually based on nothing more than rumour (except in the cases of my subjects' personal friends, people I had interviewed). I was aware while writing Hannah Arendt's biography that her youthful affair with her teacher Martin Heidegger was going to be both a crux in her story and the shocking revelation of my book, as I was aware that Anna Freud's analysis with her father was going to be a crux in her story and the shocking revelation of that biography. Both revelations were going to raise questions about how my subjects' crucial youthful experiences played out in the rest of their lives, in their later relationships, and in their work. Not surprisingly, these episodes were the most difficult ones for me to try to understand, while working through my own feelings about them, and also to write, while taking into account my own reactions and my anticipation of how my readers were going to react. In retrospect, I can see that I behaved towards both revelations in the same way, which is characteristic of me: that is, as though commanding myself, "Do not sensationalise, do not dramatise!", "Keep this episode under your control, do not let your feelings about it show!"

Psychoanalytic character study and self-study

I have been trying to indicate how, from my first biography to my second, I kept the classical practice along with the newer, more constructivist mode; kept the idea that the subject has a character that can be portrayed for the reader's edification along with the idea that character is also who a person becomes in relationships, including the interpretive relationship of another's analysing or story-telling. But just now I have indicated that my own character, which is particularly obvious in the crucial moments of both biographies, did not differ fundamentally from one book to the next even though the books are quite different: confronted with crucial, turning-point episodes in my subjects' lives, and in the stories I was telling, I behaved "in character".

Considering the character from which that characteristic response of mine arose will bring me into the territory of the characterology with which I operated implicitly as a biographer and operate now explicitly as an analyst. This is a characterology which I made explicit to myself after both biographies were published and that I wrote about starting with a book called *Creative Characters* (1991), going on to one called *The Anatomy of Prejudices* (1996), and culminating in various essays I wrote during the years of my training analysis, when my evolving sense of my own character really began to have an effect on me. In my analysis, I was able to look at myself quite differently from how I had before, and to change—to the point where I know that if I were confronted today with the task of writing about Hannah Arendt's affair with Martin Heidegger and its after-effects, or about Anna Freud's analysis with her father and its after-effects, I would write differently and much more transparently. (As far as Arendt is concerned, I have recently written about her quite differently, as I will indicate; and I am currently writing a new preface for the Anna Freud biography's second edition.)

Let me illustrate my characteristic way of confronting the crux of my subject's life by returning to the question of Anna Freud's sexual life with which I began these remarks. From the first moment when I entertained the idea of becoming Anna Freud's biographer, this question was in front of me. That was in the late fall of 1984, when Anna Freud's editor and literary executor, Lottie Newman, summoned me to her house in order to ask me to write the biography and to offer me access to Anna Freud's papers, which were at her house en route to their final destination as part of the Sigmund Freud Archives in the Library of Congress, Washington, DC. After she had shown me this daunting collection of papers—six large steamer trunks full of neat bundles, one bundle per year from 1946 through 1982—Lottie Newman served me a lovely lunch and made her proposition: she would give me access to the papers (and permission to quote them) for a biography, with no control over the result, and I would, going through all the papers, remove any that made direct reference to patients, so that these could be restricted and the patients' confidentiality preserved. During the conversation we had about her proposition and about Anna Freud's life and work, I put Lottie Newman a blunt two-part question. Was the rumour that Anna Freud was a lesbian true? And, if so, what did she, Lottie Newman, think about how biographical news of Anna Freud's lesbianism would resound in the world community of psychoanalysts, given the fact that homosexuality was then still considered a pathological condition?

Lottie Newman did not take up the second part of my question because she answered the first by saying that she was aware that some people thought Anna Freud and Dorothy Tiffany Burlingham had been lovers, but that she did not think so. She based this judgment on the many times that she and her husband Richard had stayed in the Freud house in London and travelled with Anna Freud and Dorothy Burlingham, who kept separate bedrooms at home and when travelling and were never physically affectionate or in any way lover-like with each other. At this point, Richard Newman, a psychoanalyst, who had joined us for lunch, concurred that the phrase "Boston marriage" was accurate, and asked me a wry question in his slow Texan drawl: "Now I ask you, those two ladies had a really excellent and quite *harmonious* relationship for fifty years—do you think that could be sexual?"

I left that lunch quite confused by his question, which after all implied the broader question of whether I thought *any* sexual relationship could be harmonious! His intention was clearly to get me to take account, before I even began, of my countertransference to my potential subject. But I was also confused by my own ambivalence about writing a biography *either* of the woman the Newmans had described *or* of a lesbian whose lesbianism I would be forced to expose, in the face of denials like the Newmans', to the psychoanalytic community. Even though I decided to go ahead with the biography, my ambivalence never completely disappeared. By the time I had interviewed her friends, read letters (her own and others'), and particularly interpreted several of her father's case studies and one of her own that were based on his analysis of her, I was convinced that Anna Freud had been an ascetic and a virtuoso sublimator of her sexual desires. But my reaction to this conclusion was great disappointment, because I would have preferred her to have had a less constricted sexual life and would have been quite comfortable if it had been a homosexual sexual life—despite how uncomfortable I would have been with exposing that or "outing" her, particularly to the psychoanalytic community.

I wrote into the biography an intricate, chapter-long reconstruction of Anna Freud's analysis as it can be glimpsed in the existing documentation, particularly in the case studies written by father and daughter in the early 1920s. My tone is calm; my stance, analytical. Anna Freud never abandoned her love of her father for any other love, I argued, making it clear that her analysis with him did not release her from him—how could it? In my judgment, I would not be able today to make this argument with any more precision and richness than I made it then. But I am very well aware that, later in the story, when Dorothy Burlingham came on the scene and I invoked again my argument about Anna Freud's asceticism, I would make two revisions were I writing today.

The first would be to acknowledge explicitly that a biographer cannot have the kind of certainty about the subject's sexual life that an analyst would have. I would say: "Of course, although all the evidence points to Anna Freud's asceticism, no one can say definitively what form the erotic tie between Anna Freud and Dorothy Burlingham took, as neither of them left behind a written or oral testimony to it, and it is not possible to know what either said about it in their analyses or to their surrogate analysts."

Why did I not make this simple admission, which would have saved me a lot of criticism from later readers (including the *New York Times* reviewer) who felt that I had covered up Anna Freud's lesbianism out of my own homophobia? The answer to this question is connected to the second revision I would make were I writing the biography today. In the pages I devoted to Anna Freud's analysis with her father and to the ascetic way of living she settled upon in the analysis, and partly as a consequence of the analysis and its unresolved—unresolvable— transference, I left aside the question of how Freud's followers might have reacted if Anna Freud and Dorothy Burlingham had been known to be lovers—and what this might have meant to Anna Freud herself and to her father-analyst. Was she, who spoke again and again about her concern for the good opinion of others and about winning praise, inhibited by the psychoanalytic opinion that homosexuality was a neurosis; did she fear judgment, even ostracism? I did not weave into my narrative a little one page history of Freud's own and his followers' much more homophobic attitudes to homosexuality and perversion in the 1920s or in subsequent times, up to the moment when my readers would be reading her story and questioning it.[2] Why did I not take up this topic, which had, after all, been on my mind since the day Lottie Newman asked me to write the biography?

The obvious answer is that the homophobic cultural milieu of the mid-1980s, and the continued pathologisation of homosexuality in the psychoanalytic community, inhibited me. True as this may be, it is not the whole story. The cultural story intersected with a less obvious (and to me more powerful) story, which I will come back to in a moment as I try to answer these questions about the Anna Freud biography. But first I want to turn to my Hannah Arendt biography and how I faced the crux in it of her affair with Heidegger. Here again, I would, were I writing the biography today, make an explicit admission: no one can know very much about the course this affair took or what its psychodynamic was, as there is no available oral or written testimony from either Arendt or Heidegger except what has survived of their correspondence with each other. I did not have access to that correspondence when I was writing the biography and even now that it has been published I find it unrevealing, not just because it is peculiarly abstract and opaquely poetic, but because Arendt's letters from the late 1920s are missing (for unknown reasons).

In the biography, I presented—undramatically—the facts of their affair as those could be reconstructed from my interviews with the very few people who knew about it. The person who—it seems—knew most about it, Arendt's husband Heinrich Bluecher, had died four years before Arendt herself, and, as far as I know, he did not speak about it to anyone else. But I studiously did not speculate about the affair on the basis of the facts as I could reveal them. And, particularly, I did not interpret her love for Heidegger psychoanalytically, because this seemed inappropriate given the kind of biography I was trying to write and her hatred of psychoanalysis, and because I did not, at the time, trust my ability to do so, sensing that I was missing some datum that would secure the psychoanalytic ideas I did have about it. I dreaded being a psychoanalytic amateur.

For a 2005 second edition of my Arendt biography, I wrote a new preface, and the next year, the centenary of Arendt's birth, a short book called *Why Arendt Matters*. In both these texts, I detailed how the affair had been presented in another biography, whose author had gained access to the Arendt/Heidegger letters (and permission to quote Arendt's). That biographer, a Polish woman named Elzbieta Ettinger (1995), had sensationalised the affair, constructing an obviously distorted picture of a naïve schoolgirl swept off her feet by a an older man—married, Catholic, father of two sons—who scorned her in the late 1920s and then betrayed her (and his Jewish colleagues) shortly thereafter by joining the Nazi Party. Ettinger's Hannah Arendt nonetheless slavishly stood by her man and even tried, after WWII, when she re-established contact with him, to whitewash his Nazi Party affiliation. To counter this lurid caricature of Arendt, which provoked intense interest in the affair among readers around the world, I documented how she had criticised Heidegger during and after the war in print and how she had analysed his duplicitous character time and again in her correspondence with her husband and with Karl Jaspers, who eventually repudiated Heidegger, having been unable to sustain their prewar friendship in the face of Heidegger's obstinate refusal to recant his Nazism publicly. She had no illusions about Heidegger's character; she flatly described him as half mendacious and half genuine, a great philosopher who often behaved foolishly, especially by cultivating adulators and sycophants. Had she not been so dismissive of psychoanalytic concepts, she might have called him a narcissist.

In my second edition preface and in *Why Arendt Matters*, I offered my interpretation of Arendt's motivation for re-establishing contact with Heidegger after the war and maintaining her friendship with him until her death, but I put it very succinctly, depending on her own words from letters in which she stressed how important to her was what she called "continuity". The word continuity appears again and again in her post-war letters to the three men she most loved: Heidegger, Bluecher, and Jaspers. Today, after further thought about her longing for continuity, I could develop my interpretation psychoanalytically and say with some confidence: as a twenty-year-old, she experienced from Heidegger her heart's desire, her core wish—recognition of her personhood and her talents from a man who happened to be the most talented philosopher of his generation. He did not, after their affair ended or during the war, offer anything like continuity, but he did offer it after the war, as she had hoped he would, by telling her when they met in 1951 that she was the love of his life and that she was the one person who really could understand *him*. (Narcissists characteristically single out for praise the intellectual abilities of people who can understand *them*.)[3]

I feel confident now of this interpretation of the genesis of Arendt's longing for recognition and continuity because very recently Hannah Arendt's old friend Lotte Kohler—one of the few of her close friends who is still alive—told me two stories about dreaming. These stories were, finally, the kind of material that a psychoanalytic biographer would need. When she was a child, Arendt had told Lotte Kohler, she had a recurrent dream about her father returning from the psychiatric hospital where he died and greeting her in loving recognition. Her dreams were often so vivid that she awoke not sure whether her dream had been a dream. To illustrate in another way the vividness of her dreams, she went on to tell Lotte Kohler that when she was a young woman at university she had dreamt that a well-known professor had died and then went about the next morning talking about how sad this was. People were shocked and telephoned the professor's home to check on him. When he answered the phone and assured them that he was quite alive, she was terrifically embarrassed to realise that she had only dreamt his death. Lotte Kohler's first story conveyed the original longing for recognition and return, representing continuity and integrity of self, and the second showed Arendt's dreaming that a professor living elsewhere had died and then—miraculously, in the secondary revision of awaking, in which her wish was her command—returned to life.[4]

For a woman who had lost her father early, having been so hurt first by his inability to recognise her in his paretic dementia and then by his terrible death, an older lover who could offer recognition and continuity would step into an empty place. Her husband Heinrich Bluecher later held the place much more reliably (and far less narcissistically) than Heidegger had, and for that she tolerated his flirtations with other women, who, he assured her, never supplanted her or, in his eyes, held a candle to her talents.[5] Her surrogate father, Karl Jaspers, was endlessly admiring of her and unfailingly steadfast until his death in 1969 (when she was sixty-three years old).

To me, Arendt's longing for recognition and continuity, her willingness to be loyal if loyalty was shown her, even if imperfectly, as well as her strong wish for a disruption of love to be overcome or miraculously repaired, seemed perfectly familiar. I have experienced variations on these themes in myself, and had great difficulty in my analysis coming to see them clearly or to understand their origins; I brought a variation of my resistance into my resistance towards seeing the themes in her life and clearly or confidently analysing them, much less revealing them publicly.

Today, as an analyst, I understand these themes of need for recognition and continuity as basic to normal narcissism and central to a character of basically narcissistic organisation—the sort of character that Hannah Arendt and I have in common, and have in common with many people who have felt an early loss of love. I understand narcissism of Heidegger's sort as an extreme: he seems to me a grandiose narcissist of the sort who goes so far as to try to remake reality (in reality, not just in dreams), erasing any dissent from his narcissistic wishes. It had astounded Arendt to learn that Heidegger had, in 1933, imagined himself as the house philosopher for Hitler and the National Socialists who envisioned remaking the world.

Characterologically, people like Hannah Arendt and like me, regardless of differences in intellectual abilities, want to be carefully and thoroughly right and to try to help other people live up to their views of what might be best. Speaking of myself (not her), I can say that I have always hoped to steer clear of imposing my view on others and now, as a matter of analytic self-knowledge, I actively restrain myself from imposing my view—otherwise I should not be an analyst. Nurturing or mentoring narcissists, although they want to be right, do not characteristically punish other people for being who they are, tolerating no dissent and eventually constraining others who show any independence. Before my analysis, when I was disappointed that I could not help another to be what I thought would be best for him or her, I backed off, and was afraid of any retributive feelings I felt towards the protégés. I had the same attitude to groups and, I came to understand, to groups of my imagined readers. I backed off when I felt that I would not be able to get readers to see things as I saw them. And that, it seems to me, was why I was so reluctant to be more transparent about my biographical analysing process and my judgments on the crucial episodes I have described. In my Anna Freud biography, I backed away, particularly from the psychoanalytic community's homophobia, not because I was directly inhibited by it or intimidated by it, but because I was afraid of how furious it made me. I was afraid of becoming angry in print and then being judged an angry character, not the calm, steady one I liked to be and liked to be recognised and admired for being. The same fear, more generally, underlay my determination not to be a sensationalist or a dramatist. In effect, I fearfully instructed myself: do not be a hysteric.

Not surprisingly, in the characterology I articulated in the 1990s, narcissists and hysterics feature prominently, each with variations such as the normal (mentoring) and extreme (grandiose) narcissists, the "good" and "bad" hysterics (in Elizabeth Zetzel's formulation), and each with characteristic formations along the many "developmental lines" studied so carefully by Anna Freud.[6] The third character type I described was the obsessional—Anna Freud's type, and much of what I wrote in describing the obsessional type is based upon what I learned by considering Anna Freud and her relationship with her father. In fact, the Anna Freud biography also taught me that it is important when thinking about character and characterology to adapt the "parallel lives" method practised in the classical tradition, particularly by Plutarch, who wrote studies featuring two characters portrayed comparatively.[7]

My adaptation of the method of characterological comparisons is clearest in my Anna Freud biography when I was using it to compare Anna Freud and her father.[8] Let me offer just one example of the grounds for comparison. He was a man whose narcissistic features made it impossible for him to sustain deeply self-revelatory collaborations with other men, although he tried again and again, and achieved his most decisive advances when he failed (especially with Fliess, with Adler, with Jung, with Rank, and with Ferenczi). In his last years, I think, he actually evolved into a person who could relate to his daughter's (that is, not a man's) activity collaboratively and say (in 1925) "The future of psychoanalysis belongs to child analysis." Similarly, he was a man whose narcissistic features made it impossible for him to see the significance of transference in such a way that he would have chosen not to analyse his own daughter, or would have chosen to risk allowing her to be analysed by one of his collaborators of whom he was not too suspicious (as he allowed his son Oliver—not an heir to psychoanalysis—to be analysed by Franz Alexander). In comparison, Anna Freud was a woman whose entire career was spent in collaborative ventures—nurseries, clinics, centres for clinical work and research—where she could be the leader and mentor of other women and younger men, although exercising her leadership in her characteristic obsessional mixture of innovatory and conservative ways, with her equally characteristic ambivalence in relations with peers outside her circle. She operated by "altruistic surrender" of the rewards of love and work to others—a quite controlling strategy that would not suit a mentoring narcissist like me, so I felt it as foreign. After her analysis, she was able to write the first sustained description of altruistic surrender as a mechanism of defence.

Making a portrait of a biographical subject in which these kinds of characterological dimensions become clear permits asking questions that lead on to the levels on which biography can contribute—as a case study can—to psychoanalytic theory, or, more simply, to our understanding of how people love and work. In terms of work, one might ask a question of the kind: how did a person of this character type come to work in this way? Or, as I put the question for Anna Freud, how did this woman of obsessional character, so fundamentally conservative and interested in the conservation of a legacy, become able to contribute so creatively, so originally, to the idea system she was conserving? In terms of love, one might ask a question of this kind: how did a person of this character type love—what patterns did her loves take? Did she have a recurrent love story? As far as Anna Freud was concerned, the question might go: how did this woman of obsessional character develop a sexual life—an erotic relational life—that, while it was very restricted in expressive terms, that is, while it was apparently ascetic, and while it was a clear instance of the Oedipal fixation to the parent of the opposite sex that she and her father studied so deeply, nonetheless allowed her to sublimate so intensely and be so very attuned to the sexual life of children, that is, not to be full of puritan disavowal of childhood sexuality. Anna Freud was a remarkably mentally adroit and unpretentious, curious, and witty person—a very "good obsessional" (if one might analogise to the distinction Zetzel drew between a "good" and a "bad" hysteric), who was able to make her obsessiveness into as much of a virtue as it could be.

Each of these questions presumes a portrait of a character developing and becoming consolidated in late adolescence and young adulthood, becoming, then, refined and nuanced—perhaps, in some lives, altered with experience or with a midlife crisis or bodily change, including aging. The narrative units of a biography of the sort I am describing are, in other words, the developmental units of character formation.

Notes

1. I will set it out as a proposition that there is no modern person about whom a rich and instructive biography can be created who has not himself or herself created a biography—of sorts. Perhaps only a short textual biography—a vignette—or a biography appearing as something else—a painter's description of painting a portrait, for example, or a film-maker's study of a subject's way of walking down the street—but a biography of some sort. To put the proposition in another form: only those who are interested in how other people live and how other people's lives can be presented are really rich and richly interesting to present biographically. There are no biographies of schizoids, although there are case studies.

2. Anna Freud's father did not share the idea that homosexuality is a neurotic condition, because he considered it as the opposite of a neurosis, that is, as a perversion (1905d). By my standards this is also a homophobic category when applied to homosexuality. In Freud's case study of a female homosexual, published in 1920, he notes that the girl's father might have taken the position of "lofty resignation" towards her—perhaps the one Freud himself took, although he attributes it to a

medical colleague—that her "irregularity" was "a misfortune like any other" (1920a).

3. Their relationship was continuous after the war, but became distant for a period in the 1960s after Arendt sent Heidegger a copy of her *The Human Condition*, which certainly was a full display of her abilities. She remarked to Jaspers that she thought Heidegger had been displeased, as his appreciation of her had centred on her ability to understand him. "I know that he finds it intolerable that my name appears in public, that I write books, etc. All my life I've pulled the wool over his eyes, so to speak, acted as if none of that existed and as if I couldn't count to three, unless it was in the interpretation of his own works ... Then I suddenly felt that this deception was becoming just too boring, and so I got a rap on the nose. I was very angry for a moment, but I'm not any longer. I felt somehow that I deserved what I got—that is, both for having deceived him and for suddenly having put an end to it" (*Correspondence* (1992), p. 457).

4. In her biography of Rahel Varnhagen, Arendt included a chapter on Rahel's recurrent dreams, emphasising their vividness and explaining that they constantly challenged "the continuity of the day" because they brought up Rahel's losses, her rejections, her exclusions (because of her Jewishness) from the society she wanted desperately to belong to. In the most persistent dream, two lovers who had rejected her were represented by a beautiful animal who loved her tremendously and knew how to tell her and show her that it did: "It looked at me with more love than I ever remember seeing in any human being's eyes." But eventually, as the dream changed over time, the animal which had recognised her so strongly died—and Rahel interpreted this as a sign that her lovers had been, really, heartless and untrue (Arendt, 1957, p. 109).

5. During a time when she found out about a relationship Bluecher had with another woman, Arendt reflected in her journal (October, 1950) on *Treue* and distinguished between "more or less innocent infidelity" and "the great crime of infidelity that murders that which was true ... that which one brought into the world". The crime of infidelity is "true destruction because it is only through fidelity that we are masters of our past: Fidelity's existence depends on us". This infidelity, which destroys continuity, which is a "forgetting", is ultimately "the only real sin, because it smothers truth and that which was true" (Hannah Arendt, *Denktagebuch: 1950 bis 1973*, 2002, p. 39; and see Lotte Kohler's introduction to *Within Four Walls: The Correspondence between Hannah Arendt and Heinrich Bluecher*, 1996).

6. When I use "character" as a psychoanalyst, I take into account the early Freudian emphasis on libidinal stages (particularly the anal stage

influence on obsessiveness, which is one of the most demonstrated correlations in all of psychoanalytic theory), but I put much more stress on the relational features of character, the ways in which a person habitually loves and works, and on the relational feature of character that embeds its revelation in a relationship. By this last feature I mean that a person's character is invisible to himself or herself; another person is needed to identify it—to portray it; everyone needs a biographer in this sense. Or you need another person—an analyst in a psychoanalytic setting—to help you to see it for yourself, to mirror you interactively. In this sense, you can describe a psychoanalysis as a type of relationship in which an analysand achieves (one might say performs) a self-portrait and can see herself in that portrait in the analysis. To my mind, the condition for growth and change in a psychoanalysis is the analysand's capacity to see her character and want to make the changes in it that permit further growth and development.

7. Plutarch's charming *Lives* has standard narrative units focusing on family, education, debut in public life, crucial words and deeds, and changes (*metabolai*) of fortune, and offers characterological reflections in the medium of comparisons (*synkresies*).

8. My *Creative Characters* (1991) offers a number of comparative studies in chapters devoted to narcissists (including Freud), hysterics, and obsessionals (including Anna Freud). I argue that the three character types have characteristic modes of creativity, each dominated by a metaphor: of the self channelling energy or inspiration, of one part of the self fabricating another, and of the self purging itself.

References

Arendt, H. (1951). *The Origins of Totalitarianism*. Berlin: Schocken.

Arendt, H. (1957). *Rahel Varnhagen: The Life of a Jewess*. New York: Leo Baeck Institute.

Arendt, H. (1958). *The Human Condition*. Chicago: University Press.

Arendt, H. (1968). Men in Dark Times. Orlando, FL: Harcourt Brace.

Arendt, H. (2002). *Denktagebuch: 1950 bis 1973, Erster Band* (first tape). U. Ludz & I. Nordmann (Eds.). Munich: Piper.

Arendt, H., & Jaspers, K. (1992). *Correspondence, 1926–1969*. L. Kohler & H. Saner (Eds.), R. & R. Kimber (Trans.). Orlando, FL: Harcourt Brace.

Ettinger, E. (1995). *Hannah Arendt/Martin Heidegger*. New Haven, CT: Yale University Press.

Freud, S. (1905d). Three essays on the theory of sexuality. *S. E. 7*. London: Hogarth.

Freud, S. (1920a). The psychogenesis of a case of female homosexuality. *S. E. 18*. London: Hogarth.

Koehler, L. (1996). Introduction to *Within Four Walls: The Correspondence between Hannah Arendt and Heinrich Bluecher*. New York: Harcourt.

Plutarch. *Plutarch's Lives*.

Young-Bruehl, E. (1991). *Creative Characters*. New York: Routledge.

Young-Bruehl, E. (1996). *The Anatomy of Prejudices*. Cambridge, MA: Harvard University Press.

Young-Bruehl, E. (2006). *Why Arendt Matters*. New Haven, CT: Yale University Press.

INDEX